Ghosts

Ghosts

Death's Double and the Phenomena of Theatre

ALICE RAYNER

UNIVERSITY OF MINNESOTA PRESS

MINNEAPOLIS • LONDON

Sections of chapter 3, "Objects: Lost and Found," are published in David Krasner and David Z. Saltz, *Staging Philosophy: Intersections of Theater, Performance, and Philosophy* (Ann Arbor: University of Michigan Press, 2006).

Parts of chapter 5, "Double or Nothing: Ghosts behind the Curtains," first appeared in "Rude Mechanicals and *The Specters of Marx*," *Theatre Journal* 54, no. 4 (December 2002).

Published by the University of Minnesota Press
111 Third Avenue South, Suite 290
Minneapolis, MN 55401-2520
http://www.upress.umn.edu

Library of Congress Cataloging-in-Publication Data

Rayner, Alice.
    Ghosts : death's double and the phenomena of theatre / Alice Rayner.
        p. cm.
    Includes bibliographical references and index.
    ISBN 13: 978-0-8166-4544-2 (hc) — ISBN 13: 978-0-8166-4545-9 (pb)
    ISBN 10: 0-8166-4544-2 (hc : alk. paper) — ISBN 10: 0-8166-4545-0 (pb : alk. paper)
    1. Theater—Psychological aspects. 2. Drama—History and criticism. 3. Ghosts in literature.
4. Ghosts in motion pictures. I. Title.
    PN2049.R39 2006
    792.01'9—dc22   2005035588

Printed in the United States of America on acid-free paper

The University of Minnesota is an equal-opportunity educator and employer.

12 11 10 09 08 07 06   10 9 8 7 6 5 4 3 2 1

Contents

Acknowledgments

Colleagues in the drama department at Stanford University have been exceptionally generous in their patience and support through this project. Early on, Jean-Marie Apostolides gave me particularly strong encouragement and the assurance that the work was worthwhile. His suggestions and support have been invaluable. Peggy Phelan and Harry Elam each generously read and commented on early drafts of a couple of chapters, for which I am enormously grateful. Rush Rehm has been the voice of conscience for my impulses to get carried away with language too abstruse, and the clearer parts of the writing can be attributed to that voice. I was also fortunate to have a graduate seminar with students who just happened to have an interest in the phenomenology of objects; Kyle Gillette, Rachel Joseph, and Barry Kendall were a wonderful group with whom to try out some of the ideas. All this help has made this a better work than it otherwise would be, and I feel exceptionally fortunate to have such colleagues and students.

Michal Kobialka of the University of Minnesota has been especially supportive, letting me work out ideas in lectures at Minnesota and inspiring me with his work on Kantor. I trust I have not abused that inspiration by bringing Kantor into this book.

I am also grateful to the readers from the University of Minnesota Press. In addition to an anonymous reader, Jon Erickson gave the manuscript an attentive reading that was simply astonishing. His extensive, detailed, and thoughtful comments, questions, and sources gave me a way to dialogue through the revisions, and if I have not answered all the questions and still use more Derrida and Lacan than is seemly, it is not his fault. I could not have asked for a more understanding reading.

Unwritten in the book are all the personal aspects of ghostly past and present, and it is to those personal relations that the book owes its life. Bert States died before it was complete, but to him I owe a debt that will never be paid. The integrity of his work and the grace of his mind remain with me. Jonathan Berkeley was a witness to my facing up to the blank spaces in my own memory, and he gave me his apparently unwavering faith that I was up to this task. The support of Richard Maldonado, Kevin Redmond, and Andrea Peri Rosenfield has kept me going through the writing and rewriting. Along the way, friends and relations kept me as sane as could be. To them, also, my love: Tom Caldarola, Dave Bisson, Claudia Holmes, Evelyn Gilbreath and Stanford Hughes, Andy and Kristen West, Judy Dolan and Raymond Hardie. Thanks to Brett Stewart for not reading the manuscript. Family is always the source for one's secrets and delights. I would like to think I have released the ghosts of my parents with this work. This is dedicated to those with whom I share the family secrets and history: Jeanne, Betsy, and Bill, my friend and sister-in-law Sue Rayner and family, Mike, Kristen, John, and Kelly, and, always, my son, Eric Quandt.

Doubles and Doubts

Yeah you've seen the old man's ghost
Come back as creamed chipped beef on toast
—JOHN HIATT, "Your Dad Did"

Whatever the doubts about the truth of ghosts, I would claim that almost anyone can recognize what John Hiatt means when he sings that his old man's ghost has come back as creamed chipped beef on toast. Hiatt is naming that peculiar discovery that one is repeating the habits of the long-gone parent in spite of the assumption that one leads an autonomous, independent life. That much seems straightforward: chipped beef turning into a sort of objective correlative for the recognition of a haunting repetition of the past both within the mundane and by means of the mundane. Poetic license can do that, because, as Sydney said, the poet, unlike the historian or philosopher, never "asserteth" the truth. We do not have to believe that the creamed chipped beef *is* the old man's ghost. How, then, do we take the truth of Hiatt's lines? What does it mean to take the ghost *as* creamed chipped beef on toast? What, after all, is a ghost? Is it a deluded psychological projection or a subjective delusion? Are Hiatt's lines a sign of beliefs about fathers and their demonic or culinary characteristics in late twentieth-century popular culture?

If one were to unpack the image, it would be easy to unravel a long narrative of stories about the old man, his effect on his son, and the repetition of habits in succeeding generations. To some extent, the image is a compression of such imagined narratives. The effectiveness of the line of song, however, depends upon the sudden perception and the "rightness" of seeing the old man and the chipped beef at the same time, in the same place. The rightness is a sense of revelation in the truth of the double image, but just how that image makes sense is not obvious. Making sense of ghosts is the project of this book. Unlike a metaphor, which also joins two unlike entities in a single image, a ghostly double involves secrets and a return. Ghosts hover where secrets are held in time: the secrets of what has been unspoken, unacknowledged; the secrets of the past, the secrets of the dead. Ghosts wait for the secrets to be released into time.

In this book, I am concerned with the way ghosts make their appearances in the world and with theatre as the art of appearances, or what Herbert Blau called "the dubious spectacle." The figure of the ghost accounts for a specific force in repetition and the double that cannot be identified simply as an imitation or a representation. What Artaud sought in his impossible Theatre of Cruelty was to end theatre as imitation and to give flesh to the force of the ghostly double that constitutes theatre. That force has the effect of the uncanny, which Freud described as the strangeness or "secret" aspect in someone or something familiar. In Hiatt's lines, that force effects laughter out of the disparity between chipped beef and a dead father. In theatre, the force comes as an affective response in one's captured attention to appearances that both are and are not what they seem to be. To call it doubt may be to overstate the case, for the theatrical event does not especially evoke a skeptical stance toward the event. Perhaps something closer to fascination is more apt to describe the uncanny aspect in the appearance of a double that holds the secrets of being other than what it is. In his account of the uncanny, Freud tells a kind of linguistic ghost story as he traces through the transformations of meaning in *heimlich* to show that the notion of the familiar, comfortable, tame, or at home with, comes around to mean also what is secretive, concealed, deceitful, or withheld. The word *heimlich* turns into its own opposite, *unheimlich*. This linguistic transformation gives a focus to a broader issue that connects the uncanny aspect of ghosts with theatre and the issue of the double.

In theatre since the time of Plato and Aristotle, the double has been connected to discussions of mimesis and imitation: What is original or authentic, what is real, what is false? What is the image, what is the real "thing"? Theatre has fostered that model of the double through its skill in creating illusions. Indeed, the skill in conjuring the illusions of ghosts has long served to equate ghosts with illusion and illusion with the stage. Raising spirits to visibility became one of theatre's technological specialties, a specialty that will be revisited in the chapter on film. As early as 1598, Angelo Ingegnieri's treatise on theatre included details of the ghostly effects made possible by candlelight. The ghost must appear, he writes, toward the back of the perspective scenery in order to seem hugely out of proportion with the surroundings. With a black scrim or veil stretched between screens at the back of the stage, "one sees everything that happens behind it in a mysterious way, and the hellish monster, which 'must spread around its darkness just as the holy figures shed light,' conveys to the spectators an illusion." The ghost-actor, furthermore, should be dressed in shapeless black, letting neither arms nor legs show; it should not walk but "glide on small wheels," and speak in a shrill, high-pitched voice; it should be in constant motion, then vanish suddenly, as the black scrim suddenly bursts into flame.[1] The dichotomy between illusion and reality materialized in the Italian Renaissance with the discoveries of pictorial perspective and its uses on the proscenium stage. With Renaissance stage perspective, duality materialized via the illusions of the stage picture. Ingegnieri's technical manual simply identifies one historical moment for the creation of ghostly effects. The image of a formless body floating within a veil together with a monstrous, pervading darkness is associated clearly with a Christian notion of hellishness that has become a cliché. The purpose of the instruction, apparently, is to create the wonder of the uncanny along with the uncertainty of how the wonder is created.

The history of attempts to dematerialize the physical realities of the stage is one story of ghosts. But a great deal in theatrical practice is far less interested in illusion. The earliest and most pervasive forms of ritual theatre maintain no dichotomy between reality and artifice. The symbolic aspects of a ritual mask, for example, are indistinguishable from its material aspects. The artful mask is not an illusion of the god but a version of the god, and the symbolic is not severed from either matter or significance. The mask, rather, brings them together in the same site. At issue is the refusal in the deep sense of theatre to consent to the idea that invisible, immaterial, or abstract forces are illusions, that the spirits of the dead are imaginary, or that the division between matter and spirit is absolute. To whatever extent stagecraft may be said to create mere effects and illusions, it relies on a premise that clearly divides the world into oppositions of true and false, real and unreal, visible and invisible. Theatre in its dense practices thoroughly confounds that premise on a principle of negativity or invisibility within visibility. The double in this sense is not a reflection or imitation of an original but an appearance of a dynamic contradiction or opposition that cannot come to rest in either what is visible or what is invisible. Doubling in this sense is a representational practice that does not necessarily represent or imitate anything in the world. This is why what I mean by the theatrical double is not the same as imitation or representation of something else. Yet it does not escape representation. Theatre is not simply a second world. Rather, like the linguistic tropes of metaphor and metonymy, theatrical doubling invokes two dissimilar elements and finds the points of overlap, such that the double negative "not not" and the dualism "is and is not" do not so much present an ontological truth as they indicate the limits of dualistic thought. Any point at which dualistic, oppositional thought is invoked but then breaks down might be said to be theatrical.

In the studies that follow I hope to counteract the sense that ghosts are no more than signs of illusion or imaginary projections. If an argument binds these chapters it is that theatre, in all of its aspects, uniquely insists on the reality of ghosts. On the other hand, something is fundamentally unassimilable about ghosts. It is virtually impossible to answer the question, What is a ghost? Here, ghosts share a problem with time, which Augustine expressed this way: "We surely know what is meant when we hear someone else talking about it. What then is time? Provided that no one asks me, I know. If I want to explain it to an inquirer, I do not know."[2] A ghost escapes definition because it is not a thing, yet, like time, it works in things, as things, or invisibly on things. It is easy enough to understand metaphorically how one can appear as creamed chipped beef on toast or speak from the dark or from dreams, in the voice of a stranger, or in the writing of history, or arise from the unknown realm of the dead, from unregistered trauma, from cultural memory. But to say what one *is* defies definition. The theatre loves ghosts as much as people love ghost stories. So whether or not one can say with any credibility what they are, ontologically speaking, one can try to account for their production through theatre. Theatre constantly encounters the dead, and the appeal as well as the doubtful status of ghosts goes to the heart of theatre's appeal. Ghosts, that is, pervade theatre more thoroughly than any particular instance of staging, to the extent that theatre itself is a ghostly place in which the living and the dead come together in a productive encounter. Theatre is thus fundamentally a human space where we humans encounter not only the dead who have gone before but also the images of our own mortality. As Robert Pogue Harrison writes in *The Dominion of the Dead:*

> If a house, a building, or a city is not palpably haunted in its architectural features—if the earth's historicity and containment of the dead do not pervade its articulated forms and constitutive matter—then that house, building, or city is dead to the world. Dead to the world means cut off from the earth and closed off from its underworlds. For that is one of the ironies of our life worlds: they receive their animation from the ones that underlie them.[3]

Ghosts animate our connections to the dead, producing a visible, material, and affective relationship to the abstract terms of time and repetition, sameness and difference, absence and presence. If we doubt the presence of those absent, it may be only because the abstractions are safer and more comfortable. A ghost, particularly in the theater, ought to startle an audience into attention with a shiver. Doubt rationalizes the shiver, but it also signals an encounter. Where doubt exists, there may well be a ghost. As Harrison argues, the earth on which we live is itself the home and dominion of the dead. To understand our institutional means of reflecting that dominion, theatre gives us ghosts.

Each chapter that follows addresses some mundane aspects of contemporary theatre convention and traces how conjunctions between the living and the dead can be read through ordinary and overlooked elements. Such connections cannot necessarily be proven, for they test the limits of intelligibility, but they inevitably lead to broader issues of how we see what is missing, to questions of time and history, to the lived experiences ghosted by the past, to the relations between the material objects of the present and the effects of absence, to the uncanniness of appearances themselves. These issues tend to repeat in variations through the chapters. The approaches shift among theatre practices, texts, and phenomenological speculation, often based in a psychoanalytic account. This is not because I believe psychoanalysis finds confirmation in theatre, or that theatre in some way validates psychoanalysis, but that along with phenomenology, theatre and psychoanalysis share similar epistemological problems in regard to validity. Like ghosts, both phenomenology and psychoanalysis fail tests of rationality and, often, credibility. Questions about visibility, about images that confound the real and representation, about the return of the past to the present, materiality and memory, about self-deception and action, and about the corporeality of language have dominated critical theory in recent years but have often been regarded with the kind of suspicion usually reserved for the supernatural.

These issues nonetheless trace an intellectual history back through the French poststructuralists, including Derrida, Lyotard, Guattari, de Certeau, Barthes, Kristeva, and Sollers; they appear in social philosophers such as Pierre Bourdieu, Michel Foucault, Henri Lefebvre, and Marx; they echo Freud, as well as Merleau-Ponty, Heidegger, and Nietzsche. Post-structuralism, taking its cues from psychoanalysis and phenomenology, has understandably been subject, like ghosts themselves, to accusations of self-authorizing as well as self-canceling circularity, particularly in regard to evidence and symptom. The failure of psychoanalysis as a scientific discourse has led to widespread denial of its validity, just as poststructuralism already seems relegated to the past of critical fashion or an apolitical self-absorption and is close to becoming the ghost of a critical past, which suggests it will return in another form. Within psychoanalysis, denial itself is a signal for the blind spot within consciousness. If denial, whether of ghosts or Freud or Freud's ghost for that matter, is symptomatic of an unseen or unacknowledged or unconscious truth, no positive, uncontradictory proof is ever available. In this way, psychoanalysis is an analogue to the question of whether one believes in ghosts or not. Psychoanalytic pursuits, like ghostly apparitions, seem to be chasing the very things they have brought into being by the fact of the pursuit, and belief in either one requires a radical suspension of disbelief and an embrace of doubt and denial. That is the same circularity that makes theatrical appearances suspect, but as Shakespeare has it on the discovery of twins in *Twelfth Night,* "One face, one voice, one habit, two persons; / A natural perspective that is and is not."[4] The fact of twins does not explain the uncanniness of twins. The theatrical doubles do not explain the singularity of a theatrical event, but explanation is certainly not my intent. As even Freud found, the specific, supposedly causal narratives of the origin of trauma do not constitute an understanding of trauma apart from either the multiple, overdetermined repetitions or the therapeutic transferences between analysis and analysand. The void, an absence within consciousness itself for which death is the most fundamental instance, must be experienced, and theatre, psychoanalysis, and to some extent phenomenology restore the experience better than they explain themselves. Theatre is the place to embrace doubt and denial and discover the material reality of what is not, which is to say that theatre not only "unmakes mimesis," as in Elin Diamond's apt title;[5] it also unmakes the ontological presumptions of *is*.

Similarly, a phenomenological approach threatens to produce either eccentric perception or merely obvious tautologies along with the implication of some ontological essence in its objects of study. I am painfully aware that my use of the word *theatre* here already sounds as though I am pursuing an essence, especially because there is little concern with historical specificity in my uses of the term. The desire, if not the result, is rather to cut through conventional assumptions about just what the theatrical "object" is. For I will be looking neither at movements or moments in theatre history nor at a collection of similar theatrical projects or practices. I will, rather, be moving in and out of theatre, in and out of dramatic texts, and speculating extensively on the correlations between broad concepts in psychoanalysis and phenomenology and peripheral elements of theatre practice that have rarely been considered theoretically. I hope to suggest that the ghost is not so much an essence of theatre as it is an inhabitant of all its elements. I cannot hope to prove the case but only to offer possibilities for a complex perception of theatre practice.

Herbert Blau has long identified the ghosting aspects of theatre. In the most obvious sense of the metaphor, the actor embodies and gives life to a nonliving thing and essentially erases the differences between the living and the dead to produce an uncanny spectacle in which the animate and inanimate coalesce. Whether the ghostly presence derives from a demonic mask that transforms the living body into an object or is concealed by the conventions of realism, the otherness that inhabits the actor is a prime example of theatre's traffic with ghosts. Blau writes of ghosting as the core of his actors' work in the group KRAKEN: "The missing person is recurrently there insisting that his story be told, both playing and giving up the ghost. In our work, we have tried to make this uncentering dilemma into the methodology at the heart of the story, what I have described as ghosting."[6] I suggest that with his idea of ghosting Blau is after a term for a particular affective force in the work of the actor that distinguishes an uncanny element in performance from pretense or illusion. The affective force, however, is more than just an emotional effect or attribute of the work, as though the work were an object with attributes. Rather, the affective force constitutes a form of thought, in the etymological sense that the word *mind,* from the Greek word *menos,* includes the sense of "mind, intention, and force" and has kinship with a host of other words, including *memory* and *mania.*[7] Remembrance and the force of remembrance, repetition and thought, are thus deeply implicated in one another not simply as after-effects of a practice but as forms of knowing that constitute the practice. In his work with KRAKEN, Blau was seeking from his actors something that all the most radical theatre practitioners have tried, and often failed, to create onstage: a sensory manifestation of "truth" in the sense in which truth, again etymologically, goes back to the Greek words *aletheia* or *alethes,* which relate to the sense of "unconcealed," which is to say visible. Those words also represent the negative of *lethe,* or "forgetting," as in Lethe, the river of oblivion in the Greek Hades, and hence are connected to the idea of a remembering that is contingent on forgetting. The "truth" of the practice of ghosting suggests that the actors are in some sense unconcealing and making visible what otherwise is invisible. They are unforgetting the presence of something absent, whether that be called a text or a character, history or the past. The living energy of the actors measures an absence, in work that is specifically not trying to imitate life but to engage with life in its fullest aspect, which requires contact with death.

But ghosting goes beyond the actor to the total theatre event. For Blau, what appears in theatre, as theatre, is the visible and material something that both produces and is produced by the no-thing of character, of text, of an invisible, absent, or missing reality. He is fond of quoting from *Hamlet,* "What, has this thing appeared again tonight?" (1.1.21). Theatre as a repetition of some ghostly *thing*—already an apparent duality—produces its own *thing,* the singularity of the event. The theater itself gives appearances to the unseen, the hidden, and to the chronic return of the theatrical event from nothing into something. Theatre is the specific site where appearance and disappearance reproduce the relations between the living and the dead, not as a form of representation, but as a form of consciousness that has moved beyond dualities and problems of representation without disregarding them. "What is universal in performance," Blau writes, "is the consciousness of performance."[8] The ambiguity of the preposition *of* in that sentence indicates that such consciousness is not simply a matter of a subjective agent—the audience, the viewer, the critic—who looks at a performance as though at an object. Consciousness *of* performance certainly includes that sense but also implies that performance itself is a mode of consciousness that includes performer and audience without distinction. Performance could be said to be a circulation of such consciousness: the performance aware of itself as performance in such a way that it occurs neither within the individual selves of performers or spectators nor within the staged matter alone, but through and because of all of them. In this sense, the ghost is not at all a metaphor for something else but an aspect of theatrical practice.

> When I speak, therefore, of the consciousness of performance, I am stressing the consciousness in the grain of performance—no outside no inside—which in certain kinds of performance may appear not to be there but, as in a topological warp, is there in its appearance, appearing not-to-be.[9]

The important point here is that ghosting or haunting is an aspect of theatre as a mode of consciousness in which a fully materialized reality, even a representational reality, is haunted by an appearing not-to-be—that is, by its own negation. The greatest mystery of theatrical ghosting is not that the ghosts are disembodied spirits from some ineffable realm, heaven or hell, and hence imaginary. The mystery, rather, is that they are fully embodied and material but are unrecognized without a certain mode of attention, a certain line of sight that can perceive the mysterious thing that is distinct from, yet embodied by, the theatrical object. There. Not there. The consciousness of performance is impossible without the performers, the materiality of the stage, the audience, the moment. Such consciousness is not *in* any of them, yet arises from them and in a certain sense because of their intersection. The materiality of the performance is ghostly if for no other reason than that performance event is not an object but an event of consciousness generated by repetition. I do not believe that such consciousness necessarily escapes representation, simply because upon the viewing of performance our habits and techniques for creating meaning are so persistent, our need to contain, hold, and comprehend so pervasive, that if we cannot understand, we will most likely deny or dismiss the ghost or categorize it as merely imaginary. But to draw a line between the material and imaginary is already to invest belief in a duality in which thinking and doing, mind and matter, past and present, are separable entities. Whatever meanings one may assign to a particular theatrical event in order to trap it in significance, the event itself, the performance, is a consciousness materially displaying its own absent past, its historicity, and its self-awareness of its own repetition by appearing not-to-be. That humans are representing animals cannot be avoided, but that it is possible to experience the difference as well as the coordinates between our representations and the world, between our living and our impending death, is an achievement realized in theatre performance as a form of consciousness. From one point of view, of course, the ghost *is* a metaphor for the distinction between illusion and reality, which is to say it serves to identify what we designate as real in the way a parent might say to a frightened child, "Don't worry, it was only a dream" or "Go to sleep, forget it, there's no such thing as ghosts." Pressing the case, however, the child may well want to know what it was that frightened her so.

The consciousness of performance puts "negative capability" (appearing not-to-be but also unforgetting) into a practice that is not an imitation or pretense. It lends itself to an undoing of conscious habits, of ideological formations of intelligibility, and of ontological categories. The "thing" that is theatre/performance is exactly what cannot be held in mind as either one thing or another but an uncanny double that "is not." Blau again: "It is exactly what goes out of sight that we most desperately want to see. That's why we find ourselves, at the uttermost consummation of performance, in the uncanny position of *spectators*. It is uncanny because, in some inexplicable way (though Freud comes uncannily close to explaining it), *we are seeing what we saw before.*"[10] Putting the "thing" into practice is hardly obvious and requires the rigor and dedication that often approach a religious, even delirious, fervor. Ghostly practice is almost anathema to Western theatre that remains largely imitative, but the most radical practitioners have worked with the paradoxes and consciousness *of* performance: Meyerhold, Artaud, Kantor, Grotowski, Blau, and even Stanislavski, in spite of his legacies in psychological realism. For theatre ghosts are specifically and materially different from the recycling of material, from the conscious memory of previous work, from the known past, insofar as all of such elements can be identified and named. Or rather, even if those elements can be named and identified, their effective, affective force escapes the name.

"Seeing what we saw before" implies recognition in the root sense of the word, a reknowing, and thus is related to the idea of unforgetting. A phenomenological ground for such recognition suggests the moment when one perceives that one is perceiving what has been there all along. That is to say the "world" as perceived has been there before, but the moment of perception is one in which the world appears in what Heidegger called its "unconcealedness." This is quite different from the more obvious commonsense idea of seeing what we saw before, like a television rerun or a favorite movie from one's youth revisited years later. Recognition or reknowing or unforgetting is, rather, a particular kind of perception; it is a sensation of seeing for the first time what one has seen many times before. One function of any art is to bring about that moment of unforgetting, when the familiar world suddenly seems strange and new or impossible. This function separates the world-making aspect of an art from subjective relativity, for the work of art mediates between a world that is a given, in the Greek sense of Necessity, and the world that is made by perception and representation. Phenomenology seeks to identify the moment of emergence in which the world is generated by its perception and at the same time has preceded perception, giving one the sense of both remembering and creating in the same moment. Repetition in this sense is less a matter of sameness than of difference within the same, like the river of Heraclitus. His river is the same only when it is caught in an idealizing but limited form of thought in which the "I," the subject-centered consciousness, names the things of the world. Such forms of thought obviously have their power and function in pragmatic terms; they give shape to the sense of duration. But the very "I" that speaks and names the duration and durables of the world is also caught in the processes of the world's emergence. An event must by necessity recede in time and be reconcealed, but it remains as a factual having-been-done and thus can and does return with a difference. The working of theatre art makes it possible to perceive perception, for no perception is entirely innocent or free of repetition. Rather, as a ghost, it "calls to mind" and recollects the function of perception in world making. As sociologist Avery Gordon writes, "The ghost is a living force. It may reside elsewhere in an otherworldly domain but it is never intrinsically Other. . . . The need of the dead to be remembered and accommodated . . . is inseparable from the needs of the living. In other words, the ghost is nothing without you. In this sense, the ghost figures what systematically continues to work on the here and now."[11]

Like ghosts, theatre does not have the power of action in any pragmatic sense. However much it might blur the boundaries between the real and the representational, theatre is set apart by special circumstances, which is why I choose the term *theatre* rather than *performance,* though performance is often the aspect of theatre I wish to invoke. Theatre may well move people to act; it may incite revolution. It can both represent and exhibit action, but in any political, pragmatic, or even personal sense, theatre is a force without obvious or immediate consequence, which is not to say it is inconsequential. But ghosts do not have the power of action. Hence, they call upon the living to act for them. They invest the living with the "spirit" to act, but they need the living to fulfill their demands, to respond, and ultimately to set them to rest. For Hamlet's father to call "remember me" is to demand of young Hamlet that he act for his father, on his behalf, in his name, such that remembrance is not in Hamlet's mind but in his act, such that the whole of *Hamlet* is an act of memory made visible.

The basic question I am asking, then, is, Why are ghosts so appropriate to a description of theatrical repetition, and what is lost by rationalizing them? The most obvious reply is that in some way the presence of the ghost acknowledges the reality of death, so that theatre's memory must also be somehow engaged with death and a return from the dead and the paradoxical position that the return is also a unique and singular occasion. For the actor, this means that a performance is a launching into the territory of the radically unknown. The launch into performance involves the death of a particular sense of self, of the particularity of self: a giving away of self. No matter that lines are learned or gestures repeated: the actor is ghosted by an absent text that has already produced the phantom of character, and to inhabit a character fully is to become a ghost who wears a human, living mask. It is no accident that forgetting lines in performance is called corpsing.

The less obvious answer to the question of rationalization, though no less important, is that ghosts have both a powerfully emotional effect and a crucially doubtful status. The emotional effect of the uncanny—Freud's unfamiliar familiarity *(Heimlich/unheimlich)*—is visceral: not just new or strange, the unfamiliar must in some way be a double, with aspects of both the animate and the inanimate, different from but indistinguishable from the known, the familiar, the familial.[12] The doubt deriving from this double vision surfaces in both antitheatrical prejudices against duplicity and in theatre's effectiveness as an "unreal" reality. Doubt toward the uncanny, toward the living dead, toward an impossible return, constitutes an epistemology that is fundamentally theatrical. The doubtful status of the ghost thus concerns not just a theatrical object but a theatrical way of seeing double. Such double vision recognizes both the animate aspects of the inanimate object and the death implicit in the living being.

Neither repetition alone nor difference per se generates the uncanny element in representation, so not every representation is necessarily uncanny, even if the uncanny operates at the heart of representation. Realism often tries to obscure the uncanny. Thus, Gordon Craig could call for the "return of the image—the über-marionette" that "will aim to clothe itself with a death-like beauty while exhaling a living spirit."[13] Where most kinds of realism will try to make differences between the world and its representations disappear, an image, in Craig's sense, will emphasize the differences between the animate and the inanimate, between the living body and the artifice, and move toward the sense of the object with its uncanny unity between its symbolic and material aspects. But the point is not to celebrate death as much as it is, in Craig's words, "Life, Life, Life."[14] To put this in Victor Shklovsky's terms, the function of the doubtful double is to alienate us from life, but thereby to make life itself seem strange and therefore perceptible, to feel and recognize and remember life.

From Rousseau's antitheatrical celebration of festival to Artaud's Theatre of Cruelty or Kantor's Theatre of the Dead, attempts to overcome the merely imitative double and to create a singular event, unrepeatable and unrepresentational, have been both fleeting and perpetual. And clearly, not all theatre practices try to negate imitation. Realism in particular tends to exploit it, but does so by pretending to erase the differences between art and life. To some extent any representation implies doubleness and difference, whether that representation is simply a physical perception represented in the brain, an abstract idea, a piece of writing, a work of art. Even the broad notion of performance as a cultural or personal enactment that produces a culture or a subject cannot wholly escape the mental habits of duality that distinguish a here from a there, a now from a then, life from death, a real from an imaginary, an event from significance. If duality is an aspect of human fate, a fate that theatre embraces, then theatre also demonstrates that such a fate does not condemn us to always being apart from ourselves. For theatre also insists that its dualities, like dualistic thinking itself, are only representations that mask the nothingness—or what thought imagines as nothing—and which Suzan-Lori Parks has called "the Great (W)hole of

History"—out of which representations themselves arise. The artifices that alienate and divide the living from the dead also return us to life by demonstrating the limits of our representations. Ghosts arise not from the *idea* of the double but from the perceptible presence of an absence that the double outlines and gives shape to. No rational articulation can re-create the ghosts whose very symptoms are uncertainties about their status. It can only name the experience and accept the limits of articulation itself.

Under scholarly scrutiny, in other words, ghosts tend to become safely domesticated by our turning them into significance rather than experience. I am anxious, however, to suggest a way of looking for them that is distinctly not a rational one. A ghost is no-thing. It is not the sort of object that can be examined, unearthed, analyzed: there is nothing to be dissected, parsed into constituent elements, revealed, or critiqued. Instead, a ghost appears only from an oblique perspective and emerges only from the sideways glance at the void of death or the blanks in memory. When a ghost acquires meaning it is at the cost of denying its origin in another dimension, the dimension of no-thing. Marvin Carlson's book *The Haunted Stage,* for example, demonstrates quite clearly how theatre practice, reception, space, and history are all infused with repetition and remembrance. Taking the notion that theatre is fundamentally a ghosted practice, he shows how theatre recycles the past in the present of performance. He notes that repetition, recycling, and memory are well-recognized conditions of theatre, citing the work of Blau, Joseph Roach, Elin Diamond, Richard Schechner, and Bert States. But Carlson identifies ghosting in the aspect of theatre that "presents the identical thing that [audiences] have encountered before, although now in a somewhat different context. Thus a recognition not of similarity, as in genre, but of identity becomes a part of the reception process, with results that can complicate this process considerably."[15] If the returning thing is identical to what was encountered before, it doesn't seem to me to carry any aspect of the uncanny but is rather part of an identifiable historical memory that is fully available to consciousness. If the ghost is the same as what was seen before but simply appearing in a new context, it is no different from a history of ideas and practices that is already a selection based on the terms of intelligibility, more like the television rerun than the unconcealing of being. In historical terms and records the ghosts of the past are quite safe. At the very least, the ghost becomes a knowable entity rather than a disturbance in the fabric of what is known and a force for unforgetting. Making full use of the terms *ghost* and *haunting* involves, it seems to me, their remaining in the realm of uncertainty. As Margery Garber writes of the customary approaches to old Hamlet:

> The difficulty of holding an essentialist view of the Ghost, or of *a* ghost, is implicit in and intrinsic to the nature (if that is the word) of ghosts themselves. To instate a meaning, or a dramatic effect, is to divest it of some of its power, the power that inheres in the sequence "'Tis here! 'Tis here! 'Tis gone!" It is the nature of ghosts to be gone, so that they can return. When they are predictable, when they are no longer uncanny, they are no longer ghosts, but characters, capable of being inscribed in stage history.[16]

Theatre's ghosts, when they are present, induce another force entirely, something close to the fearful astonishment or even vertigo in the radical unknowing and lack of explanation for what appears: the effect that Ingegnieri wanted to produce for his audiences. The ghost is known only by its affective presence, when one asks from a state of wonder, What am I seeing, how does this happen, where is this coming from, this "thing" happening before my eyes? If words are successful in naming the ghost, there is no ghost. If the experience of the uncanny does not precede the argument about its undoing of ontology or the repetitions of history, it is only an idealization. My insistence on this admittedly undermines this project, turning this book into a memorial tribute to unspeakable experiences that are, nonetheless, real.

Horatio in *Hamlet* speaks to the ghost, but the ghost will not speak back to him. Why? Perhaps because Horatio is a scholar, and the ghost needs the haunted actor, Hamlet, who will perform and carry out his demands in action. The actor is haunted only to the degree that he or she presents an image that combines the animate and the inanimate, like Craig's Übermarionette. Such a combination constitutes the artfulness of the actor that is something other than imitating or pretending. For the artfulness of the actor, like the artfulness of theatre, is the dimension of the work that exceeds signification and meaning, which for Craig involves ceremony and which I would call the double negative of the actor's presence: not that, and not not that, yet fully perceptible. That dimension belongs in the "perceptual impression theatre makes on the spectator," in Bert States's phrase. "This site is the point at which art is no longer *only* language."[17] So this book about ghosts puts me more in the position of Horatio, a witness who lives to tell the tale, a tale that is fractured, repetitious, doubly redoubling its elements, and, finally, continually open to interpretations that always miss. Ghosts make their presence known symptomatically, in personal and social behavior, in beliefs, in writing, in performance. The ghost needs to speak to Hamlet, not Horatio; but Hamlet needs Horatio to speak for him, and Shakespeare needs the ghost to speak through him. The movement of return and repetition between these figures, Shakespeare, Hamlet, and Horatio, traces the critical differences between the ghost and the living, the discursive and the imaginary, the pragmatic and the productive imagination. Yet they all cooperate in producing each and every *Hamlet.*

In order to "broach" and speak to the ghost, then, as Gordon says we must, we have to recognize it in its living presence, and that requires a certain way of looking that is not a perspective or a "position" vis-à-vis an object but a kind of stereoptic double vision that sees thing and no-thing at once. If a ghost is seen at all, it is with a perhaps clouded eye that is open to time, death, and repetition as they inform our living experiences. To see the ghosts in the empirical world is to remember the dead and their legacies as well as to experience a logically impossible event, one that is both unique and a repetition, singular and double. Such double vision is a vital constituent of theatre, which takes its shape as a double of the world, which appears, disappears, and reappears through performance: each time a singular event; each time a repetition with a difference. Most of us, most of the time, I suspect, are more like Gertrude than Hamlet. "Do you see nothing there?" he asks. "Nothing at all, yet all that is I see." The empiricist has an unclouded eye. To dismiss Hamlet's vision of his father's ghost as a mere symptom of a private pathology, however, is to rationalize and erase those conditions of inheritance and grief that make Hamlet a paradigmatic figure of both modern subjectivity and theatricality itself. On the other hand, to dismiss Gertrude's statement as that of an empiricist is to ignore the strange if not awesome truth in what she says when she says she sees "nothing." The double that is theatre's worldly condition is also a double play between appearance and disappearance; theatre history may stabilize its ghosts by empirical methods, but in performance its ghosts are everywhere.

Ghosts have made the transition between poststructuralist critical theory to postmodern culture. Not only have they become central figures for emerging critical, philosophical, and social epistemologies, they have also made appearances in an array of disciplines: in history, philosophy, anthropology, and sociology, not to mention literature, literary criticism, and literary history. As Rebecca Schneider writes, "Ghosts are particularly postmodern entities."[18] They serve not only to disturb the certainties of empiricism and the confidence in mastery over a field of inquiry but also to complicate distinctions between the scholar and her object, between subjects and objects, personal and political, the past and the present, the living and the dead, materiality and imagination. Schneider's ghosts are "explicitly disembodied signifiers": that is, they have arrived from the Lacanian unconscious to become critiques of culture in which thought, language, narrative, and materiality engage with issues of the real and the representational. These ghosts disturb disciplinary certainties in the distinctions between reality and illusion, truth and falsehood. For if ghosts were patent illusions on the Renaissance stage, they have joined the realm of the real in postmodernism. As a sociologist arguing for complexity in studying the lived effects (and affects) of the past in present experience, Gordon writes, "Haunting is a constituent element of modern social life. It is a generalizable social phenomenon of great import." Furthermore, "ghostly matters are part of social life."[19] The commonality among theatre, ghosts, poststructuralism, and postmodernism lies in the sense of a lack or loss that initiates a crisis of belief.

Perhaps the incursion of ghosts into critical consciousness is simply a sign of millennial anxieties and fears over the "end of history." The marker of year 2000 seems to have brought about a historiographic consciousness of anomalies and problems in the ghostly constitution of history itself. Ghosts began appearing throughout academic writing in the last twenty years of the century: in Avital Ronnell's 1986 book *Dictations: On Haunted Writing;* in Margery Garber's 1987 *Shakespeare's Ghost Writers;* Michel de Certeau's 1988 *The Writing of History;* Terry Castle's 1993 *The Apparitional Lesbian;* and Jacques Derrida's 1994 *The Specters of Marx.* Derrida, of course, has long been interested in ghosts, and his appearance as himself in Ken McMullen's 1983 film, *Ghost Dance,* effectively allowed him to ghost himself. Ghosts appeared in theatre and performance criticism in Elin Diamond's *Unmaking Mimesis,* 1997, as well as in Joseph Roach's *Cities of the Dead,* 1996; Spencer Golub's *Infinity (Stage),* 1999; Jeanette Malkin's *Memory-Theater and Postmodern Drama,* 1999; and, of course, Marvin Carlson's *The Haunted Stage: Theatre as Memory Machine,* 2001. But even earlier than all these, as

Gordon points out, Horkheimer and Adorno had appended a note, "On the Theory of Ghosts," to their 1944 *The Dialectic of Enlightenment*, projecting the need to account for the terrible repetitions of destruction through the twentieth century.

In these scholarly frames, ghosts represent an epistemological or methodological corrective to forms of thought that reduce the world to series of oppositions in order to clarify and control. In an attempt to move into the complexities of lived, affective, sensory, and imaginative experience, combined with the economic and social dimensions of global capitalism, of systematic racism, and gender discrimination, performance studies in particular have moved away from theatre to focus on the material reality of the event rather than illusionistic staging. Yet theatre practice remains, almost a ghost itself, haunting the general sense of performance with its transformations of "action" into art. And it is through art that the paradoxes are felt in the most vital way. What theatre adds to critical thought by virtue of its artfulness is the force of affect, the "perceptual impression" that is indistinguishable from its substance. To put it another way, the ghosts of theatre are perceptions without content. Precisely because theatre is made of sensory but doubtful visibility, doubling and disappearance, matter, memory, action, and speech, it undermines the abstractions of meaning. Deep doubt and its extremity in the confrontation with nothing that is something, with the unintelligible mystery of death, is more than a conceptual position for theatre. The artfulness of theatre needs to raise the hackles of doubt and produce the pleasurable pain of tension between what is and what is not comprehensible, what is and is not living.

One of the dilemmas in using ghosts as a critical trope is that, on the one hand, they remain imaginary figures and can thus be dismissed as imaginary and that, on the other, these figures represent realities so horrifyingly real either personally or historically that the trope may trivialize those realities. In moving from superstition to critical figures, from hair-raising creatures to discursive legitimacy, ghosts are in danger of losing their affective force. The best of the work using a ghost as a critical figure are themselves artful, which is to say they set out not simply to describe or argue but to demonstrate, through either the qualities of prose or the incorporation of multiple kinds of styles and examples. Given a century of an apparently unprecedented scale of violence and mass destruction, the unimaginable torture and annihilation in the Holocaust, the devastation of the atomic bomb in Japan, followed closely by mass exterminations in Stalin's Russia, in Cambodia, Central and South America, Bosnia and Rwanda, to mention only the best known, reality has exceeded imagination. Any distinction between the real and the imaginary is haunted by millions of dead. It can hardly be surprising that at the turn of the millennium there are grateful technological escapes into virtual realities, where the simulation of violence, torture, and death is preferable to the real thing. Nor can it be surprising that there is a contemporary attunement to the voices of the dead calling "Remember me."

The last decade of the twentieth century also produced a great number of books dealing with death, memory, and trauma. In popular psychology as well as the popular press, interest in repressed memory was stable fodder for the 1990s. Inhabiting the twentieth-century landscapes of the dead, where ever fewer survivors of the Holocaust, of Hiroshima and Nagasaki, can tell their stories, the demand to remember is increasingly imperative lest the reality of the terror be forgotten and turned into mere fact. For whatever their value as correctives to idiosyncratic, speculative, or manipulative rhetoric, facts are already signs of forgetting as they provide legitimacy, order, selectivity, and false assurance against the indeterminacies of the lived relations between past and present, the dead and the living. While soothing, facts are themselves spectral, having lost the productive and constituent force of the paradoxical position of doubleness, of "is and is not." Through facts, reality fades through a comforting series of apparent certainties or an apparent ground for opinion or action. The demand to remember, however, cannot depend on facts as they are written, recorded, and archived. The efforts to legitimate repressed memories by subjecting memory to rules of evidence and the law, for example, may at any given historical point rightly designate oppressor and oppressed, perpetrator and victim. The historical and legal determination of what actually happened to people importantly puts some ghosts to rest and serves to prevent the revisionist history that might deny genocide. There are crucial contexts for identifying the differences between ghostly illusions and reality, and I do not want to underestimate those contexts and values. But law is also contingent on historical factors and does not necessarily teach us how to live with ghosts. Ghosts are soon domesticated by law and logic. The twentieth-century history of death has already made a call for an epistemology that can incorporate the incomparable losses that the world has endured, an epistemology that does not explain away the losses, does not comprehend the incomprehensible, does not fill in the blanks, but incorporates those losses with an embodied ethics that does not rely on rationalist principles of an absolute and imaginary justice but is not without reason, an ethics that recognizes both complicity and innocence.

Ghosts and phantoms supply a vocabulary for such an epistemology. Ghosts define the conditions that have become thematic in poststructural thought. But they also make a demand to resist the flattened affect of abstract thought and to stay close to the shiver of the uncanny, the dread, and their uncertain call. Theatre brings them out of their safe confines of thought. Still on the periphery of the more central academic disciplines of philosophy, history, literature, psychology, anthropology, and sociology, theatre has nonetheless become a metaphor within those disciplines. *Performance,* more particularly, has become the term with which to identify a wide and unwieldy range of practices and ideas, from tribal ritual to urban myth, gender constitution to political action, folklore to fashion, identity to impossibility. In turning to theatre and performance as metaphors or analogies, the discourses of those other fields have tended to pass over theatre practices themselves, as though commonsense notions of theatre were sufficient. Judith Butler, for example, has denied that her sense of performance comes from theatre and attributes it explicitly to J. L. Austin's notion of performative speech acts. Yet beginning actors learn that dialogue— speech—is always an action, always doing something, always performative, and wonder what the fuss over Austin is all about. The insights of philosophy, psychoanalysis, and cultural studies have often ended up repeating what theatre has long practiced, as though discovering performance for the first time. Theatre academics, conversely, have often failed to recognize the importance of theatre within an intellectual community and have remained isolated with a kind of willful innocence about doing shows. Theatre has an important place among the thematic concerns of poststructuralism, not because it makes plays about those concerns, but because it is constituted by them. That is, theatre is not so much *about* visibility, doubling, repetition, matter, memory, pretense, action, and speech as it is *made* of them.

In keeping with my sense that ghosts appear in the most ordinary and material circumstances but are generally unrecognized, each chapter considers some overlooked aspect of theatre that harbors what I find to be fundamental issues of ghostly theatricality: repetition, the double, matter, and memory. In the sense that the phenomenon of memory is contingent on what is forgotten or absent, these issues will rehearse the correlations among trauma, death, and the unconscious, between the visible and the invisible, the past and the present. Although each of these is a distinctive set of circumstances and has a very particular set of affective consequences, they will often seem interchangeable to the extent that they meet at the point where the known world turns unfamiliar, uncanny. But theatre itself is a place for turning the elements of a known and familiar world into something unfamiliar, if only to "make them strange."

Chapters 1 and 2 consider time not as it is represented in theatre, but as theatre employs phenomenal time in its multiple aspects of presence, duration, and passage. Both also use the notion of the crypt, as it is used in the psychoanalytic analyses of Nicolas Abraham and Maria Torok, to identify the way in which time can be held still. More than simply a matter of some repressed event or content, and not a matter of some perverse willfulness, the crypt accounts for secrets held back from the flow of time. The crypt is an image for what Walter A. Davis identifies as "the psychic register of those primordial anxieties and affects that we build other psychological theories in order to repress and deny."[20] The image appears in several chapters for the obdurate resistance and encoded mystery that keep the secrets of memory in an unapproachable psychic vault. In "Tonight at 8:00" the issue concerns an individual's encounter with a point in time as it characterizes the resistance of a real present to representation. In "All the Dead Voices" that encounter moves to a broader scope through the idea of repetition and its consequences in matters of historiography and public memorials. Chapters 3 and 4 deal with objects, the properties that make up the material details of theatrical performance. "Objects" looks generally at stage props as objects in transit from a kind of suspended animation on the prop table into motion and meaning. It considers how collection of items like props might model a materialistic historiography that connects the past to the present through the sense of touch. "Empty Chairs" looks specifically at chairs and their functions onstage in relation to memory. Chapter 5, "Double or Nothing," tries to go more directly into how ghosts are produced, or rather how they are the products of the curtain that supposedly divides a real world from an imaginary one. "Ghosts Onscreen," chapter 6, takes the logic of the curtain to film as a technological extension of the question of the seen and the unseen.

"Tonight at 8:00: The Missed Encounter" begins with the fact that most theatre events presume a beginning point in time. Even those experimental pieces that play with an open-ended beginning implicate the convention of a starting moment by their very resistance to one. The arbitrary but practical use of designating when the event begins sets up one of the temporal dimensions that frame a theatrical event. The chapter explores the temporalities of loss that the convention of a given "curtain time" conceals. The agreement between an audience and the stage to begin at a precise moment elides the actual slippage of time. The measure of punctuality, set by a clock, interrupts the self-same flow that constitutes individual dream and somatic time. It punctures the flow with a demand to believe that there are *points* in time. The puncture may be scarcely felt, yet it is a break created by the demand to "be" on time. Any demand to conform to the measurable yet conventional public time of the clock is a demand from something other than the time of the body and the time of the unconscious, which have their own temporalities. The mechanistic governance of time requires an audience to act in accordance with that time by showing up at a named "now." The exactitude implied by the clock idealizes time in such a way as to make a real encounter with now impossible, which is to say it shows an encounter with the real to be impossible except through a representation, which is always in syncopation with now. The demand, however, remains, like the demands of the ghost of old Hamlet to remember and avenge. To encounter the real of a now designated by a clock is thus to encounter a ghost of now that escapes the moment it appears. The ghost remains only in the syncopation of temporal flow, as though the syncopation of time gives time a space in which the now has a kind of duration within which the encounter may be experienced. The model for this syncopation appears in Lacan's account of the "missed encounter" as it occurs in a dream. Exploring Freud's example of a father's dream of his burning child, Lacan outlines a territory "between perception and consciousness," which includes both perception and consciousness but is identical to neither. When he writes that Hamlet is "always at the hour of the Other,"[21] I take it to mean that Hamlet's deferred action has something to do with being caught in the temporality of an impossible demand, a paternal demand, that holds his attention and suspends him in time like a "John a-dreames." When his time becomes his own, which is to say when his consciousness turns from the demand to his own "readiness," he begins to live his own life. The dream aspects of theatre in these terms occur when one recognizes the impossibility of ever really being in time for the beginning, either because the moment of beginning is always about to be or has already been. *Hamlet* is again an enactment of the dilemma in the way that the moment of the father's death has passed and the future act of revenge is deferred, so the play goes on in the duration, which is the syncopation between the past moment and the future moment, which are both moments of nonbeing. The precise moments of death, of that past and future, are known only through the representations of the play, which are the materializations that constitute an audience's encounter with the ghosts of time. When a moment is marked not by an immaterial and ideal sense of time but by a sound, like the bell that alerts Winnie in Beckett's play *Happy Days,* it wakens consciousness from its drift in the real world. In the theater, the bell that calls to the audience to take its seat wakens the audience to the dream reality of the representation. It announces, in effect, as it does to Winnie, we are not yet dead, and sets off another round of memory and recovery.

"All the Dead Voices: Memorial and History" takes up repetition as an alternative to imitative representation and as a form of memorial that does not result in forgetfulness. The historiographic problem of a rupture between past and present and the creation of an other, which Michel de Certeau describes as the foundation of intelligibility in the writing of Western history, is answered theatrically through a repetition and its ultimately spatial encounter with transience. The specificity of voice in a production of *Waiting for Godot* is a way to consider how voice both incorporates and generates an "Irish" identity and history that is not static, conceptual, or whole but perceptual, particular, and cumulative. This leads to a discussion of the sources of identity in performativity and then to a consideration of the way that memory and history turn into spatial images through writing. It suggests that identity categories are imaginary projections of an idealized wholeness that encrypts the mimetic and living transmissions of cultural memory. Theatre is a unique historical medium in which the intersections of text and performance engage both the spatiality of writing and the temporality of speech. That intersection in turn relates to how each element—speech and writing—serves to encrypt the other, each burying the other's memory in its own form of materiality. Writing buries the voice, but voice conversely buries writing, such that each is ghosted by the other. The psychoanalytic concept of incorporation, defined by Nicolas Abraham and

Maria Torok, identifies both a personal pathology and the conditions of cultural inheritances. The image of the crypt thus relates to the writing of history as a spatialized memorial to a lost reality. In theatre, the recovery of writing through the voice of the performer gives a second life to the memory buried in the text.

"Objects: Lost and Found" considers the tactility and three-dimensionality of objects onstage to be a distinctive factor that separates theatre from other visual arts. I use the prop room and table to suggest the suspended, archival situation of objects in transit between worldly usefulness and staged signification. That transit between attachment to the world and isolation on the stage situates objects in a scheme of object relations, wherein the departure or loss of an object is the foundation for the contours of a subject, its attachments and its bereavements. Touch is a mode of both memory and knowledge in a register that attaches the hand and body to other times, places, people. As such, it further suggests an alternative modality for history that does not depend on the "rift" of intelligibility, even while writing supplies the sense of authenticity that informs the touch. The chapter touches on object relations to identify some aspect of the pleasure of touch and its relationship to loss.

The stage object can be seen, then, as a version of subject-object relations not only in a private imaginary stemming from infancy but also in the public and cultural imaginary that constitutes the subject of history. This suggests further that props may also function as memorial devices within the economy of object relations. Using Suzan-Lori Parks's *The America Play*, with its representation of a recovery of history through the recovery of artifacts, the chapter looks at how the material fragments collected from the past are available to the authentication of writing and telling as well as to the commentary of retelling and rewriting history. I look briefly at the way Tadeusz Kantor's work brings fragmentary objects together with the textures of objects as a way not to represent history but, as Michal Kobialka says, to respond to history. Then a look at the theatricality of two objects of very different scale: an installation called "Defenestration," by Brian Goggins, in which furniture flies out the windows of a huge building on a San Francisco street; and "Shattered Anatomies," which is a cardboard box of items assembled by Adrian Heathfield, containing remnants, signs, notes, pictures, and documents of performances by various artists. Both works signal the memorial function of objects.

Finally, the chapter takes the suspended state of prop objects not as an archive alone but as a way of speaking about Heidegger's distinction between an object and a "thing." His discussion brings an alternative view on things, a view that does not use the traumatic sense of loss or forgetfulness, which objects memorialize, but uses an existential sense of things, coming from a void and constituting an elementary emergence of the world in continual change.

The chapter "Empty Chairs: The Memorial Double" examines three uses of chairs to delineate the way in which their staging exemplifies the theatrical double specifically in relation to death. As ubiquitous theatrical props, chairs can identify an aesthetic and social history of staging. But further, from the Oklahoma City National Memorial to Ionesco's play *The Chairs* and finally to Tadeusz Kantor's last work, *Today Is My Birthday,* chairs provide a material site for an intersection and exchange between the living and the dead. They quite literally give a place to situate and recognize the missed encounter of trauma, of death. Abstracting the human form into an object built to receive a human body, chairs both represent the body and resist representation. This chapter begins with a phenomenological meditation on chairs as analogues of human bodies, having character, history, materiality, and identity. Chairs also stand out in the medial position of a body, halfway between a position of authority and one of collapse. An empty or uninhabited chair makes obvious the absence of the human body to which it would give rest, so ghosts are especially apparent in an empty chair. With that absence apparent, these examples show chairs serving as memorial devices, as locales for imaginary projections and social critique, and as doubles for death and loss.

As memorial devices, chairs find their way to the Oklahoma City National Memorial in a different kind of medial position, halfway between memory and forgetfulness. Framed within a designated minute of clock time, those chairs both preserve the impossible moment of meeting death and, upon exit from the space, release the survivors into time. In another context, Eugene Ionesco implicitly employs both the phenomenal presence and the trope of analogy in his play *The Chairs* to stage a critique of bourgeois imagination that is ghosted by his tendency to universalize an existential position toward isolation and death. This section is a close reading of the play in which the very devices Ionesco uses to critique a bourgeois imagination turn around to reveal his own assumptions about universal subjectivity. Kantor appears in this chapter with the chair onstage for the posthumous production of *Today Is My Birthday*. An uncanny representation of the missed encounter with death, his chair onstage, like his double onstage, an actor, was no mere representation of his death and our loss. The final exit of the actor who stood in for Kantor left his chair onstage, creating the moment in experiential time, not clock time, of a real encounter through the vehicle of the double.

"Double or Nothing: Ghosts behind the Curtains" offers some relief from the dominance of psychoanalytic notions in the previous chapters. An early and very different version of this chapter, entitled "Rude Mechanicals," was published in *Theatre Journal*. That version focused primarily on the intersection of the technical laborers who make theatre and the representation onstage. It looked at Marx and at Derrida's commentary in *Specters of Marx* as well as considerations of the ethical relationship between technicians and both onstage performers and far offstage critics and interpreters of drama. Here, the focus is far more directed toward the phenomenon of the curtain, which materializes the concepts of differences between the inside and the outside, true and false. When such dichotomies are produced spatially, they instantiate a sense of reality, or the Real, which is always hidden, but it is the hidden, or the veil, that produces both a momentary pleasure in revelation and the ghost of the Real. The textual example of this is *A Midsummer Night's Dream*, with its infinitely regressing, bottomless dance of reality and representation. That there is nothing—or nothing more than more world—behind the curtain breaks up the conceptual dichotomies and dualistic thought and brings the laborers who make theatre and the public representations of theatre into the cooperative and productive relationship they actually have. The "rude mechanicals" who do the labor of theatre are in a position to see the contradictions and to offer an antidote to ghostly haunting through laughter.

The excursion into film, "Ghosts Onscreen: The Drama of Misrecognition," takes off from the curtain and goes to the screen, where there really is nothing lurking behind. Film is both all production and all image. The chapter also returns to some of the issues of chapter 1, on the missed encounter, with the idea that what we project onto film is constituted by what we miss seeing in ourselves, our blind spot. Three films, George Cukor's *Gaslight*, M. Night Shyamalan's *The Sixth Sense*, and Hitchcock's *Vertigo*, all offer the opportunity to discuss how narratives and technologies of visibility coincide both to represent and to materially exhibit the "missed encounter" and the traumatic void in consciousness through the devices of the blackout and scenic cutting. This chapter is also a reading of the films as ghost stories. It examines the way that a traumatic void syncopates an investigation that moves forward in time against a recovery process that moves backward in time. That process generates images and objects that manifest not simply the return of the repressed but the return of the real in the guise of the unreal, which is the "truth" of ghosts. The encounter with a second or double version of an unknown or unrecognized original reveals the necessity of a second death for an encounter with a real death. The Judy/Madeleine figure of *Vertigo* must die twice in order to reveal Scottie's own trauma and his projections onto the woman, which concealed the real death of the other, unseen woman. It is a story of misapprehension and misrecognition that is ultimately recognized *as* misrecognition, a story that is duplicated by an audience watching the films, in which, like Malcolm Crowe of *The Sixth Sense*, we recognize ourselves as ghosts only after the fact.

Ghost stories told around a campfire will certainly do more than these chapters to say what ghosts are. Such stories are successful because they already displace ghosts from the ordinary world and find them in the atmospheric glow of dim light. But if ghosts hover where secrets are kept and demand that secrets come out from the crypts of time, they are everywhere. Family secrets, the secrets of a heritage, secrets of the past, secrets of oneself, the secrets of time, of life and death, all wait to be unfolded. Some secrets can wait forever. Some compel their ghosts to appear, and the ghosts are impatient for the living to set them right, do them justice, and release them into time. Theatre is where ghosts best make their appearances and let communities and individuals know that we live amid secrets that are hiding in plain sight.

chapter 1

Tonight at 8:00
The Missed Encounter

> You heard the buzzer. You looked at your watch.
> —PETER HANDKE, *Offending the Audience*

The time printed on a ticket may say 8:00 p.m. The more punctual members of an audience will be in their seats waiting while others drift in. But they know that the printed time is a loose approximation for an agreement to meet at a given place and time. The agreed upon time is simply part of modern social cohesion, a conformity that lubricates the mechanisms of social order. The actual curtain time—whether or not there is a curtain—is less exact than the clock, as the house manager waits for latecomers (or any comers), as actors are slow to dress, as a prop (or an actor) goes missing or a costume needs pinning. The buzzer sounds and the audience looks at its collective watch, comparing the clock time with the printed time, comparing the present moment to the moment when the play starts. Handke, above, implies that something rather Pavlovian is at work in the response to the buzzer. The sound stimulates anticipation and the audience asks, "What time is it?" as though the buzzer were not enough to tell them or as though the information on the watch would make some difference. The watch may satisfy some need for comfort or security in knowing what time it is, or perhaps it legislates that special sense of righteousness in determining that the performance is late. The watch is an impartial judge. No matter that each watch might be slightly different. A belief in objective time seems sufficient.

Showing up at the theater on time seems hardly cause for comment. But if it is not strange to play one's part in the social order of time, it is a bit odd to hear about it, as the audience does in Peter Handke's *Offending the Audience.*

Before you came here you made certain preparations. You came here with certain preconceptions. . . . Your thoughts were one step ahead of time. You imagined something. You prepared yourself for something. . . . You went about dressing in a different way. You approached this location from different directions. You used the public transportation system. You came on foot. You came by cab. You used your own means of transportation. Before you got underway, you looked at your watch. . . .[1]

We look at our watches and seem to accept the orderliness if not the necessity in the good manners of being on time. We (the same "we" that is addressed as "you" by Handke) wish to be present at the beginning of the show. We correlate our actions to an abstract measurement of something called time, which eludes definition but works by agreement. "The buzzer sounds" and we go, docile, into the theater. Handke's "offense" makes us self-conscious of our consent to sleepwalk into the theater in hopes of being awakened to *something* in a play or performance but not awakened too harshly. It is not always clear that an audience wouldn't prefer to sleep through a play in self-satisfied, postprandial digestion, and Handke means to wake it up. If performance is always in the present, Handke demonstrates that it is not so easy for an audience to be in the present rather than in the dreamlike state of waking life.

Offending the Audience clarifies how time, especially in the theater, is almost always "out of joint." Multiple time frames tend to intersect as the present of performance meets time past, as when a narrator tells a story, or time future, as when the prologue announces what is about to happen. *Offending the Audience* reminds the audience that their own pasts are included in the present of the performance. It begins with the speakers speaking in the past tense, narrating the audience to itself: you were, you went, you came, you looked. Gradually, this becomes a narrative of a future tense: "You will think of tomorrow. You will gradually find your way back into reality. . . . You will lead your lives again. You will no longer be a unit."[2] And finally the speakers move into the present in the tenseless form of invective, "You deadbeats. You phonies. You milestones in the history of the theater. You historic moments. You immortal souls. You positive heroes. You abortionists. You anti-heroes. . . . You comrades you, you worthy listeners you, you fellow humans you."[3] Handke accomplishes here a rare conformity between the speech and presence. The representation *to* an audience *of* the audience's presence is spoken in the form of name calling. Verbs disappear, as though speech were outside the frame of time. The play brings the present into conscious articulation by initially using and then discarding the temporal forms of narrative that generally give shape to the present of performance. In doing so, it implicitly argues for an erasure of time.

Toward the beginning of the play, the speakers—for there are no characters here—outline what amounts to a history of mimesis and the many roles that theatre has played.

> Time was played. Since time was played, reality was played. The theater played tribunal. The theater played arena. The theater played moral institution. The theater played dreams. . . . Instead of time staying out of play, an unreal and uneffective time transpired. With the unreal time an unreal reality was played. It was not there, it was only signified to you, it was performed. Neither reality nor play transpired here. If a clean play had been played here, time could have been left out of play. A clean play has no time. . . . But since reality was part of the play here, there were always two times: your time, the time of the spectators, and the played time, which seemed to be the real time. But time cannot be played. It cannot be repeated in any play. Time is irretrievable. Time is irresistible. Time is unplayable. Time is real. It cannot be played as real.[4]

The play Handke seems to prefer would be in real time, as football games are. His indictment against bourgeois theatre and its representation of an imaginary past is perfectly apt, and the way Handke brings the audience around into the present by eliminating verbs altogether is at least theoretically successful. A question worth asking, however, is whether or to what degree the present time of the audience is ever fully free of past and future. What does it mean to say "Time is real?" Clock time may easily be seen as arbitrary, and the past represented by a play may be easily seen as imaginary. The harder question is whether there is anything real to measure or to falsify in the first place.

Another way into the question is through the interval between the sound of the buzzer that calls an audience into its seats and the beginning of the play. "You heard the buzzer. You looked at your watch." What is the relation between time as an interval composed by the buzzer and the play's slippery beginning on the one hand and the point marked by a watch on

the other? What is the *sense* of an interval of time? One speaks of it in spatial terms, as though an experience of duration were a fragment marked
out on a line of time. More than simply an abstract temporal shape, however, the interval marks a difference between a sensory stimulus or bodily
perception and a representation of the present on the face of a watch. That
is to say the interval is the temporal space that takes elements from both
the present of physical sensation (perception) and the remembered or the
anticipatory consciousness that knows or, rather, represents time. The relation between the two, physical and conceptual, is syncopated in the interval, an interval that Gertrude Stein particularly hated about theatre as it
unfolded dramatic stories through time, demanding that the audience both
remember and anticipate. We tend to elide the difference and the syncopation in the practical world, and narratives have their own kind of pleasures,
as Roland Barthes pointed out in *The Pleasure of the Text*. The play of time
in theatre, however, works through the paradoxes of time in the difference
between the present and its syncopations with the calculations of time that
are contained in the present. As Nelson Goodman asked about art in general, *when* is it theatre? The present is real but also not entirely available,
thanks to the difference between somatic and mental representations of
time. Objective time exists only as a representation of something that escapes
objectification. Such an absurdity is the dilemma of time, which is both
where and how ghosts appear. "But in all that," says Beckett in *Waiting for
Godot,* "what truth will there be?" What do we know by knowing what time
it is? Time is a duplicitous phenomenon. Virginia Woolf in *The Waves* puts
it this way:

> But it is a mistake, this extreme precision, this orderly and military progress;
> a convenience, a lie. There is always deep below it, even when we arrive
> punctually at the appointed time with our white waistcoats and polite for-
> malities, a rushing stream of broken dreams, nursery rhymes, street cries,
> half-finished sentences and sights—elm trees, willow trees, gardeners sweep-
> ing, women writing—that rise and sink even as we hand a lady down to
> dinner.[5]

It might be nice to believe that only one thing happens at a time, but as
Woolf's array suggests, not only do many things go on all at one time, but
things are also rising and sinking, coming and going, falling away and

repeating themselves like waves, and one moment succeeds to the next. Social niceties and the conveniences of punctuality tend to wash away the multiplicities of time and space. Nonetheless, to ask any questions of time leads to difficulties.

Augustine put his dilemma of time this way: "Take the two tenses, past and future. How can they 'be' when the past is not now present and the future is not yet present? Yet if the present were always present, it would not pass into the past: it would not be time but eternity. If then, in order to be time at all, the present is so made that it passes into the past, how can we say that this present also 'is'? The cause of its being is that it will cease to be."[6] The further dilemma for Augustine is that we speak meaningfully of a long or short time: "But how can something be long or short which does not exist?"[7] He goes on to ask, "If future and past events exist, I want to know where they are. If I have not the strength to discover the answer, at least I know that wherever they are, they are not there as future or past, but as present."[8] Thus, for Augustine neither past nor present exists except as part of the present, or more exactly as "a present of things past, a present of things present, a present of things to come."[9] He supplements the notion of a "threefold present" with the idea of measuring time through an "extension" of sound as it makes a sense impression and is held in mind. With a sound that begins, resonates, and ends, one measures not the time but the "space of time" or extension it created, that is, the "distance" between beginning and end. That measurement can occur only after the sound has ended, so what one is measuring is the *memory* of the sound. The length of an ongoing sound is impossible to measure because it has not yet ended. With alternating lengths of time—long and short syllables in a hymn is his example—come the possibility of comparison or difference. But what finally is measured is not the syllables but their duration taken from sense impressions and held, again, in memory. "The impression which passing events make upon you [mind/memory] abides when they are gone. That present consciousness is what I am measuring, not the stream of past events which have caused it. When I measure periods of time, that is what I am actually measuring. Therefore either this is what time is, or time is not what I am measuring."[10] Time may thus still not exist as a thing independent of the consciousness that experiences and holds it. The measurement of time is a measurement of consciousness.[11] How, asks Augustine, could the future become consumed or the past increase, "unless there are three processes in the mind which in this is the active agent? For the mind expects and attends and remembers, so that what it expects passes through what has its attention to what it remembers."[12]

Time exists for Augustine but presents untenable paradoxes when he tries to apprehend it as a thing in itself. It appears, like a ghost, from the consciousness that perceives it, which is to say it is both real and imaginary, a projection from consciousness, but necessarily and materially real. It is a capacity of consciousness to perceive difference and duration, to anticipate and recollect. Past, present, and future are not attributes of time but our means of perceiving change and duration. From this perspective even the disappearance of performance is a perception. This is a discomforting, enigmatic proposition, because disappearance happens and time exists. How could a perception be a perception of nothing? One is inclined to say with Augustine, "My God, protect me and rule me. [Or with Hamlet, 'Angels and ministers of grace defend us' (1.4.39).] Who will tell me that there are not three times, past, present and future, as we learnt when children and as we have taught children, but only the present, because the other two have no existence?"[13]

Can there then be *only* a present of performance? Augustine's logic says that if there were only the present, it would not be time but eternity—a logic he argues against. Can there be a present that does not also hold the memories and anticipations and therefore the disjunctions of the perception of time, past, present, and future? Can there be, in Handke's words, a "clean play"? To put it another way, can the three temporalities of consciousness, past, present, future, fully coincide? Can psyche and soma temporize in anything but a syncopation?

One of the most fruitful areas for examining such questions, or for raising further questions, is in the relationship between the world of real time—of time in the world and all its arbitrary measures—and the world of dreams. The question of the relationship between what is actual and what is represented in dreams concerned Freud since the time of his first major work, published in 1900, *The Interpretation of Dreams*. Initially, that work seems to avoid questions of temporality. What mechanism, he wonders, could refer to known events in daily life and at the same time transform them? In naming the psychic mechanisms as condensation, displacement, and substitution, he invokes the connections of language to experience, words, images, and affects. He also uses that dream work to develop his theories about the transformations between the real world and individual psyches. Late in *Interpretation,* he cites what he calls a "model dream." But rather than leading to the methods of interpretation he had developed up to that point, Freud cites this dream as an indicator of the "incompleteness of our psychology of dreams." Where interpretation does not present a problem, he says, one can look beyond meaning to the clues that the dream gives about more general functions of psychical processes. "There is no possibility of *explaining* dreams as a psychical process, since to explain a thing means to trace it back to something already known, and there is at the present time no established psychological knowledge under which we could subsume what the psychological examination of dreams enables us to infer as a basis for their explanation."[14]

Moving into unknown, unexplored territory, Freud is about to articulate his theories of censorship, repression, and regression. The dream as he reports it is well known:

A father had been watching beside his child's sick-bed for days and nights on end. After the child had died, he went into the next room to lie down, but left the door open so that he could see from his bedroom into the room in which his child's body was laid out, with tall candles standing round it. An old man had been engaged to keep watch over it, and sat beside the body murmuring prayers. After a few hours' sleep, the father had a dream that *his child was standing beside his bed, caught him by the arm and whispered to him reproachfully: "Father, don't you see I'm burning?"* He woke up, noticed a bright glare of light from the next room, hurried into it and found that the old watchman had dropped off to sleep and that the wrappings and one of the arms of his beloved child's dead body had been burned by a lighted candle that had fallen on them.[15]

In citing this dream, Freud takes for granted that its meaning is clear, if overdetermined. He assumes it must derive from a combination of real events before the dream, events during the dream, and the dreamer's "wish" to stay asleep in order to keep the image of his son alive. Dream content, like the other elements of the psyche, cannot be traced to a single source or work in the linear flow of time from the future through the present into the past. Rather, the dream comes from multiple sources in the multiple psychic times: some identifiable, actual, somatic; some a matter of memory, and all its faults, from the past; some from the imaginary and emotional processing. It is likely, he says, that the phrase "I'm burning" might well have been spoken during the child's illness and that "Father, don't you see" could easily have been a repetition of "some other highly emotional situation of which we are in ignorance." At the same time, the wish to keep the image of his son alive, as he appeared in the dream, kept the father from waking to the real fire, even while the real fire was creating part of the dream images. "If the father had woken up first and then made the inference that led him to go into the next room, he would, as it were, have shortened his child's life by that moment of time."[16] Having already made his case for the meaning of dreams to be found as "wish-fulfillment" and their content to be formed by condensation, displacement, and substitution, Freud then uses this dream to indicate the power of the psychic censor that prevents unconscious contents from coming to consciousness. He begins his argument by claiming that the common experience of forgetting one's dreams signals the activity of psychic censorship that operates even more emphatically in waking consciousness.

Jacques Lacan takes up this same dream to explore the ways in which the trauma of a missed encounter is repeated. He first writes of his own dream that was formed around an actual knocking at his door before he woke from a nap. "And when I awake, it is in so far as I reconstitute my entire representation around this knocking—this perception—that I am aware of it."[17] In other words, the somatic perception of the knocking is known by consciousness only when it is recovered through its representation *in* the dream. The body hears, but consciousness registers the sound only from within the dream. The knocking woke him, but he stayed asleep long enough to dream of the knocking. The time between dreaming and waking is unknown, unexperienced, if indeed there is any time between them at all. The unconscious can be apprehended only in terms of a "non-temporal locus," and the "experience of rupture, between perception and consciousness." The question for Lacan is how the dream, "the bearer of the subject's desire, [can] produce that which makes the trauma emerge repeatedly?" The dream is an explicit space, he says. "Reality is in abeyance there, awaiting attention." The dream state is "another locality, another space, another scene, *the between perception and consciousness.*"[18]

If a fundamental desire in dreams is to prolong sleep, what is it that wakes the father to his burning child? The call to wakening, Lacan answers, comes from within the dream itself, from the speech of the child, "Father, can't you see I'm burning?" He goes on:

> Is there not more reality in this message than in the noise by which the father also identifies the strange reality of what is happening in the room next door. Is not the missed reality that caused the death of the child expressed in these words? . . .
>
>   . . . Is not the dream essentially, one might say, an act of homage to the missed reality—the reality that can no longer produce itself except by repeating itself endlessly, in some never attained awakening? What encounter can there be henceforth with that forever inert being—even now being devoured by the flames—if not the encounter that occurs precisely at the moment when, by accident, as if by chance, the flames come to meet him? Where is the reality in this accident, if not that it repeats something actually more fatal *by means of* reality, a reality in which the person who was supposed to be watching over the body still remains asleep, even when the father re-emerges after having woken up?
>
>   Thus the encounter, forever missed, has occurred between dream and awakening, between the person who is still asleep and whose dream we will not know and the person who has dreamt merely in order not to wake up. . . .
>
>   . . . Desire manifests itself in the dream by the loss expressed in an image at the most cruel point of the object. It is only in the dream that this truly unique encounter can occur. Only a rite, an endlessly repeated act, can commemorate this not very memorable encounter—for no one can say what the death of a child is, except the father *qua* father, that is to say, no conscious being.[19]

"No conscious being" implies that consciousness itself is always in some sense false consciousness to the degree that consciousness is a representing mechanism and is always somewhat retarded. The delay between perception and consciousness, that is, composes an interval of time. The sound of the actual fire, in other words, is less real than the reality of the message from within the dream, because the father is unconscious of the sound while he is occupied in the dream. The somatic perception, claims Lacan, is less effective in waking the father than its representation in the dream. The call to wake up to the immediate fire is already too late, but the tardiness of the message repeats the tardiness that makes it impossible to be present in the moment of the death of the other. The reality of that impossibility repeats in some never attained awakening. Simply because one has to take notice of the death of the other, that notice cannot coincide with the moment of death, which in any case is not in a single moment but in a slower leave-taking that has no absolute point in time, only a before and an after, which are representations of the moments surrounding death. More significantly in that passage, the actuality of the fire becomes the means by which the reality of the failed encounter repeats itself, like an automaton, in reality.

If I set Lacan's always dense articulation next to the sharper paradoxes of time in Augustine's queries, the reading of the dream comes quite close to the position that the present cannot exist because "the cause of its being is that it will cease to be"; that is, it would not be time but eternity. Where Augustine goes on to present the capacities of the mind or human consciousness to be the source of time's threefold present if not the source of time itself, the psychoanalytic addition of an unconscious presents a further dimension to time that might be close to an "eternal present," or at least an atemporal absence of differentiations between past, present, and future. A psychoanalytic view of the unconscious suggests that time not only flows in and out from future through present into past but is also held "in" the unconscious, as the unconscious. Though it is difficult not to think of the unconscious as a containing space, even Freud tried to articulate its operations as something closer to what might now be said to have "emergent" properties. That is, the unconscious is not a reservoir but a set of potentials that are activated under certain conditions. If the moment of the father's encounter with his child's death must be missed because the present of consciousness continually ceases to be, it is nonetheless permanent in the potentialities of the unconscious that "knows" no time; it is constant for the body that is always in the present. This reflects the psychoanalytic idea that there is no time in the unconscious.

The relation between time's passage in consciousness and time held as a set of potentials in the unconscious thus involves a gap or syncopation. That gap or void acts as a kind of vacuum to pull the missed present out of the unconscious into repetition via dreams and images, to be repeated not as the "same" present but in the present *again*. This may help to explain why Lacan can say there is "more" reality in the dream than in the sound of the flames next door. It is the mind's awareness not of the world but of the representation of the perception—the knock on the door, the smell of smoke—from within the dream that wakes the dreamer to the world. Rather than clarifying a distinct difference between being awake and being asleep, however, the temporal syncopation confuses their order like a chicken and an egg. We easily slip into the paradox of the butterfly dream of Chuang-Tzu (Did Chuang-Tzu dream he was a butterfly, or did the butterfly dream he was Chuang-Tzu?) or the question of Vladimir in *Waiting for Godot:* "Was I sleeping while the others suffered? Am I sleeping now? Tomorrow, when I wake, what shall I say of today?"[20]

Cathy Caruth elaborates on Lacan's reading of the "Father, can't you see" dream by saying that the call to awaken from within the dream "represents a paradox about the necessity and impossibility of confronting death. . . . Waking up in order to see, the father discovers that he has once again *seen too late* to prevent the burning. The relation between the burning within and the burning without is thus neither a fiction (as in Freud's interpretation) nor a direct representation, but a *repetition* that reveals in its temporal contradiction, how the very bond of the father to the child . . . is linked to the missing of the child's death. To awaken is thus precisely to awaken only to one's repetition of a previous failure to see in time."[21] Caruth is talking here about the syncopation of the gap. It is the gap, the absence of consciousness, or failure to coincide, that gets repeated as a structure more than with any particular content. The dreamer's emergence and reentry to the "zone" of Lacan's "between perception and consciousness" demonstrate that the core of the missed encounter with an origin, as with an end, is a temporal syncopation, because (in Augustine's terms) the present cannot be measured while it is happening. The zone between perception and consciousness is the present that is always missed. Awakening to the burning child, the dreamer is already late. He can no more perceive the start than he can the end, for both events are in the present. Both beginning and end are representable only through repetitions that never fully match the present actuality of what happened. Only in accepting the reality of trauma and the absences it creates within representation does one awake to the reality of repetition as a difference that comes from within. What becomes most crucial in this acceptance and awakening is—for the analyst as much as the audience, not to mention for the creators of theatre—how to come into contact with the other and how to suture the space of difference between consciousness that can represent the present only as past or future and the somatic present.

Freud, Lacan, and Caruth each interpret this dream to illustrate the mechanisms of a profound psychic absence. Freud uses it as a premise to explore the psychic censorship at work. He brings it into *The Interpretation of Dreams* where he wants to show that forgetfulness signals not simply an absence but a meaningful function in psychic dynamics. He is also in the process of developing his interpretive techniques and the value of free association that will become one of the hallmarks of psychoanalysis. Regarding dream interpretation, he says that "the very thing whose value we have undertaken to assess may slip completely through our fingers."[22] Freud asks the patient to repeat the dream. The repetition enables him to take special note when the language used to describe the dream changes. He calls the change a sign of a weak spot in the censoring mechanism. The censor takes pains to deflect attention to the meaningful parts by omitting some aspect or demurring to the significance or doubting memory. Where the dreamer doubts memory, the analyst notes resistance to analysis. Doubt is seen as a protective cover to the dream's secrets. The most vulnerable aspects of the dream are those that do not carry the manifest emotional intensity or most symbolic elements. Doubt thus locates the very issues that have been hidden.

Freud's own account of the burning child dream, however, could easily be an example of the principle of censorship. One of the strangest aspects in all the accounts of the dream is that the original dreamer is completely unknown.

> It was told to me by a woman patient who had herself heard it in a lecture on dreams: its actual source is still unknown to me. Its content made an impression on the lady, however, and she proceeded to "re-dream" it, that is, to repeat some of its elements in a dream of her own, so that, by taking it over in this way, she might express her agreement with it on one particular point.[23]

Each commentator uses the burning child dream to express agreement with it on one particular point, but none seems to attend to the absent dreamer. The real dreamer becomes the ghost within the series of narrative machineries that endlessly displace his reality at the same time that they seek to recover it. The dream is mediated by a lecturer, by the lady patient, by Freud, then by Lacan and Caruth, and here, by me. Out of the text in each case comes the ghost of the dreamer, who is hiding in plain sight as the unre-coverable origin of the missed encounter. Also hiding, however, is just that one particular point with which that lady patient agreed. The transference of the story of the dreamer from one narrator to another, from lecturer to lady, from lady to Freud, is a series of displacements from the missing dreamer. Each one repeats the missing encounter in the act of telling the story of the missing encounter. In other words, there is more to each inter-pretation than the manifest content of the dream. Each time the dream is told, the origin is missing, and its absence lies between the telling and the interpretation. The poignancy lies not only in the terrible identification with a parent who has lost a child and wakes from a dream of burning to find the child's body burning but also in the repeated absence of the real dreamer.

The lecturer, the lady, Freud, and subsequence critics and interpreters: we each displace the story onto an imaginary other, yet each of us carries the story along as though identifying with the missing dreamer. More sig-nificantly, however, in what way can a present reader resist turning that original loss into an object belonging to another? The alternative is to rec-ognize that loss constitutes not just the other or the self alone but also the common intersubjective space. This recognition is the demand put to the reader, the analyst, the audience. The content of the story or the represen-tation is a screen whose opacity both conceals and reveals the lost traumatic origin. These multiplying unknowables, however, are replicated in the absences in Freud's narrative but also confirm his assertions that the source of dreams is overdetermined by multiple time frames and multiple repre-sentations; that the sources are both actual and imaginarily transformed; and that the psychology of dreams is incomplete.

The method that Freud derives thus concerns giving attention to all those elements that seem to be accidental, trivial, doubtful, without significance. He cites such phenomena as assonance, verbal ambiguity, temporal coinci-dence, and associative links without apparently meaningful (rational) con-nections as the means for tracing the pathways through a psychic apparatus. Those peripherals carry the latent content that is in excess of conscious contents, for consciousness is already a selective mechanism that winnows out the details of perception in service to significance. Consciousness func-tions in relation to memory and relies on memory traces to provide a sys-tem for the creation of significance. Those memory traces, what might now be called more simply long-term memory, consist in permanent modifications of the elements of the systems.[24] If, Freud says, the perceptions available to waking consciousness lead progressively to motor functions (to doing something about it), the perceptions within the dream lead regressively toward the sensory end.[25] In characterizing the relation of sensory perception to conscious and unconscious systems, he differentiates between systems that retain permanent traces and those that remain open to modification. "We shall suppose that a system in the very front of the apparatus receives the perceptual stimuli but retains no trace of them and thus has no memory, while behind it there lies a second system which transforms the momentary excitations of the first system into permanent traces."[26] In an exploratory way, Freud is opening the way to identifying the form of trauma as an unrecorded but repeated event that he will later develop in "Beyond the Pleasure Principle." Here, in the dream work, he is still concerned to develop a quasi-scientific basis for the function of verbal and imagistic anomalies that give him clues to the operation of the psyche. And he has left his own traces of doubt, accident, and omission in the details of the work. While he failed to follow up on the admission that the actual source of the burning child dream is unknown, he also revealed its significance in his recognition of incompleteness, censorship, and regression. That is, Freud's own work repeats the failure to complete a theory that matches the experience of his patients and of his work with those patients. His desire to find the laws that govern that reality tend to be revealed in the absences between what calls him to such laws and what confronts him in practice.

Frances Yates opens her scholarly work *The Art of Memory* with the story of Simonides, the Greek poet who invented the "art" of memory. At a banquet of the wealthy Scopas, Simonides had honored both his host and the twin gods Castor and Pollux with a lyric. Scopas responded by saying that he would pay for only half the poem of praise. The other half of the payment, said the host, would have to come from the gods. Shortly after, Simonides received a message that two young men were waiting for him outside and wanted to see him. Leaving the banquet hall, Simonides looked for the two, but they were not to be found. While he was out, the roof of the hall collapsed, crushing all the guests beyond recognition. Simonides then helped to identify the remains of the bodies by remembering where they were sitting in the hall.

From this story, the art of memory came to be associated with the devices of placement in space and images. Like the later *Ad Herennium,* the classical techniques of memorization involved an image of a space or building with various rooms and the objects they contained: forecourt, bedrooms, parlors, statues, niches. But a major factor in the story of Simonides apparently has little to do with the art of memorization and has no place in the later commentaries of Cicero or of Yates herself. That is the mysterious intervention of the invisible twins, Castor and Pollux. They are present in the story only in the form of a message that lures Simonides away from the space. The source of the message is left to imagination and supposition and to the logical irony that the twin gods did indeed give payment to Simonides by saving his life. Those unknown visitors, as the Greek gods in general, signify a fatality that may bring salvation or destruction. The key issue here is both the absence of the gods and the absence of Simonides from the disaster that struck the banquet hall. In focusing on the story as an example of the spatialization of memory, Yates leaves out the contingency of the development of memory on the initial, if miraculous, absence from the disaster. Memory and its arts are thus the specific talents of the survivor of the disaster. Recollection of who and what went before are contingent on the miraculous absence of the poet and his escape from the disaster itself. He remembers the past but was not present in the moment of devastation. And he reconstructs the past in order for the dead to be identified and buried, since the disaster erased all the particularities of its victims. Memory and its artful devices are thus the bridge that spans the disaster, a bridge that is unnecessary except for the disaster. In this sense, memory is a repetition of space and place that encompasses the very absences and placelessness that made it necessary and possible. Castor and Pollux are the wonders or marvels that make the story uncanny but are quickly dismissed as the story of memory turns to the pragmatic aftereffects of developing the art. They appear in an interval of the story by not appearing, which is to say, like the absent dreamer in Freud, they are the ghosts who haunt the representations of the living.

The superficial, unlikely, trivial, meaningless, omitted, even formal, elements similarly provide the irrational, marvelous, or wonderful character of dreams as well as the clues to their sources. They trace the associative paths toward the trauma that cannot otherwise reveal itself, because it was never set into representation at its originating moment. This is precisely where the aspects of words and images generally relegated to formal aesthetics enter the domain of a call to awakening. Freud concerns himself largely with the latent content of dreams in *The Interpretation of Dreams,* but manifest and formal elements offer the character and clues to sources that exceed any rational or translatable content. Found in poetic language as well as the poetry of the stage, those aspects loosely known as style locate the excess that for Julia Kristeva, among others, constitutes "desire in language." In other words, regardless of the conclusions that Freud reaches concerning censorship or regression, or the perceptual-memory system that he further develops in *Interpretation,* he is telling us where to look, what to listen for, and how to trace the reality of what is left out of representation, as though that absence were an excess. That excess is irreducible to content, but it nonetheless carries cultural history, the traces of a past, and the trajectory of desires. It comes from and leads toward the repetition of the traumatic break between consciousness and experience. The manifest or obviously symbolic content of a dream, as of a play, is the easy part, for in grasping that meaningful content we satisfy an element of the pleasure in mastery over the objects of the world. We can dominate, hold, and use that content, however provisional. Didactic content in particular places us in the happy position of being both in control of the other and unconcerned with our responsibility to the other. What exceeds the grasp of meaning, however, are those corporeal elements (such as poetic language and the sound of a bell) that divorce the object from significance and yet are played, like foreign agents, within and against the field of significance. For the theatre maker as much as for the patient, it is often the interference of consciousness that censors the play of these elements in the creation of the public dream. The function of the play in theatre is thus to serve as an awakening to the real from within the dream of the fiction. Theatre, that is, occurs when we wake to the present to find that seeing is seeing *as.*

As Caruth works out the enigma of the psyche's relation to reality, she cites a passage from Lacan at the opening of her essay, "Traumatic Awakenings": *"Les désirs entretiennent les rêves. Mais la mort, elle, est du côté du rêveil"* (Desires sustain dreams. But death, that, is at the edge of (on the side of) awakening).[27] Caruth attributes to Lacan the recognition that "the psyche's relation to the real [is] not a simple matter of seeing or of knowing the nature of empirical events, not as what can be known or what cannot be known about reality, but as the story of an urgent responsibility, or what

Lacan defines, in this conjunction, as an *ethical* relation to the real."[28] This, then, becomes the story of the relation of psychoanalysis to the real, but also of psychoanalysis as an occasion for the creation of an intersubjective space and a relationship of transference, of love. That transference is real and concrete but, as in theatre, is also founded on an absent relationship and a relationship to absence, or the space of difference. It is a relationship founded on not simply the real of the analytic or of the theatrical occasion but that occasion as a repetition of the loss at the edge of or alongside consciousness. Repetition offers possibilities for intersubjectivity through representation conditioned by memory, recovery, and recognition on the part of the audience. The demand is that we recognize the reality of ghosts and haunting. It is not theatre in general that necessarily or inevitably elicits those ghosts, but it is also not without theatre, the effigy of the real, that they appear—hence the theatricality of the analytic encounter in the move from transference to symbolization. The space between analyst and analysand repeats the reality of the syncopation between what really happened and what is recorded; the theatre of the analytic event opens up to the moment of awakening from the trauma to consciousness in a symbolization of the loss that is being repeated but without a known or knowable origin.

> The relation to the real that is to be found in the transference was expressed by Freud when he declared that nothing can be apprehended *in effigie, in absentia*—and yet is not the transference given to us as an effigy and as relation to absence? We can succeed in unraveling this ambiguity of the reality involved in the transference only on the basis of the function of the real in repetition.[29]

This demand to recognize loss at the edge of awakening seems utterly abstract in the language of psychoanalysis, though it is concrete in practice. Certain works, however, can place the demand, the recognition, the awakening, in its context of mundane reality, where it actually belongs. François Ozon's film *Sous le sable (Under the Sand)*, with Charlotte Rampling, is one such work. In that film, a comfortable, middle-aged married couple go on vacation to the family home near the ocean. The husband, possibly depressed, possibly not, goes for a swim while his wife sleeps on the beach in the sand. When she wakes, he is gone; he has disappeared without a trace, without a witness. She goes to the police, she waits at the house, she drives back to Paris. In the next scene, she is at a dinner party, teasing the host about his lack of exercise and urging him to join her husband at the gym on Saturday. It should be a flashback scene, but it quickly becomes clear that she is in denial about his loss. The husband, however, appears in the very next scene, and she talks to him about the dinner and the host. While Rampling's character, Marie, puts away dishes in the cupboard, there is a shot of her face, in shock. She recovers, sits at the table, and butters toast for her husband, Jean, telling him she does not want to go to work but to stay home with him. Yet we see her teaching, reading from Virginia Woolf's *The Waves*. With Vincent, her eager suitor, she speaks of her husband in the present tense. Alone, on a bed, she feels the hands of both her husband and of Vincent caressing her. When told that she must declare her husband dead in order to get access to money, Marie says she will speak to him about it. She ignores a call from the police to return to identify a body that has washed up. She discovers, however, after paying for his prior visit to a doctor, that he had been taking antidepressants, and when she reports to his mother that he may have committed suicide, we no longer know the extent of her denial or the extent of her acceptance, for she slips almost seamlessly between absolute certainty of his presence and practical actions based on his absence. The mother, with aged, vicious spite, tells her that in Jean's family "we do not commit suicide" and also that Jean had said he was no longer in love with Marie, that he wanted to leave her. Eventually Marie returns to the seaside. She demands not only to identify the swim trunks and watch recovered by the police but also to see the bloated, putrefied body that was found. As the police hand her a watch, she laughs and says, "No, absolutely not, this is not his watch." "But Madame, it is exactly as you described it to us." "I am his wife and I should know." Returning to the beach, she weeps. But looking up, she sees a man in the distance. In the long final shot, she runs toward him, her footprints tracing a curved line in the sand. The camera, however, foreshortens the distance, and it is impossible to get a sense of how much space is between them and whether she might be running toward him or past him.

The film's use of Woolf's book *The Waves* and the return of the watch give clues to this story beyond the obvious issue of a woman in denial. In one sense the film is a clear example of the missed encounter with her husband's disappearance. Marie's bafflement at his loss is not just whether he is alive or dead, whether by suicide or by accident, but the bafflement of death that must always seem an accident, impossible to comprehend, impossible to locate in a moment. It happens only when one is not looking, because it cannot be seen. The contrast between that moment and the endless repetition of waves sets out the mixtures of temporalities. Making up the substance of that story are the visual and tactile details of everyday life: spaghetti in a pot of boiling water, the buttering of toast, a red dress. These are set against repetition in images of sameness: the long horizon of the shoreline and the steady march of waves coming in to shore. Death is the bar between the comfort of daily objects, ordinary desires, and the vast space of the ocean, its repetitious sameness. In refusing to take the watch as his, Marie keeps time attached to her husband, indefinitely. Whether she will run toward that infinity or past it and back to daily life remains open at the end. Yet it is also her own death, projected into the death of time in the death of the other, that keeps her suspended, refusing to mourn. The alternation between kinds of time, the time of things and that of infinity, both locked by the missed encounter with death, connects the film to Woolf's book.[30] Locked there, life occurs but is suspended in the time of the other, under the gaze of the specter of death.

The knock on the door, the smell of smoke, the sound of the buzzer, the feel of objects: sensory perceptions are supposed to wake us up from sleep or bring us into the theatre to pay attention. Rather than a definitive division between perceptive wakefulness and imaginary dreaming, however, the more common state of quotidian life is already "somewhere between" perception and the waking habits that keep us half asleep to reality. Handke makes the audience notice that state. Samuel Beckett will have us observe it. In Beckett's play *Happy Days,* Winnie, the woman buried to her waist in a mound of dirt, cannot fall fully asleep, but neither is she fully awake. Her habits keep her going and keep her only half aware that "grain upon grain" her days are drifting away in time. As Beckett put it to James Knowlson:

> Well I thought that the most dreadful thing that could happen to anybody, would be not to be allowed to sleep so that just as you're dropping off there'd be a 'Dong' and you'd have to keep awake; you're sinking into the ground alive and it's full of ants; and the sun is shining endlessly day and night and there is not a tree. . . . There'd be no shade, nothing and that bell wakes you

up all the time and all you've got is a little parcel of things to see you through life.[31]

A bell wakes the figure of Winnie at the beginning of each act and rings throughout the second. At its sound she opens her eyes. Each time she is about to nod off in the second act, it sounds. Waking again and again, she handles the things that make up her daily regimen: the toothbrush and paste, her handkerchief, her spectacles, her parasol, her medicine, her mirror, her lipstick. She reminisces about the past, sitting on Charlie Hunter's knees, her old loves. She passes time looking for responses from Willie. She counts the time and anticipates an end: "It is perhaps a little soon—to make ready—for the night . . . and yet I do—make ready for the night— feeling it at hand—the bell for sleep—saying to myself—Winnie—it will not be long now, Winnie—until the bell for sleep."[32] Closing her eyes in remembrance, it rings ("hurts like a knife"); calling to "the eye of the mind," the bell rings and she opens her eyes.

> Long pause. A bell rings piercingly, say ten seconds, stops. She does not move. Pause. Bell more piercingly, say five seconds. She wakes. Bell stops. She raises her head, gazes front. Long pause.[33]

Ten seconds is a very long time to hear a piercing bell. It is an effective assault on the sense of hearing. It effectively, phenomenally, marks the moment of awakening—and of sleeplessness—not just for Winnie, but for the audience as well. It marks the singularity of that moment but does so from within the fiction/dream of the stage representation. Does the audience wake up too? Winnie's bell marks the moment for the sudden awakening from within the dream. In a certain sense, it is louder than an everyday bell, because it is framed by the play and is therefore a repetition or representation of itself. It is entirely possible to hear Winnie's bell and not hear it as a repetition, of course. Even the senses can be coerced by denial, by habit, by the refusal to be affected by phenomena when they are framed within representation. An attentive audience that is attuned by grief to the losses in/of time may wake up from within the dream/representation to the sound of the different bell that is the same; it may wake up along with Winnie to its own repetitious habits that get us through a conventional day while, bit by bit, grain upon grain, we are buried by the present. From within the representation of the play, that wake-up bell makes the kind of demand on Winnie that daily life insists on: endlessly repetitious until the anticipated end. Each bell is always the first one, however, because it marks a beginning, even if that beginning is a return or a repetition. The sound marks the difference between waking and sleeping, but this happens only if one actually hears that second bell *as* the second one. As Jesus said, in what might be read as a phenomenological mood, in the gospel of Mark (8:18), "Having eyes, see ye not; and having ears, hear ye not; and do ye not remember?" It is entirely possible in the theater to hear the bell and not hear it by leaping ahead toward its significance and to dismiss it as only a pretend bell, important only in the field of significance. But it is also primarily in the theater that we might most fully hear doubleness and difference in the sound.

Conditioned to the conventions of time, we ignore the daily coercions that we submit to, like Peter Handke's Kaspar, who is also trained in the ways of the world by the sound of a bell. In *Kaspar,* the play based on the story of Kaspar Hauser, the eponymous character is socialized into language by the brutal Pavlovian conditioning of a bell that rings intermittently through the play. In spite of its phenomenal reality of the sound, it is possible to hear and not hear at the same time when meanings dominate sensory perception and conditioning leads to an active response. The bell within the representation is on the one hand less audible to the extent that it signifies within the play but on the other hand more audible precisely because it is within representation and not simply an instrumental sign sending us to our seats after the intermission. Is it within representation that a bell can be more fully heard as a bell rather than as a signal to act? That question is implicit in the speeches in which Winnie speaks of two bells, the one for waking and the one for sleep. The bell for waking implies the bell for sleeping, as morning implies night. But the bell for sleeping will never be heard. We may all, like Winnie, anticipate such a bell, but if it were ever to ring, we would already be past it, already long gone. The audible bell is given only to waken, available only to bring us into consciousness, a consciousness that recognizes that representation and survival go hand in hand. For the bell is heard only by the survivor. It is therefore always a repetition of a first bell, the bell of a beginning, not the last bell of an ending. It awakens to a certain kind of failure to be present at the moment of death, but that failure is also an awakening to life.

Winne's suspension between life and death nevertheless seems significantly different from a character such as Hamlet, who is held in suspense by the death of another and who can be seen to suspend desire. For habits do get Winnie through the day and put her into existential time that moves along. Hamlet, on the other hand, cannot move in time but holds himself and is held in what Lacan called "the time of the Other." In his essay on *Hamlet*, Lacan identifies what this means psychoanalytically.

> I have said before that hysteria is characterized by the function of an unsatisfied desire and obsession by the function of an impossible desire. But beyond these two terms the two cases are distinguished by inverse relationships with time: the obsessive neurotic always repeats the initial germ of his trauma, i.e., a certain precipitancy, a fundamental lack of maturation.
>
> This is at the base of neurotic behavior, in its most general form: the subject tries to find his sense of time *[lire son heure]* in his object, and it is even in the object that he will learn to tell time *[lire l'heure]*. This is where we get back to our friend Hamlet, to whom everyone can attribute at will all the forms of neurotic behavior, as far as you want to go, i.e., up to character neurosis. The first factor that I indicated to you in Hamlet's structure was his situation of dependence with respect to the desire of the Other, the desire of his mother. Here now is the second factor that I ask you to recognize: Hamlet is constantly suspended in the time of the Other, throughout the entire story until the very end.[34]

What exactly is the time of the other? Lacan defines the ways in which hysterical symptoms can be oriented in two directions in time: the future and the past. Both suspend the subject in time. The orientation of desire toward a future holds an unsatisfied desire, whose lack constitutes a denial. The orientation to a past holds a desire that may at one time have been satisfied but has been repudiated. The lack of satisfaction in the first instance separates the subject from her object at the same time that it binds her to her object. The repudiation in the second instance bars the fact of loss from any representation in consciousness: a self-repudiation and foreclosure of desire. It equally binds the one who desires the other, but the binding is to an interior other, a kind of absolute. The time of the event is literally incorporated as an encrypted event of repudiation of desire and of the impossibility that the original satisfaction be repeated in the very same event.

Sameness is the impossibility, because the present slips into past. In order to keep from manifesting that impossibility, the origin and the forgetting are held as a permanent memorial in which time does not move at all. The origin is the blank space of repudiation. That is, the subject does not and cannot know the trauma itself. The desire is memorialized, however, in the form of an encrypted denial of desire that is actually a holding of the object in a timeless interior zone. The therapeutic coming-into-mourning is coming into recognition of the loss, a separation from the object, and a gradual expansion of the psyche toward the inclusion or introjection of the lost object that allows the living psyche to enter the time of the body and the body to enter time. Mourning is impossible, however, while the encrypted denial remains hidden in the timeless zone of encrypted desire.

Maria Torok defines the unawareness of loss as incorporation. Incorporated, the encryption makes access impossible, because it is "a memory . . . buried *without a legal burial place.*"[35] In *Under the Sand,* where the vacation idyll with her husband turns into an impossible-to-know loss, Marie is unable to speak of him as gone. She is incapable of mourning. There are important differences between the filmic representation of such a loss and the clinical version. The most important one is that, for Torok's cases, the idyllic scene itself is forbidden and thereby maintained as a "preservative repression."

> The memory is of an idyll, experienced with a valued object and yet for some reason unspeakable. It is memory entombed in a fast and secure place, awaiting resurrection. Between the idyllic moment and its subsequent forgetting (we have called the latter "preservative repression"), there was the metapsychological traumatism of a loss or, more precisely, the "loss" that resulted from a traumatism. This segment of an ever so painfully lived Reality—untellable and therefore inaccessible to the gradual, assimilative work of mourning—causes a genuinely covert shift in the entire psyche. The shift itself is covert, since both the fact that the idyll was real and that it was later lost must be disguised and denied. This leads to the establishment of a sealed-off psychic place, a crypt in the ego.[36]

Lacan points out that all kinds of neurosis can be attributed to Hamlet. But in the specific sense of his "obsessional" mourning, Hamlet is suspended in time. That is to say he is outside his own time and held by the other time that is within, the time that has no movement because it has no markers: it is inhuman. It is the time of the traumatic loss of the other experienced as a renunciation of the impossibility of repeating the idyll. By holding on, a repetition of the same is, for the psychic imaginary, just possible. The refusal and the hope are contained in the premise of an identity that "I and my Father are one" (John 10:30), just as Hamlet cannot distinguish his name from that of his father, Hamlet. The renunciation is the internal crypt and encryption of impossibility, of desire, of loss, and the loss of desire, held as a permanent moment in the figuration of the psyche. Motionless, inert, a permanent fixture of time that "passeth show," that crypt cannot be recognized by Hamlet himself, by other characters, or by generations of interpreters, except as that which is uncannily persistent in the appeal of the play. Most easily conceived of as a space, the crypt is the thing of otherness; but equally a temporal "object" that takes up no space, it holds the entire psychic economy in suspense, waiting for the miracle of a resurrection. "That within that passeth show" is the phantom of a memory that never occurred for the subject, because it was inherited as a gap in speech and belonged to the time and the unconscious of the other, primarily the parental other. Torok writes: "The buried speech of the parent will be (a) dead (gap) without a burial place in the child. This unknown phantom returns from the unconscious to haunt its host and may lead to phobias, madness, and obsessions. Its effect can pass through several generations and determine the fate of an entire family line."[37] That unknown phantom is passed along also to the listener(s), the analyst as much as the audience, in the form of an unknowable absence in the discourse. It is thus not just Hamlet's obsessional mourning for his father but also the impossibility of his relinquishing the absence of his father that keeps him in suspended animation. Abraham and Torok's psychoanalytic perspective on Hamlet sees not that he was simply acting out an Oedipal conflict but that he inherited the secrets of the family as an "awareness—un-awareness" and that the ghost's story of his murder is a subterfuge that conceals a further enigma and guilty secret that belongs to old Hamlet in the unknown past.

> Produced by the secret, the gaps and impediment in our communication with the love object create a twofold and contrary effect: the prohibition of knowledge coupled with an unconscious investigation. As a result "haunted" individuals are caught between two inclinations. They must at all costs

maintain their ignorance of a loved one's secret; hence the semblance of un-awareness (nescience) concerning it. At the same time they must eliminate the state of secrecy; hence the reconstruction of the secret in the form of unconscious knowledge. This twofold movement is manifest in symptoms and gives rise to "gratuitous" or uncalled for acts and words, creating eerie effects: hallucinations and delirium, showing and hiding that which, in the depths of the unconscious, dwells as the living—dead knowledge of *some-one else's secret.*[38]

The exorcism of the phantom comes from the expression of its secret in words. The "Phantom of Hamlet" is in one sense such an expression with the goal, for Abraham, "to spur the public to react unconsciously to the enigmas that remain and to backtrack toward an equally unstated yet no less imperative goal: breaking down the 'phantom' and eradicating its effect, the uneasy state of knowledge-unknowledge responsible for the unconscious conflict and incongruous repetitions . . . to cancel the secret buried in the unconscious and to display it *in its initial openness.*"[39]

The sense of an unknown inheritance turns, then, from an individual fate into a public, historical, and cultural fate through the history of Western theatre. We go to the theater and enter the fatality of its unspoken history that is acted out on every stage in the various articulations of particular dramas, performance styles, approaches. Performance in the theater is the condition of "initial openness," because it is the condition of repetition within an event, not a matter of speech. As an event, the play carries the enigma of otherness within participatory sameness, seeking from the audi-ence a recognition of the enigma of otherness of time from within its own historical losses. Performance itself is the encryption of an origin passed on as an enigma. To interpret a meaning for *Hamlet* is to murder its otherness and explain it away. To undergo the experience of *Hamlet* is to participate in the enigma of otherness *and* to understand the nature of the enigma of time through its expression in performance.

The reach of the ghostly enigmas of this play extends far beyond its bor-ders. It tends to haunt history. Its part in the thought of Marx and Freud is well documented. In pointing out that "remember me!," the injunction from the ghost, "encodes the necessity of forgetting," Margery Garber takes particular note of its echo in Nietzsche's idea of "forgetting history" and his meditation in "The Uses and Abuses of History": "Hamlet's own meditation

on revenge and bestial oblivion is so close to Nietzsche's that we may wonder whether Nietzsche's complex of ideas, from revenge to the ghost to the
beast to the gravedigger, does not derive in some way from Shakespeare's
great untimely meditation, and in particular from the soliloquy in Act 4
scene 4."[40]

> Is *Hamlet*—as I have suggested above—the play that articulates, or represents,
> the construction of the modern subject?
>   I think that [this question] can be answered, tentatively, in the affirmative,
> and that this accounts at least in part for the befuddlement and irritation some
> contemporary critics demonstrate when they are asked to come face to face
> with the play. It is too close to us. What look like critiques, analyses, imple-
> mentations of *Hamlet* to make some other point (philosophical, political,
> psychoanalytic) dissolve to bring us back to the play itself, not as referent,
> but as origin—or marker of the unknowability of origins, what Freud called
> the navel of the dream: "There is at least one spot in every dream at which
> it is unplumbable—a navel, as it were, that is its point of contact with the
> unknown."[41]

Between the event, out of which history can be written, and the writing
of history, is the something that is neither in nor apart from representation,
and therefore may be nothing. That something is the interval in time within
which the real is missing. The missing present creates a paradoxical relation
between the human and the inhuman, a Möbius strip that one can follow
on the inside-outness between effective, empirical human reality and the
idealism that would say that the name or idea of a thing *is* the thing, that the
time on the watch *is* the time, or that the representation is transparent to
the object. The missing origin, however, has the character of a fact, of something done, of the irrevocable passage of events in time and the inevitable
persistence of the fact of having been done in time, in reality. Reality in time
is the *means* of theatre. Performance returns the event to its original condition of passage and persistence, of being unrecoverable and a repetition.
This is why the writing of history, whether of persons or nations, cannot be
more than notations covering the loss of the real. Performance, whether
located in personal behavior, in the public forum of theatre, or in poetry,
enacts the experiential and temporal conditions of historical events even
while it may falsify details. Written history is generally a writing away from

trauma. Performance, on the other hand, particularly in the "talking cure," speaks and embodies the specific relatedness out of which the trauma arose in the first place; it therefore works toward trauma. Trauma is characterized by the impossibility for an event, in its singularity, to enter any representation. But that is not the same as saying it is as good as never having happened. It remains as a fact that is unknown and unknowable to consciousness, like the present. And that is not to say it is unknown. Rather, the absence that constitutes history's trauma becomes the ghostly part of any individual performance, in behavior, gesture, obsession. It has a constitution that can be *done* but not consciously known, and thus cannot be remembered in the way one recalls a nice day at the beach. It is remembered and experienced otherwise. It is remembered in and as performance that, not having been experienced, can be witnessed only as a demand to revenge. The witness carries the memory of the performance and holds the trauma as close to consciousness as it can come and still remain unknown. It feels like vertigo. It is the promise of a future that wears the past like a mask.

Unlike the present, both past and future extract impossible promises from the living: that the future will revenge the past and that the past desire will continue in the future. Hamlet's desire is inevitably thwarted, because revenge cannot undo murder. Like capital punishment, it can only produce another death, again, and again, and again. Revenge links the subject's desire to loss. His father-other ghost is that present past time, then, represented as a ghost, that encompasses Hamlet; it locks him into inaction, is incorporated. If/when he releases the past into the present, he forgets the ghost, and it will not return. Hamlet is the tomb of past time, where the character harbors the past masked by an antic disposition that encrypts its dead presence and forbids a historical reading of the present. It is an inhuman other, that time, because it is fixed time that remains in him. It is an undead presence that he will not relinquish until, by accident, rescued by pirates, he returns from his own death sentence to leap into the grave of act 4.

If Hamlet were to speak back to Lacan, he might say, "So you're telling me that for most of this play I have been 'always in the time of the Other,' that I elided and thereby eluded the time of my own action. You imply that I hold not to the memory of the man, my father, but to the memory of his loss. You're telling me that my resistance to being at the right time in the right place, why I couldn't kill Claudius that time, was resistance to my own unsatisfied and impossible desire and the crypted memory of loss.

You're telling me that my desire for revenge is a pretense that covers my fury at the loss of—whom? mother or father or both? You're telling me that it's what? a lack of maturation? What's that? A failure to enter into my own time, the present of the body. I live rather only in my consciousness, where I foreclose desire and abuse Ophelia. I'm quite certain I do not love my mother and that I hate my stepfather, and you're saying that my certainty is itself a symptom? You're telling me I haven't been feeling what I thought? That the thought was always different? You're telling me I have been doing away already with the desire to be present, which is the desire to act? You're telling me I didn't really want revenge? Because to take revenge I would have to acknowledge both my desire and my lack? You say I want to kill that Other, whose time rules me, who obligates me to take revenge on my own desire, which is why I couldn't do it? That for four acts I insisted that the impossible desire would not inhabit Me. My 'I' will stand apart. My 'I' will stand against the brooding fury against the Other, who will not accommodate my desire. I repudiate It to repudiate my Own, and I repudiate my Own, to repudiate It. We were a perfect circle, empty. But I refused, finally, to die in the Other, in my own desire of the Other. I will die as myself. I'm done. I'm ready. I shall live the life of my body. I'm going to the theatre." Where, of course, he will die and come to repeat himself.

The appointment with theatre demands that one not only witness a missed encounter but also act it out. I already know I will miss the exact time of a play's beginning. When did that event actually begin? When I stepped inside the building; when the curtain opened? It asks me to be a witness to that imaginary moment of the beginning when the curtain opens and reveals the other place in the same space, or, lacking a curtain, when the lights go down, or, lacking lights, when the first word is spoken, or, lacking words, when the first motion is made. The appointment with the curtain time is not, in fact, like any other appointment, because it demands not just that I encounter the missing of the real but that I witness that lack of encounter as a repetition. Still, the bell startles, like a trauma. It is brief trauma that I will more than likely ignore and repress, perfectly happy to slide through the impossible now and construct it as a past. Nonetheless, that call to witness, as Lacan and Caruth suggest, is a call to an impossible demand. More particularly (and more possibly) it is the demand not to reduce that impossibility to a finite meaning, because in reducing it to meaning I reduce the other to an object and fail to acknowledge the other as another, separate subject. The desire to reduce the real to an empirical fact is a violent desire to murder the present and take revenge on the passage of time, "whose being is that it will cease to be." The mark of time always fails to stop time, which flows on around it. The mark, however, persists as a memorial.[42] Eight o'clock announces the intersection of ritual repetition with an empirical moment on the clock, but it is a moment that the audience will pass through without noticing. Passing through the moment, the audience misses the impossibility of knowing any absolute now marked by the representation of the clock. For the now is an unconscious point that everyone knows and is both within and apart from. Pretending to mark a point in time, the clock disguises its own failure and conceals the moment of the missed encounter (the now), where past is exchanged for future, reality for the dream. Nonetheless, as an event, the moment also works as an alarm, calling for an awakening to survival.

> How can we fail to see that awakening works in two directions—and that the awakening that re-situates us in a constituted and represented reality carries out two tasks? The real has to be sought beyond the dream—in what the dream has enveloped, hidden from us, behind the lack of representation of which there is only one representative. This is the real that governs our activities more than any other.[43]

By going to the theater at a certain time, I enter a space in which a repetition is planned but still open to accident. I make a bargain to be present at the site of a trauma that is being resurrected in the symbolic dimension of the real. By doubling the present, theatre represents the present in its own terms in an *almost* self-canceling mode. In Augustine's sense the present is always traumatic to the extent that it can be represented only in terms of past or future, ever elusive in itself. The "almost" is the difference between seeing and seeing as. Theatrical catharsis might well be the transformation of trauma through its entry into the material symbols of loss or, rather, into the difference between those symbols and their materiality that nonetheless appear coextensive. That is, the catharsis is an awakening to the nothing of the present within the material and temporal artifices of theatre. This may well be a version of the purging or cleansing aspect of catharsis implied by Aristotle or more and less articulately by Oedipus when he cries upon recognizing the ghost of himself, "O, O, O, O, O."

That is not to say that such awakening always happens in the theater, but when it does happen, it's theatre. Catharsis is, especially for Freud, remembrance, but in theatre we do not remember an event, an object, or even a relationship as much as we remember having forgotten and wake to our own forgetfulness. This is what makes an appointment with the theater different from just any appointment. It is already a promise to witness repetition taking the risk that the performance will be no more than a reproduction. Simply to reproduce an event, that is, to do the same play, night after night, is the certain death of theatre, and to the extent that any given theatrical event is a scripted play, that death occurs as deadliness, as a kind of vampire or the living dead. And it bores to death. But repetition in the psychoanalytic sense is the structuring of a recognition of the failure of awareness. It is the awakening to the fact that remembering loss must be new, accidental, since the loss itself is an accident, the sudden blow to consciousness that forecloses any entry of an event into representation. There is the promise, then, that in the context of even the most deadly reproduction of a play, the theater itself will make accidents happen. The utterly contagious pleasure of an actor laughing, out of character, moving between a scripted, choreographed part and an uncontrolled outburst, is the shared syncopation between the deadly script and the real. The utterly terrifying frisson of an actor forgetting lines, losing the place, turns actor and audience alike into momentary corpses. "Where am I," asks Catherine Clément, "in syncope?"

> Physical time never stops. That may be, but syncope seems to accomplish a miraculous suspension. Dance, music, and poetry traffic in time, manipulate it, and even the body manages to do that by an extraordinary short circuit. . . . People vie to describe the cause of syncope—circulatory, nervous system, neurovegetative; a cure can be found—cardiac massage, smelling salts, a slap. But inside, what is going on? Where is the lost syllable, the beat eaten away by the rhythm? Where does the subject go who later comes to, "comes back"?[44]

A character dies into the mortality of the actor, both falling into the nothingness between. I heard once of an actor who corpsed so thoroughly on stage that no amount of prompting from either fellow actors or the stage manager helped. The actor had to stop the performance and say, "I'm sorry, ladies and gentlemen, but I have completely forgotten where I am. I have to stop." Another actor tried to help. "We'll start wherever you want," she said, as though in an effort to bring her partner back to the life of the play. But he was beyond reach. They started again at the beginning of the act. But for that moment of utter collapse, in the frisson of reality, the actor and the audience were together, were *with* one another in the catastrophe, at the very moment of the forgetting, in the event of the lapse they had no choice but to share.

We submit to the theatrical bargain simply by showing up at the designated time, and we agree to recognize that we get more than we can see. We agree to accept the reality of the ghosts that shadow the material reality with their very nothingness and lurk in the unrepresentable origins and unknowable destiny of that moment. When Hamlet insists that his father's ghost is present, Gertrude replies that she sees nothing at all, adding, "yet all that is I see" (3.4.132). On the one hand, this speaks to a Gertrudian lack of imagination. Like many theatergoers, Gertrude sees only what is physically present and hears only what is said aloud. Other theatergoers, however, do see the Nothing that is present at the theater: the Nothingness of death that resides in every living thing, that turns actors into the masks of their own death, and appears only to those who, like Hamlet, are almost ready to keep their appointment. The Nothing appears to everyone in the corpsing of lines, in the spontaneous, hysterical laughter of the actor whose laugh comes out of nowhere.

We submit to the bargain to endure through a course of time of something called a performance. To be present to what happens *while it is happening*. That, of course, is the difference between a psychoanalytic session and reading about psychoanalysis through Caruth, Lacan, or Freud. Being present at the theater is *when* one could hear the call to the impossible, real present of the body. The agreement to endure that present is an agreement to be the witness of the repetition of an impossible real, in the space of transference. Impossible because chance, the accident, *tuché,* that Lacan called "an encounter with the real"—an encounter with the present—is encountered through the mask of convention and fiction, a mere dream of passion that can fashion a conceit to bring real tears, real laughter. Impossible because the theater is a designated space—planned and used for repetition—that invites the accident in which the present is supposedly known while it is happening. The impossible present is made possible in the theater by the copresence or transference of performance, which is something an audience accomplishes along with performers. In other words, rather than the spatial metaphor of a duration of the present, which passes from future through present into past as though a fragment marked out on a line, the copresence of performers and audience creates a kind of temporal mirror for the present in which what is passing is known while it is passing. The copresence in the theater is not *just* about real live bodies being in one another's presence but about experience itself as a form of knowing the trauma of the impossible present as it passes, of *being there* when it passes, if it passes, and when love occurs, if it occurs. To show up on time is to agree to witness the time of the other in representation with the possibility of seeing the representation of our own investments in the time of the other. We agree to act the part of Horatio for the duration, both part of Hamlet's drama and witnesses to it. That is, we enter the dream in order to be wakened from within the dream to reality. In return we get the repetition of a trauma that is no longer effectively outside time but represented through time. We agree to be surprised by the flashes of death and commit ourselves to, indeed hope for, accident, not just to share an embarrassment with the performers, but to be there when the real breaks through and allows us to share the knowledge of the bargain and an appointment almost kept.

chapter 2

All the Dead Voices
Memorial and History

They make a noise like wings. Like leaves. Like sand. Like leaves. *Silence.*
They all speak at once. Each one to itself. *Silence.* Rather they whisper. They
rustle. They murmur. They rustle. *Silence.* What do they say? They talk about
their lives. To have lived is not enough for them. They have to talk about it.
To be dead is not enough for them. It is not sufficient. *Silence.* They make a
noise like feathers. Like leaves. Like ashes. Like leaves.

—SAMUEL BECKETT, *Waiting for Godot*

"In the sepulcher which the historian inhabits," says Michel de Certeau,
writing of Michelet's *History of France,* "only 'emptiness remains.'"[1] Western
historiography, de Certeau goes on to say, is effected by a series of ruptures
between past and present, between labor and nature, between discourse
and the social body. The writing of history relies, in other words, on a break
that creates an other, which is "the phantasm of historiography, the object
that it seeks, honors, and buries."[2] The gesture of writing history "posits
death, a breakage everywhere reiterated in discourse, and . . . yet denies
loss by appropriating to the present the privilege of recapitulating the past
as a form of knowledge."[3] The rupture, in other words, is a condition for
the intelligibility of Western historical writing, which recovers from the
very losses it installs by appropriating the past, nature, or the body into
the present in the forms that count as knowledge. De Certeau contrasts the
rupture that inaugurates uniquely Western historical writing with various
traditions whose historical sense comes from an accumulation of time, a
"co-existence and re-absorption" in relation to the dead, in which the dead
leave a "legacy of ears" and "memory by mouth."[4]

Theatre provides a unique venue for historiography insofar as it is
composed of both writing and repetition. If dramatic texts count as the

discursive elements in writing that is severed from both past and present, then the repetitions of performance constitute a kind of living memorial in which the ghosts of history are animated. In theatre, the dead whisper to the living through repetition. Repetition is not an easy or obvious thing to understand, if only because it does not come as an accustomed form of historical knowledge. Repetition, like de Certeau's notion of historiography, implies a gap and a difference between one instance and another. But instead of creating the phantasm of the other as an object of knowledge, repetition is paradoxically an instance of a singularity. Following is an exploration of how repetition composes theatre's way to memorialize the dead and makes theatre itself a memorial where the dead can speak "traditionally" through the legacy of ears and memory by mouth.

It is probably fairly common to envision memorials as solid objects in public spaces: statues of a war hero astride a horse or GIs raising a flag; phallic monuments or triumphal arches; buildings. In such monumental works, the durability of marble and metal seems suited to the desire to make memory endure; and the singular, realistic figure, to the sense that the one can stand for the many. The material and style attempt to do justice to the dead. Since the appearance of Maya Lin's Vietnam Veterans Memorial in Washington DC, however, the forms of memorials have become both more abstract and more particular, seeking to account for individual lives among vast numbers of the dead and to do justice to both. Other work by Lin goes even further toward the elemental, with the use of water. Her design for the Civil Rights Memorial in Montgomery, Alabama, takes Martin Luther King's paraphrase from the Bible in his "I have a dream" speech: "until justice rolls down like waters and righteousness like a mighty stream"; she uses water flowing over a large, round, flat surface marked by moments in the Civil Rights movement. Both transient and ever-flowing, a permanent base with a moving surface, that memorial captures history in elemental terms. Similarly using water, the design by Michael Arad for a memorial at the World Trade Center captures both the vast scale and the singular particularity of the catastrophe there on September 11, 2001. Called Reflecting Absence, the memorial outlines the two square acres of the two towers' footprints; two square pools of falling water fall twice to deeper, smaller square pools. A ramp from the surface leads to an interior space of bedrock behind the second pool, where names of the dead are inscribed on a low wall and the sound of falling water fills the space.

The designs of both Lin and Arad counteract the statuary memorial in which the one stands for the many, an intelligible signifier for the person or people it represents, a frozen image that substitutes and reproduces a likeness. Such statues have the intelligibility of realism, like a datum of historical knowledge. Statues tend to become invisible artifacts in the public landscape. In other terms, the memorial statue is an idealized Signifier that supposedly holds all particulars in its grasp but quickly empties of its signifieds. As the joke about Lord Nelson's monument in Trafalgar Square goes, Lord Nelson is a great lover of pigeons. Arad's design (not built as of this writing) uses silence in the inscription of names and the sound of falling water as a means to remember. But remember what? It suggests that what needs remembering is loss itself, loss without further signification, loss without answer. Reflecting Absence is an empty space that is replete with memory of loss, which is the antidote to the emptiness of the Signifier. Where the Signifier, whether as concept or statue, encrypts the trauma and authorizes an escape from memory, Reflecting Absence gives space to the trauma by a repetition of loss. With a double play on the sense of reflection, it spatializes a return of thought to emptiness, or what Kierkegaard called the dimension of repetition that is "reflecting into itself." That is, it memorializes the unthinkable with all the particularity of names, those irreducible signifiers of individual people.

In his essay "Why Is Every Act a *Repetition?*" Žižek correlates the Lacanian terms *Imaginary, Symbolic,* and *Real* to Kierkegaard's triad of aesthetic, ethical, and religious stages in his extended meditation *Repetition.* A kind of fictional autobiography of thought written in the first person by "Constantin Constantius" and in letters from "A Young Man," *Repetition* poses the question of whether repetition is possible. The notion of repetition, Kierkegaard says, is a contradiction that occurs in a collision between reality and consciousness. In early notes on the idea, he writes that for either reality or consciousness (ideality) alone, there can be no repetition because,

> in reality as such, there is no repetition. This is not because everything is different, not at all. If everything in the world were completely identical, in reality there would be no repetition, because reality is only in the moment. . . . In ideality alone there is no repetition, for the idea is and remains the same and as such cannot be repeated. When ideality and reality touch each other, then repetition occurs.[5]

The impossibility of repetition—that is, encountering the same thing twice—varies between philosophical stages for Kierkegaard, and these stages connect to particular life experiences. In the aesthetic stage, his narrator fails to experience the same pleasure he once had visiting the lodgings, theaters, cafés, friends he knew previously in Berlin. It is not that the places and people were not the same but that he could not repeat his experience. In the ethical phase, more mature, the narrator has learned to find comfort in the return to the theater, to his same lodgings, in seeing old friends. He invests in neither nostalgia for the old (that it will be the same) nor hope for the new. Yet at that stage, repetition is also impossible, he finds, because there is no moment, no ideal point in time between nostalgia and hope, because that point (cf. Augustine) is "never present as such." It is present only in the mode of hope or memory, not in reality. Having described a moment of waking up absolutely elated, virtually walking on air, when "all existence seemed to have fallen in love with me," Constantin is suddenly irritated by a speck in his eye that sends him into "an abyss of despair." "Since that time, I have abandoned every hope of ever feeling satisfied absolutely and in every way, abandoned the hope I had once nourished, perhaps not to be absolutely satisfied at all times but nevertheless at certain moments."[6] That impasse leads Kierkegaard to the next stage, the religious, which Žižek identifies as "reflection into itself."

If repetition is impossible in both the aesthetic and ethical stages, it is possible to repeat the experience of impossibility, which is the failure to know the present, or what Žižek calls "the failure to attend the Object," that is, the obscure object of desire. Here, he brings in Lacan's distinction between the repetition of a signifier, which repeats the symbolic mark of an idealized object (e.g., the sign of the present or the past in memory or anticipation), and the repetition of trauma, which "designates precisely the reemergent failure to integrate some impossible kernel of the Real."[7] If the repetition of a signifier is akin to the remembrance designated by the war memorial statue, the repetition of trauma is closer to that of the flow of water over the memorials by Lin and Arad. Elemental and real, the water neither designates nor signifies the "objects" that are lost. Remembrance and repetition render very different forms of history. Remembrance is a way to look back on the past from a distance, across a gap, and to account for what took place. The stationary object stops the flow of time. It loses the character of "becoming," in which the openness of the present is, for Kierke-gaard, an abyss of "free decision."

Kierkegaard's example for a figure in that religious stage of repetition is Job, and his ordeal is an encounter with what Lacanian psychoanalysis figures as the Real.

> This category, ordeal, is not esthetic, ethical, or dogmatic—it is altogether transcendent. Only as knowledge about an ordeal, that it is an ordeal, would it be included in a dogmatics. But as soon as knowledge enters, the resilience of the ordeal is impaired, and the category is actually another category. This category is absolutely transcendent and places a person in a purely personal relationship of opposition to God, in a relationship such that he cannot allow himself to be satisfied with any explanation at second hand. . . . Job is not a hero of faith; he gives birth to the category of "ordeal" with excruciating anguish precisely because he is so developed that he does not possess it in childlike immediacy.[8]

Knowledge about the ordeal is aesthetic, ethical, or dogmatic because such knowledge is constituted over a gap of difference by the discourses of art, law, or religion. Direct "contact," or being within the ordeal, by contrast, cannot be known by customary forms of intelligibility. And knowledge "firsthand" from God, by implication, also surpasses understanding. The end of Job's story, when "the Lord gave Job twice as much as he had before" (Job 42:10), is therefore unimaginable for Kierkegaard. "When everything has stalled, when thought is immobilized, when language is silent, when explanation returns home in despair—then there has to be a thunderstorm." Repetition here is thus a conformity rather than a contradiction between consciousness and reality, in which consciousness does not produce knowing about or representing the ordeal. It occurs for Job "when every *thinkable* human certainty and probability were impossible."[9] Every explanation of his suffering from his friends, he rejects; every call to accept it as punishment, he refuses. In that sense, when he says he repents "in dust and ashes," he is not submitting to the Law but choosing the limit of knowledge: "therefore have I uttered that I understood not" (Job 42:3).

Žižek's example for the repetition of the "impossible" encounter and free choice is Antigone. He starts with the premise that to enter the symbolic community of language entails a "forced choice," because to choose other than the symbolic community is to lose the possibility of choice, which clinically is psychosis. In "choosing" to enter the symbolic community, a subject sacrifices the incestuous Object of desire. But that object is paradoxical, because it comes to be only by being lost (not unlike the Augustinian present).[10] That is, the sacrifice and the appearance of the Object of desire occur simultaneously: a self-canceling formula in which the subject gives up everything (the Object of desire) that is nothing. The consequence of that forced choice is inclusion in the community where a symbolic exchange of meaning and distributive justice can operate. Žižek points out that the psychoanalytic theory of incest prohibition is unique in its focus on the impossible paradox that the Object of desire comes to be only by being lost. Similarly, the psychological accounts of developmental phases identify a period of change when the child sacrifices primary narcissism in order to be included in a social community. The psychoanalytic version of renunciation/prohibition is "pure," because the subject gets and gives nothing. Yet, says Žižek, that "pure negative gesture of withdrawal . . . constitutes the space of possible gains and losses."[11] Antigone is an example of one who repeats the impossible situation of the forced choice, "an act which reaches the utter limit of the primordial forced choice and repeats it in the reverse sense. . . . Antigone is 'free' after she has been excommunicated from the community."[12] He goes on to point out that Lacan's sense of Antigone's act is not simply to counter Creon's arguments with her own arguments. She does not simply argue the validity of one kind of law against another. She simply insists tautologically, "It is so because it is so"—the logic of Saul Kripke's "rigid designator."[13] The "rigid designator" is a signifier like a name that designates the "real kernel" of an object, which remains the same object regardless of its variable properties. This suggests why the inscribed names on the Vietnam and World Trade Center memorials are so powerful. They are the irreducible designators of the irreducible particularity and reality of real people.

What remains the same and is repeated singularly in trauma is the unthought, the unthinkable, the arrest of knowledge, in which the real nonetheless occurs. But such a real kernel is just past the limit conditions of both speech and writing. Antigone's stance, like Job's, emerges between the law as written and spoken, as a reality that can be designated only in negative terms, for it is neither in the written inscription nor in the speech alone but in an empty coordinate or point at their intersection. It cannot answer the question, Why? because it is beyond the forms of intelligibility but is nonetheless a material gesture. Perhaps it is best named as the ghost that repetition produces.

Between writing and speech, a ghost is more easily found, though no less strange, in theatre. Here is a testimony. In October 2000, the Gate Theatre of Dublin brought a production of *Waiting for Godot* to the Zellerbach Playhouse at the University of California, Berkeley, with Johnny Murphy as Estragon and Barry McGovern as Vladimir, Alan Stanford and Stephen Brennan as Pozzo and Lucky. The effect of that production on me was a sense of uncanniness that is ultimately unprovable and inarguable, but I felt that I had finally seen onstage the ghosts I had always thought, but never believed, were there. I have no idea if the rest of the audience sensed these ghosts, but I have been trying ever since to identify what was "there" and what I heard in the voices of the living actors.

"Nothing to be done." A first line so familiar, it echoed from the stage to my undergraduate past and back again through at least six other productions and countless class periods and lectures on the play. The sound of Johnny Murphy's voice was inseparable from the image of Estragon on his mound and Vladimir at the back, staring into the mottled backdrop. My view was oblique from the obstructed sides of the mezzanine, so I could never see the play properly, with a straight-on view. Perhaps it was the improper perspective that made a ghostly effect. The actors produced the words effortlessly, as though the words were being said for the first time and carrying no more weight than someone saying, "The sun came up today." Ordinary and banal, they were hardly the signs of "the greatest play of the twentieth century," according to some lights. When Barry McGovern replied, "I'm beginning to come round to that opinion," I felt I might be hearing a conversation in an Irish pub. No longer famous, yet also not forgotten, the speeches had the plainness of a celebrity wearing rags, familiar but anonymous, with no aura of specialness. No sense of dream or unreality, the words were there and then voiced onstage in the dim light, but the words and the voices were not alone. They were inhabited, if by nothing else, by my memory, not only of the text itself, but also of echoes of the same speeches in other times and other places, other productions. Yet they were also other than my memory, because they were being spoken in the present. The voices of other actors in other productions, by comparison to what was being spoken then, seemed in

retrospect full of the weight of effort to be meaningful, the effort to communicate, to make me understand, to show off an intelligence, a sensitiv-
ity, a comic virtuosity, an interpretation. In the mouths of Murphy and
McGovern, the words dropped all that weight. They put me in the middle
of an ordeal, testing both me and theatre to explain.

The effortlessness and ordinariness seduced me entirely. I knew there
must be great craft in creating that ease. In other productions, I could assess
the actors' work: they did their jobs more or less thoughtfully, feelingly,
convincingly, humorously, carefully. The work of these actors seemed imper-
ceptible, yet they were still intelligent, feeling, believable, funny, and precise. This performance had the same ease, the same lack of effort, that in
sports makes a home run seem inevitable after it is hit—an easy thing and
almost necessary the moment it crosses the fence. In both the performance
and the game, the hope (for a home run) turns into fact as though the
right thing, the necessary and inevitable thing, has just happened and always
would have happened. In the Gate Theatre performance on that day, an
event between hope and accomplishment collapsed into a sense of fatality,
as though what happened was both necessary and inevitable. The event
was so "perfect," which is to say so actual and simple, that I wondered how
all productions of *Waiting for Godot* had not been that way. That sense of
perfection immediately made me acutely aware of the disappearance of the
performance, of the absence of any instant replay, and of the fact that even
if I were to see the production again, it would neither be nor feel the same.
I would turn into a critic, as I do when I see the videotape of the same production, for reproduction is not repetition. I felt a terrible longing to hold
on, to keep that sense of perfection going, but also awed by its departure.
I felt myself caught in the "bliss" (not the pleasure) of the text, which was
this performance, in which I could only, as Roland Barthes put it, "enter
into a desperate plagiarism, hysterically affirm the void of bliss."[14]

Pleasure can be expressed in words, bliss cannot.

Bliss is unspeakable, inter-dicted. I refer to Lacan ("What one must bear
in mind is that bliss is forbidden to the speaker, as such, or else that it cannot be spoken except between the lines . . .") and to Leclaire (". . . Whoever
speaks by speaking denies bliss, or correlatively, whoever experiences bliss
causes the letter—and all possible speech—to collapse in the absolute degree
of the annihilation he is celebrating").[15]

Those actors, McGovern, Murphy, Stanford, and Brennan, as best as I can say it, seemed to have brought the text "home." They seemed to have put Beckett's text into something of a native habitat, which, of course, is simply putting a text into performance, into space, sound, and light. But even more specifically, they seemed to me to have put the text into the native habitat of the sound of a language, nominally English, but locally Irish. In that habitat, everything is gathered in the sound of the voice, yet everything remains between the lines. "The text of bliss is absolutely intransitive."[16] "It" goes nowhere, like the text or the tactic, which is simply the strategy of the written play ("It's terrible. Nobody comes, Nobody goes."). But in this case, the text is intransitive, which is to say it seemed self-fulfilled in the present of enactment. The text, both written and structural, was, hysterically speaking, all there, then, in that place, before my eyes, trying to communicate with me, but incapable, intransitive, uninterpretable, present. Hysterically I could affirm only: Did you see them? Did you hear that? They (who? what?) were there, between the words, in the space that held the figures onstage, and in the voices. Ghosts were there. I can testify only as witness to a dream now but was more certain of what I witnessed than I am of most things I see. But whose ghosts were they? What ghosts? What was their demand? Was it that of old Hamlet: to "remember me"?

In the reviews of this production, also seen in Dublin, London, and New York, critics took note of the "Irishness" of the interpretation. Walter Asmus's direction was deliberate in its emphasis on the sound of speech. Some critics apparently found that too referential to British colonial history, since Pozzo, by contrast to Didi and Gogo, was distinctly English. References to colonial history were found not in the words but in the accents of the actors: Irish brogue for Didi and Gogo, posh English for Pozzo. The text, of course, does not make specific references to accents but does not disallow them. Presumably, to those complaining of too much "explicitation," the performance ought to stick to the words as written, which seems to mean they must seem abstract, formal, universal, unlocal, without hinting at the long history of Irish-English history. The problem with such an idealization of the nonlocal and unhistorical, however, is that the nonlocal and unhistorical cannot exist: they can only be idealized in the realm of a fantasy of textuality and writing. Praise for the production, on the other hand, as Karen Fricker wrote in the production notes, comes from the sense of "how natural the lines sound being spoken in Irish cadence, how unexpectedly full of humor." Other productions that are not so at home in the speech have their own kind of local and historical specificity, which adds a certain weight to the text. The conformity I heard between text and speech, however, added no sense of interpretive excess, no syncopation between speech and meaning, which is what I mean by habitat: an interplay of speech and text that encompasses a long historical trajectory in the moment of performance. The performance held and released the ghosts of Irish history into presence on the stage. There was a sense of a tradition being spoken.

The sense of Irishness noted by critics correlates to Judith Butler's sense of performance that constructs categories of identity through repetition. While she takes the sense of repetition as "iteration" and "re-iteration" from the linguistic model of J. L. Austin, the more fully theatrical sense of performance comes from mimesis and therefore includes the somatic, physical, sonorous, and optic fields. In this case, Irishness comes through as a mimetic reproduction of the sound of a voice that reads as a cultural inheritance and locality. What the voices of the actors brought home could be called the ghosts of history that constitute Irish identity, not in the form of written history, but in the form of tradition. The voices carry history through the body into the world. Such history is not a matter of documentation or information but a matter of imitation and performance that embody both material specificity and the gaps that arise in the process of imitation and repetition. Without reference or interpretation, history is present in the voice, carried in rhythms, cadences, and accents that are reproduced somatically from a specific somatic context of lived experience. But history itself is a ghost that rises from the gap of repetition. Neither the original nor the copy, neither lost past nor performing present, the history-ghost makes the past perceptible in the present but is made by what it is not. The "sanctions and taboos," which Butler identifies as the regulating forces of performativity, begin somatically even while they are entangled by cultural and historical readings and perception. Voice and body render qualities that further constitute *attitudes,* the style of a shrug, the rhythm of a phrase, the hesitations of thought. Identity categories such as "Irish" are shorthand readings of those qualities: the signified concepts that stabilize the variations and differences that occur in mimetic processes. History in this sense is the presence of a past inherited mimetically by the speaking body and altered by the very processes of mimesis. Somatic attitudes are not spoken about;

they are spoken *by* rhythm, cadence, accent. Attitudes are thus historical and variable. They are the perceptible sediments of the past, gestured by the language of the body and the body that is voiced.

The function of language, Lacan insists, "is not to inform but to evoke."[17] One need not take this statement as an absolute, since language also clearly carries information and submits to purposes or intentions. Its power to evoke, however, begs the question of just what is being evoked. The Gate Theatre production of *Godot* evoked "Irish"; it called out a history of English-Irish relations; it even evoked the written text to the extent that I was tempted to say it was how the text was "meant" to be played—though in fact I believe no such thing. But is it enough to say that the production was therefore an interpretation of *Godot* as a version of colonial history? One could say that, of course. But such a meaning does not account for the "bliss" of the performance. The processes of imitation that produced those particular voices, with their specific timbres, rhythms, tones, and accents, combined with the words of the text, evoked more than what was manifest, in the same way a dream image will evoke latent associations. The specificity of the voices brought out, but did not enclose, a broad history of habits that might include many pints of Guinness and nights in the pub and politics and murders and the Troubles and Sein Fein and home rule and the Catholic Church and Protestants and famine and emigration and national trauma of colonials and colonialism and the traumas of nationalism and family violence and abandonment and gypsies and a sense of humor and rules of polite behavior and expressions of aggression, irony, anger, and grace; of green and the sound of words and the bloody English and Yeats and the Abbey and the bullet-marked post office in Dublin and pots of gold at the end of the rainbow. These are not a matter of essence or essential Irishness but a matter of continuity, of sedimentations, of lived habits, imitation, and absorption. For all the identifiable elements of Irishness that the voices evoked, however, they also carried elements of traumatic loss and the radical absence that constitutes repetition. This particular production is one of the few that has ever demonstrated for me the difference between reproduction and repetition in relation to a text.

When actors speak the dialogue of a text in a particular way, and when I hear it from the "blissful" mode of repetition's real, which, in Kierkegaard's words, "is hard to say in any human language,"[18] a question opens: Who is speaking? Am I hearing Irishness or Beckett, an absent text or an actor, a person or a ghost? Lacan's answer is that all of them speak from "where there is pain."

> "Logomachia!" goes the strophe on one side. "What are you doing with the preverbal, gesture and mime, tone, the tune of a song, mood and af-fect-tive con-tact?" To which others no less animated give the antistrophe: "Every-thing is language: language when my heart beats faster when I'm in a funk, and if my patient flinches at the throbbing of an aeroplane at its zenith it is a way of *saying* how she remembers the last bomb attack." . . .
>
> . . . One began to repeat after Freud the word of his discovery: *it* speaks, and, no doubt, where it is least expected, namely, where there is pain.[19]

The conformity of voice and text that I am claiming for this production is rather a site of a common trauma: the space of a pain that binds the multiple differences among Irish history, Beckett, writing, and individual actors, yet leaves each to its own distinct pain, its own access to an unconscious that nevertheless speaks through them all. Pain was encrypted in the language of sound and gesture as well as text. The Irishness of the production, so obvious to all the critics and, presumably, audiences, was a marker for an otherwise indecipherable encryption of a lost history, a history of loss, a history built around trauma, a history that cannot be reduced to or remembered by information. Encrypted by language, it is both present and secret, hidden in the auditory presence of the words of a text. Not to be decoded into an informational communiqué alone, "*it* speaks" through the language of the play, ready for an audience to decipher. "The distinction [between decoding and deciphering] is that a cryptogram takes on its full dimension only when it is in a lost language."[20] The lost language here in the production is the lost "letter" (read, lost, absent Thing) in the unconscious dimension that supports a conscious idea of "Irish"—the "thing" present as an absence, trauma.

In the syncopation between the performance and its identification as Irish, there is space of memory. And memory is one form of the symbolizing process by which the facticity of the past and the concept meet. Memory, as a set of ideations or thoughts, is always faulty; there is always something missing, something absent that is unavailable to consciousness: the missing X of trauma, around which all symbolizations occur. Memory as the reality of what has been persists in the body and voice *as* that missing piece. To put it another way, the body is the memory of what is otherwise forgotten. It serves as a placeholder for the blanks in consciousness. Somatic memory persists in the material representation of representation, which is the very thing that, in Lacan's terms, is repressed, unavailable to consciousness, but utterly manifest in ordinary reality. The traumatic foundation of the signifier "Irish" hides in plain sight in walking and talking bodies where a traumatic history is performed.

Between the traumatic foundation and the idealization of an identity comes the symbolizing process that mediates between the living flux of bodily life and the fixations on the Signifier. The fixations of the imaginary are found, among other places, in the projections of the image, which of course can also be a word. In the imaginary field, the notion of Irish (as of Gender or Race) is a fixation insofar as it is used as an identity term. But in the process of symbolization, the fixation on identity works only to the degree that it is an empty signifier. Žižek elaborates on the way that such symbolization is the middle ground between the fixations of the imaginary and the flux of the real:

> The very plasticity of the signified content (the struggle for what democracy "really means") relies on the fixity of the empty signifier "democracy." What characterizes human existence is thus the "irrational" fixation on some symbolic Cause, materialized in a Master-Signifier to whom we stick regardless of the consequences, disregarding our most elementary interest, survival itself: it is the very "stubborn attachment" to some Master-Signifier (ultimately a "signifier without signified") which enables man to maintain free flexibility towards every signified content. . . .
>
> . . . The self-transcending plasticity and freedom of man is grounded in the distance between "things" and "words," in the fact that the way we relate to reality is always mediated by a contingent symbolic process. Here again, however, a certain excessive fixity intervenes: according to psychoanalytic theory, a human subject can acquire and maintain a distance towards (symbolically mediated) reality only through the process of "primordial repression": what we experience as "reality" constitutes itself through the foreclosure of some traumatic X which remains the impossible-real kernel around which symbolization turns. What distinguishes man from animals is thus again the excessive fixation on the trauma (of the lost object, of the scene of some shattering *jouissance*, etc.); what sets the dynamism that pertains to the human

condition in motion is the very fact that some traumatic X eludes every symbolization. "Trauma" is that kernel of the Same which returns again and again, disrupting any symbolic identity.[21]

Thus, the very Irishness that the critics both blamed and praised in that production of *Waiting for Godot* was, in fact, a play between the real (the facticity of history: what *really* happened) and the impossibility of its recuperation, except at the level of a symbolization process, which was itself in the act of disappearing: performance. The notion of a universal text will always be a projection of the imaginary, as will the notion of a stable text. The text itself, however, mediates at the level of the symbolic between the imaginary projection of a universal, whether it is the universal Irish or the universal Human, and the particularities (or peculiarities) of any given performance. Conversely, the specificity of the actors (now, any actors) finishes off the instabilities of the text by grounding them in the materialities of performance. But the instabilities will not really die off; some aspect of textuality will remain left over in words that, like Falstaff's "honor," can return to fight another day precisely because they are only words. In the Gate Theatre production, the real that the Irish actors belong to and that belongs to them, simply conformed to the symbolic play of the text, transforming their own real (uncontrollable, unrepresentable) into the symbolic play (material, present, representable) of the text in performance (aka theatre). That is what distinguished the performance from any old conversation in an Irish pub but also from almost all other productions. All the surfaces of this performance—the rhythms of speech and body, scene and visibility— played against any fixed concept of Irish, yet *Waiting for Godot* was rediscovered as Irish.

Between the surfaces of performance and the idea of Irish, other memories could flood the gap, and these memories were the ghosts I encountered. Transparent, they had no bodies of their own; they were incomplete, fragmented, but real. Loss was immanent and, like Pozzo's "accursed time," always the same. "One day, is that not enough for you, one day he went dumb, one day I went blind, one day we'll go deaf, one day we were born, one day we shall die, the same day, the same second, is that not enough for you?"[22] Apparitional, the ghosts came out to me through what was visible and auditory, yet they were not "there." Had I tried to point to them, others might only have seen the stage and actors. Ghosts are not objects to be pointed at. They appear only as a consequence of a certain manner of attention, and everything reasonable says to pay no attention. This is not to say they exist only as imaginary entities in the way that Ideas, Causes, Meanings, or Identities are imaginary. The losses are real. Ghosts are, in fact, everywhere but rarely recognized. Throughout the performance, I could sense my own traumatized grandfather, the starving masses of the famine, Beckett, my Irish friends, not all yet dead, yet all ghosts who were massing at the sound of the words. Their lights gleamed an instant and were gone again.

Joe Roach once gave a lecture, subsequently published in Chaudhuri and Fuchs's book *Land/Scape/Theatre,* in which he traced elements of the Irish famine into *Godot*—in other words finding the traumatic history of Ireland informing the text. After the lecture someone remarked, "But that is not what the play is about." This, of course, is the point. The somatic memory, whose imitation and persistence over time constitute one dimension of history, is neither a topic nor an issue for discourse, because it is unwritten. It is a performative presence registered by the body and/or the textual unconscious of writing. It is a question not of being "about" the famine but of sustaining the trauma of famine among the living, which, rather than a topic or an argument, is a manifestation of the unavoidable facticity of all that is lost but maintained as "all the dead voices" are heard in the speaking body, the voices that "reflect absence."

As Beckett's lines quoted above suggest, the dead speak in whispers or murmurs, soft noises on the far side of words, in the body of language. To hear the voices of the dead in the text, in distinction to the voices of the actors, one must hear the voices that whisper in the figurations of language. The corporeality of language, its body, is found in its formal figures, its poetic devices, and its rhetorical turns that encrypt what it cannot otherwise say. Figural language, in other words, is constituted by the absences it holds, which is to say by the absences of direct correlations (however conventional they are in the first place) between word and thing. Like leaves, ashes, feathers, sand—Beckett offers words referring to a natural world. That means not that the voices of the dead are "in" nature but that between the sound of the signifying word and the signified world, in the unarticulated space between them, the space of comparison, the space of "like," the voices are heard both in the present and from elsewhere but reside in neither. The voices of the dead remain other than those words, other than the sounds, but their reality is posited by their very absence, which of course is the reality of the dead, the absent presences who are and are not here. The words themselves whisper and rustle as they are voiced. The figurative embodiment in their sound registers the presence of an absence. Between language spoken and language signifying, the otherness of the dead emerges to inform both materiality and semiosis, without being heard or named in either. It is in that space between the voice and the signifier that the figurative element of language (analogy, simile, metaphor) does its figuring, making a reality—an imaginary whole—out of the nonexistent thing it designates.

Onstage, a theatrical reality is similarly posited in the space between the spoken words and the text, between the written and the spoken. What is designated by the word *play* or *performance,* then, is an imaginary whole made up of fragments of writing and fragments of speech, which together function as a figurative device that configures space and time around and through an absence. In attending to the differences between the written and the spoken, one can hear or even see that absence, which is to say can hear "all the dead voices" or see the ghosts that shadow the living, the absent ghost of one author and the many who inhabit the one, of the imaginary person who haunts the configurations of character. A classroom litany so often taught to students is that a character is not the same as a person, however much people (their qualities, their characteristics, their situations, their habits) are the referents for character. In performance, a character is also not *not* a person. The paradox implicitly sustains the projected ideal of an imaginary whole, as Žižek explained above. That whole is pointed at but not composed of the fragmentary pieces of writing called a dramatic text. That whole remains imaginary even in the concrete performance, which is itself made of fragments; it is neither in nor of the text, neither in nor of the projections of an audience. The sense of wholeness, whether of character or of a play, relies on the sense of duration through time, but a whole *thing* is a projection that does not exist altogether, all at once. Wholeness is an effect of the imaginary that binds the fragments, the text, and the voices together even while they remain distinct. Thus, theatre is the privileged arena where nonbeing—the absoluteness of absence—shows itself as being or, in Beckett's terms, is heard. It rustles, whispers, or murmurs across silences, like the notes of music Miles Davis became famous for not playing. It is also within this space of nonbeing that theatre practice implicitly becomes an occasion for the possibility of mourning.

Of all the configurations of character that inhabit the history of theatre, perhaps Hamlet and his father's ghost most fully demonstrate the configuration of fragments of text and performance, writing and voice, that compose the imaginary wholeness of character, author, and play and most fully place them in the context of mourning. One scene in particular is emblematic of the multiple elements that tie the fragmentary aspects of text, writing, and character to mourning and the imaginary wholeness of Hamlet and *Hamlet*.

After the ghost tells his story to young Hamlet and exits with the words, "Adieu, adieu, adieu! remember me" (1.5.91), a stage direction is sometimes inserted, though it does not appear in either Quarto 1, or Quarto 2, or the Folio. Swearing "from the table of [his] memory" to "wipe away all trivial fond records" (1.5.98-99), Hamlet says eight lines later, "My tables—meet it is I set it down / That one may smile, and smile, and be a villain! / At least I am sure it may be so in Denmark" (107-9). Then, the stage direction says, "He writes." This note was added by the editor Nicholas Rowe in 1709 and has appeared in most printed versions since, whether they are based on Q2, Q1, or F. The general habit of losing this piece of business in performance is understandable. It is presumably difficult to find the rationale for Hamlet running off to meet his father's spirit while carrying his "tables" or, for that matter, a piece of paper and writing tool. If any such tablet were previously set onstage as a handy prop, it could certainly be a version of the Renaissance commonplace book used to record the various *sententiae* of learned wisdom. It is not particularly easy to situate the conversation within reach of writing materials, however, since young Hamlet has just followed the ghost from the battlements to some presumably private place.

What does Hamlet write? Anthony Dawson assumes it is the commonplace idea that one may smile and smile and be a villain. Or is it rather the dozen or so lines he will eventually give to the players? Maybe the very text of *Hamlet* within which he will find himself acting? Or, "note to self: remember ghost"? On his newly blank tablet of memory, in which "all saws of books, all forms, all pressures past / That youth and observation copied there" (1.5.100-101) have been erased, what new pressure imprints the page? There is some possibility that he might write the whole story of Claudius and Gertrude he has just heard, for just after the direction he says, "So, uncle, there you are" (110), suggesting he might be putting a period to his writing. On the other hand, he might simply write down the ghost's demand to remember—"Now to my word; / It is 'adieu, adieu! remember me.' / I have sworn it" (110-12)—given the short time for writing between the direction, that last line, and the entrance of Horatio and Marcellus. Onstage, the action of writing might well wear the patience of an audience. Henry Irving notably restored it in the nineteenth century. But as Anthony Dawson notes, Irving did not, "like many a minor Hamlet of his day, inscribe his banal thought 'with grand deliberation and careful pose'; rather, he took them from his pocket and wrote in 'an outburst hardly distinguishable from hysteria.'"[23] Irving established by this the motif of Hamlet's writing, so after the line "The play's the thing" (2.2.633), he put his notebook against a pillar "and began as the curtain fell, 'to scribble hints for the speech he mean[t] to write.'"[24]

As a direction indicating the motifs of words, of writing and remembering, and of promising and acting, that run through the play, however, the moment and its curiosities enact the problematic status of written texts within any performance. What is that writing but an example of how writing itself is haunted by events, unless it is an example of how events are haunted by writing, as performance is haunted by texts. For writing itself is a ghostly act. The hand that writes is invisible, absent from the graphic signs on wall or page; but so also is writing absent from the staged performance. It returns to the stage if the Hamlet actor takes the moment to write. But whether or not he actually does the bit of business or keeps the focus on his mind and the "table of memory," this is a moment in which the writing of the script is staged. Nigel Alexander has suggested that he writes his "word" "adieu, adieu! remember me" as a mnemonic device, in a sense related to a motto or emblem that would trigger the memory of a whole.[25] In other words, it is the fragment or trigger for the memory of the whole story. A sign for young Hamlet's own awareness of forgetfulness, his writing is a reminder not only of his anticipated failure to remember what really happened but also of his failure to know in the first place.

The ghost's story, then, is the medial territory between an original lack and an anticipated forgetfulness, a territory similarly bridged by figurative language but also by the analogous connection between written text and spatial enactment, that is, the space of theatre. That text and space coexist without being identical, however, leads further to a kind of mixing of metaphors. Thus, Jonathan Goldberg takes this mixed metaphor right to Hamlet, suggesting the space that characterizes his mind is a scene of writing:

> Hamlet's memory is a theater, the "distracted globe," and a scene for the inscription of character. Remembering is at the same time erasing "all pressures past." For the memory to be supplemented, it must also be supplanted. The mind is a locus of *copia;* it is a book. There is, in Hamlet's mind, a scene of writing, and it is the one staged with the ghost in this scene of inscription.[26]

Margery Garber points out that this same scene of writing in *Hamlet* identifies a difference between what Hegel called *Erinnerung,* or "inner gathering and preserving of experience," and *Gedächtnis,* or the "words considered as names [that] cannot be separated from the notation, the inscription, or the writing down of these names."[27] Here, Hamlet's interior recollection is an awareness of loss, which is to say a blank space in memory. Not until he hears the ghost's story is he able to fill the blank with words, narrative, and judgment: "O most pernicious woman!" (1.5.105). Before writing, he promises to erase his own memory, to "wipe away all trivial fond records." Thus, "he both inscribes and constitutes the paternal story of a past which, in its pastness, is necessarily fictive, since it is only experienced *as* past, a tale, as narrative."[28] The double absence of a past in the present and the present in the future is supplemented by writing, *Gedächtnis,* thus making writing the sign of mourning for the double loss. The present, with Garber quoting Derrida, is "fabled . . . including all the figures of death with which we people the 'present,' which we inscribe (among ourselves, the living) in every trace (otherwise called 'survivals'): those figures we inscribe because they can outlast us, beyond the present of their inscription: signs, words, letters, this whole text whose legacy-value, as we know, 'in the present,' is trying its luck and advancing, *in advance* 'in memory of.'"[29]

Hamlet's doubt is thus the most likely response to the demands of the ghost. But it is that very doubt that inhabits the space of theatre and constitutes its strange enactments of writing. In other words, if writing, either literally or figuratively, is an inscription that creates memory, its enactments vivify memory in a present constituted by the fable, a pre-text. The double lack of past and future remains. They are supplemented by actions in a present, but those actions are themselves a doubtable working out of a textual inscription. So Hamlet is not simply a paradigmatic actor; he is the impersonation of theatre, insofar as theatre is a space for working out complex relations between remembering and forgetting. In the first instance, this remembering involves not *what* has been forgotten but *that* something has been forgotten. In other words, the ghost's information about Gertrude, Claudius, and his murder is as fully figurative and doubtable as the ghost itself. Hamlet certainly acts out of that doubt, but he is also acting out of the fact of the unknown, of the forgotten. His theatre—the microcosm of his mind and the macrocosm of the Globe—presents its images of remembrance for the fact of forgetfulness, and the fact of that forgetfulness or absence is a vital constituent of the theatre. Hamlet/theatre is a space based in a doubtable origin, a missing and forgotten story. But what is missing nonetheless entails a certain responsibility to act; the missing origin both belongs to and is separate from its positive images and actions; like Hamlet, theatre thus contains its own doubleness, its own otherness.

This spatial image for this strange doubleness actually reformulates the questions of memory posed by Augustine. Augustine imagines the memory as a cavernous space, sometimes as a great hall, with nooks and crannies, mysterious compartments, and infinite profundity. Some elements enter through the senses, he says, but other elements in memory are learned skills, rhetorical and mathematical principles, and ideas, which do not have an origin in the senses and therefore are not images but "realities":

> Memory's huge cavern, with its mysterious secret, and indescribable nooks and crannies, receives all these perceptions, to be recalled when needed and reconsidered. The objects themselves do not enter, but the images of the perceived objects are available to the thought recalling them. But who can say how images are created, even though it may be clear by which senses they are grasped and stored within. For even when I am in darkness and silence, in my memory I can produce colours at will, and distinguish between white and black and between whatever colours I wish. Sounds do not invade and disturb my consideration of what my eyes absorb, even though they are present and as it were hide in an independent storehouse. . . . With my tongue silent and my throat making no sound, I can sing what I wish. . . .
> . . . But these are not the only things carried by the vast capacity of my memory. Here also are all the skills acquired through the liberal arts which have not been forgotten. They are pushed into the background in some interior place—which is not a place.[30]

This placeless place, for Augustine, contains further paradoxes. For, he says, memory also contains forgetfulness. "Unless we could recall forgetfulness, we could never hear the word and recognize the thing which the word signifies. Therefore memory retains forgetfulness. So it is there lest we forget what, when present, makes us forget. Should the deduction from this be that, when we are remembering forgetfulness, it is not through its actual presence in the memory but through its image? If forgetfulness were present through itself, it would cause us not to remember but to forget. Who can find a solution to this problem?"[31]

Forgetfulness is of the mind, "in" the mind; however, in remembering forgetfulness, the mind is not forgetting but remembering the "thing" that is part of itself. How can forgetfulness be both the thing itself and an image of itself, which can be remembered? he asks. Forgetfulness must have been a reality in order for it to be remembered, but how did it inscribe itself in memory if by its very presence it erases what is found there? How do I remember what I have forgotten? Augustine takes the issues in other directions, toward the memory of his conversion and the certainty of his love of God. In other words, he solves his paradoxes by an escape to the imaginary oneness of a God who encompasses all paradoxes. The paradoxes he presents are apt here to the extent that he is interested not simply in memory based on a variety of recalled experiences but in how an experience of erasure (forgetfulness) can "inscribe" a positive image or knowledge of itself without erasing itself. In response to that question, memory, or what one could call the "scene" of inscription, could here be understood in terms of inscription that, like Hamlet's, stands in the medial territory between the anticipation of forgetting and the experience of a failure to know in the first place.

In Hamlet's scene, the memory's metaphors of writing and space become mixed, as they did for Augustine. In spatial terms, Hamlet's memory is a cavern, a hall, full of nooks and crannies. As Frances Yates points out, the classical techniques for the "art" of memory were almost entirely spatial. Recall the story of Simonides in chapter 1, who identified the victims of the catastrophic banquet by where they had sat. Later, in the Renaissance, techniques of memory were specifically theatrical. Recounting the lessons from the first-century document *Ad Herennium,* Yates details the tradition of using images of large, empty buildings and architectural detail for situating and ordering the memory. Particularly useful for the rhetoricians, elements of a speech could be recalled from the images of various sites or places in the building or identified with certain objects: the forecourt, the "parlor," or bedrooms, corners, or niches that might hold statuary. The image of a theatrical scene could likewise be used either to remember the details of a whole situation or as associational devices for words and names. Since images are more easily retained than specific words, the first element for remembering things or words is to give them a location in space or association with an object. But even at this early point, there seems to be an analogy between these places for memory and writing. "The art of memory is like an inner writing. Those who know the letters of the alphabet can write down what is dictated to them and read out what they have written. Likewise those who have learned mnemonics can set in places what they have heard and deliver it from memory. 'For the places are very much like wax tablets or papyrus, the images like the letters, the arrangement and disposition of the images like the script, and the delivery is like the reading.'"[32]

Such analogous ways of thinking of the similarity between writing and images of things and place seem to be attempts to render a kind of wholeness that subsumes differences in the modes of delivery: material objects, words, images, meaning. The vast and intricate system of correspondences between macro- and microcosms, between heavenly and earthly realms, among ideas, words, and images, between myth and history, typifies later Renaissance thought influenced by the Hermetic tradition and its incorporation of elements of Neoplatonism, the Jewish Kabbalah, and the writings of Hermes Trismegistus. The occulting of differences between spatial images and writing nevertheless retains the particularity of each element while placing it in a vast and diverse system of, once again, an imaginary wholeness that is accessible to the mind through memory. The images of physical spaces or objects are seen as analogous to writing in the *Ad Herennium,* presumably because they both externalize and specify details for use by what is called the artificial memory, that is, that which is learned and studied as opposed to that which is a "natural" capacity.[33]

The combination of scenic spaces and writing was concretized in Giulio Camillo's Memory Theater, built in the sixteenth century ostensibly for Francis I of France. This was a large wooden structure that could apparently hold two "spectators." Inside, in the shape of a Vetruvian amphitheater, a reconstruction of the theater plan by Yates shows seven tiers of seven rows arranged in a semicircle. Each row was identified with a planet, each tier with a gradation through the stages of creation, from the gods, to "primal matter," the elements, the interior (mind and soul) of humans, the union of soul and body, to "all the operations which man can perform naturally, without art," and finally to the Promethean grade, concerning "all the arts and sciences, religion and law." Based on the occult traditions but "never perfected," this Memory Theater purported to contain "the Ideas of all things both in the celestial and in the inferior worlds."[34] Compartments in each of the seven rows on each of the seven tiers were painted with images related to the meaning of the grade in the hierarchy. The emblematic and spatial arrangements, however, were just the façade of these compartments. For behind each door was a container with masses of written documents supposedly based on the works of Cicero and related to the subjects indicated by the images. Yates comments, "When one thinks of all these drawers or coffers in the Theatre it begins to look like a highly ornamental filing cabinet. But this is to lose sight of the grandeur of the Idea— the Idea of a memory organically geared to the universe."[35] While there are documented reports from those who saw Camillo's Memory Theater, and it served his reputation as a genius of the time, it was never delivered to Francis I and, by 1550, had disappeared. Only written reports and *L'idea del teatro dell'eccellen M. Giulio Camillo* remain. The latter work was published in 1550 after his death. And it was not, apparently, even written by Camillo but dictated to Girolamo Muzio "on seven mornings" when Camillo worked in Milan. The grand labor of imagination and wood, his Memory Theater, comes through history in writing alone, its concrete manifestation unfinished and, like the dictating voice, lost. Camillo's own dead voice whispers through the leaves of manuscripts like ashes, and the vast memory system containing all learning remains, at most, a lost possibility of the whole.

Performance is obviously, chronically haunted by writing. In the most conventional sense, a play text precedes performance as a disembodied demand for action and embodiment. It is the patrilinear authority of the word that requires both interpretation and adherence to its nevertheless questionable authority. Yet, whatever authority the word may demand through its patriarchal lineage, its authority is full of holes and ambiguities, subject to misreading, misinterpreting, mistakes. The word is open, like a text, and its authority is never unequivocal, precisely because it does not disappear in the way that performance does. The words remain, and in remaining they become subject to endless permutations of use: reinterpretations, re-references, temporal distortion. The authority of the word is largely help-less without both the belief and the instrumentality of the living. Like the ghost of the father Hamlet, it can haunt, it can terrify, it can tell stories, it can demand. But its status is questionable, for it can also lie and act as much as an agent from hell as a minister of grace. The writing ghost of words, like the "authority" of the text, makes its appearance and calls on the inter-pretive Hamlets to do it justice, but that very authority is subject to ques-tion. The ghostly invocations of the word call for parity between the writing and action, between the past and the future, between intention and recep-tion, which are all modes of justice. But such parity is an impossible ideal in the translation from word to deed, from the disembodied spirit of the letter to the embodied acts of the flesh.

In the space of the difference between events and writing, there is a third party who is called on to do justice to each. That third party, call it reader, interpreter, critic, or actor, mediates between them by a specific act. The subject must become a subject first by interpreting the meaning of the tex-tual demand—the hermeneutic gesture—then by transcribing that mean-ing into the fleshly forms of social praxis. There are thus three elements in the haunted situation: the haunting ghost, the material scene/event, and the agent-subject who is called on to carry out their mediation and, in doing so, to produce a new iteration, a new subject. As Barbara Johnson points out in her essay on three texts, Derrida's commentary on Lacan's commen-tary on Poe's story "The Purloined Letter,"

> Any attempt to do "justice" to three such complex texts is obviously out of the question. But it is precisely the nature of such "justice" that is the ques-tion of these readings of the act of analysis. The fact that the debate prolif-erates around a crime story—a robbery and its undoing—can hardly be an accident. Somewhere in each of these texts, the economy of justice cannot be avoided. For in spite of the absence of mastery, there is no lack of effects of power.[36]

In this sense, the haunting of performance by the words of a text presents the problem of justice that belongs as much to theatre as to law, criticism, history, and hermeneutics. And unlike the primarily verbal fields of criti-cism, history, and hermeneutics, theatre and the law are more distinctively haunted because the effects of power involve the simultaneity of the seen and unseen, of real bodies and absent texts, and of material, performative events held in check by the authority of words.

The haunting of actions by words, however, is reversible, for words are also haunted by the absent realities they record, realities that reappear as the repetition of structure, which has the uncanny effect of both familiarity and strangeness. Haunted space collapses temporal linearity among past, present, and future. It suggests that the apparent permanence of words, a permanence that renders events intelligible, is haunted by loss and the unintelligibility of the Real, of the unrepeatable Now that constitutes the criminality of time and the uniqueness of what Maurice Blanchot calls "the disaster." Even though a performance is preceded by writing, its singularity remains, and like the historical real, it too calls out for further justice through writing. Performance calls out to be documented and matched by the words that would save it from the loss of reality, the loss of itself. A real performance haunts the failure of words to equal the deeds to which they refer, even while the words haunt the performance they engender. Between these two kinds of ghosts, the subject must find itself in and through action. Just as absent writing haunts the acts onstage, the stage performance haunts the words on the page. Ghosts of both kinds appear through the temporal disjunction, demanding justice through the agency of a subject, a justice that is impossible to fulfill. For as Johnson points out, the only recourse for the delivery of justice, whether for critic, jurist, or historian, is through paraphrase or quotation. To this I would add the recourse for justice to the text in performance through the pretenses of the actor, who, by virtue of pretense, becomes the representative of representation, the false face that is real. For the actor is both haunted and haunting, both quoting and speaking. The scholar Horatio cannot converse with the ghost ("Thou art a scholar; speak to it, Horatio," says Marcellus [1.1.42]); only Hamlet, the paragon of actors, can both speak and be spoken to.

How do we hear the voices of the dead? What kind of attunement do we need to hear them? And how do we make sense of those voices that whisper and rustle like ashes and leaves? Writing is said to have a voice. Yet where, precisely, is the voice of a text? Or rather, what does it mean for a text to have a voice? Whose voice is it? The absent author's? The reader's? That of language itself? We are back to the question, Who is speaking? Voice has timbre, resonance, tone, grain. If writing is a memorial device for and by an absent author, its voice must be a kind of echo coming from within the text, an echo produced not necessarily by an originating body but by the body of the writing itself. Unvoiced, words sift into the mind from the vast territories of the dead, as Beckett describes them: faint rustles from all the words that remain unheard, unremembered. Shape and rhythm emerge into the sense of individual words. Voiced, as in performance, words recover the sonorous resonance and particularity of a body. In the performance, words return from the dead to the voices of the living, and the voice of the text is transfigured; it remains yet becomes other than itself. A text, in terms of the voice, then, stands silently between its future emergence into a body and the echo of its own voice.

Historical writing tends to tame its ghosts. History as a collection of written documents banishes ghosts from three-dimensional space and regulates them into the norms of narrative and facts, exorcising the uncanniness of an absent past that is present. The enclosed space of a theater building, however, materially contains its own past and refuses to release it. It becomes the self-representation of its own history of representation and in that sense becomes a preservative space, like a monument or a tomb. The emptiness of its space is crucial to the double, if contradictory, function of preservation and release into time. The space gathers time through its continuity and releases it in performance like a continuously filling and emptying vessel. As quoted above: "In the sepulcher which the historian inhabits, only 'emptiness remains.'"[37] De Certeau understands writing history more theatrically than most: he understands writing both to refer to and to create a "making, a doing." For him, the writing of history is spatial, a discourse that is simultaneously internal and external to its object but still contingent upon ruptures:

> This relation of discourse to a "doing" is internal to its object since, in one fashion or another, history always deals with tensions, webbings of conflicts, or plays of force. But it is also external to its object, insofar as modes of comprehension and types of discourse are determined by the greater sociocultural ensemble which defines the particular situation of history. Stable societies allow history to favor continuities and tend to confer the value of human essence upon a solidly established order. In periods of movement or revolution, ruptures of individual or collective action become the principle of historical intelligibility.[38]

The enclosure of theatre space, its unique containment, does not draw a line between the internal and external relation to the other of history—the past—that discourse draws, because it releases discourse into an event. The event of a performance, that is, has the same instabilities as an "original" event. Theatre thus encompasses both rupture and repetition. Theatre space is both a scene for other histories (i.e., the representation "of" something other, some historical subject/object) and the scene of its own history (i.e., the trace of self-representation representing itself), which is another scene, a scene of otherness. Thus Shakespeare's Chorus in *Henry V* can only wish for "a Muse of fire . . . / A kingdom for a stage, princes to act, / And monarchs to behold the swelling scene" (Prol. 1–4), for the theatre space both fails the original scene and reanimates it. The status of theatrical representation, more material, real, and concrete than discourse alone, refuses, unlike much historical discourse, to assert its truth too far beyond its materiality. It "honors" the dead by bringing them to life and making them disappear again in performance. But it also asks the audience to "entertain conjecture of a time" by shaping imagination around the contours of what has been lost, "when creeping murmur and the poring dark, / Fills the wide vessel of the universe" (4. prol. 2–3).

> After having successfully passed through the *History of France*, the shadows "have returned less saddened to their tombs." Discourse drives them back into the dark. It is a deposition. It turns them into *severed souls*. It honors them with a ritual of which they had been deprived. It "bemoans" them by fulfilling the duty of filial piety enjoined upon Freud through a dream in which he saw written on the wall of a railway station, "Please close the eyes." Michelet's "tenderness" seeks one after another of the dead in order to insert every one of them into time, "this omnipotent decorator of ruins: O Time beautifying of things!" The dear departed find a haven in the text *because* they can neither speak nor do harm anymore. The ghosts find access through *writing* on the condition that they remain *forever silent*.[39]

The ghosts of history may enter time through the duration of performance, but on their exit from performance they enter the "sepulcher" of the theater's space itself, the space in Michelet's terms, of the historian who traffics in ghosts. Whatever noise occurs in its daytime activities or dazzling light of public performances, the theater goes silent in its after hours and allows the ghosts of the past to return to the timeless zone of the dead and to haunt the empty space. Edith Wharton insisted that ghosts require silence and continuity, and it is in the silence and the dim ghost light of those after hours that the history of the space becomes a palpable presence, though in the absence of a living human that presence is unfelt, unrecognized, and unknown. An empty theater's space contains the reality of those unknowns and keeps the secrets of the dead in its silence. The same could probably be said of any architectural space. After hours in a contemporary office building or a schoolroom can be as unsettling as the isolated, aged manor house of gothic tales. What sets a theater apart from other institutional spaces is not so much that it is haunted as that it produces ghosts by design. Related but not identical to the raising of the dead by historical discourse, performance brings them to life on the site of their entombment, the theater.

If history, according to de Certeau, is a discourse from within the sepulcher of the dead, if it traffics with the dead, it is also a murderer. But de Certeau sees the writing of history, implicitly, in terms of performance:

> Writing speaks of the past only in order to inter it. Writing is a tomb in the double sense of the word in that, in the very same text, it both honors and eliminates. Here the function of language is to introduce through *saying* what can no longer be *done*. Language exorcises death and arranges it in the narrative that pedagogically replaces it with something that the reader must believe and do. This process is repeated in other unscientific ways, from the funeral eulogy in the streets to burial ceremonies. But unlike other artistic or social "tombs," here taking the dead or the past back to a symbolic place is connected to the labor aimed at creating in the present a place (past or future) to be filled, a "something that must be done." Writing gathers together the products of this labor. In this way it liberates the present without having to name it. Thus it can be said that writing makes the dead so that the living can exist elsewhere. . . .
>
> As a substitute for the absent being, an enclosure of the evil genius of death, the historical text plays a performative role.[40]

In its performative aspect, writing does have a body and a space; for history, that does make writing a corporeal interment of a living past. But de Certeau already identifies a couple of differences between writing's performance and what occurs in the space of theatre. First is the difference between saying and doing. In theatre space, history is done, not said, and done again, repeated by bodies in a trajectory of mortality that is identical to that done in the original instance. Always, as Herbert Blau has said, "someone is dying in front of your eyes."[41] In theatrical space, performance does not inter the past so much as raise the dead, in a ghostly repetition that is the same insofar as it is mortal. That is, it raises the dead from within the paradoxical space of sameness and repetition, sameness and difference. It must be haunted if it is to be effective. It must take the ghosts from the tombs of written memorialization and return to an audience the affective sorrow of experience rather than the sealed tomb of memorialization that leads not only to forgetfulness but also to the further violence of congealed nationalism. Second, if writing creates a space in the present for something to be done, then performance in the theater is such a doing, just as the writing of a dramatic text implies the historian's imperative to the present: a demand for something to be done.

Theatre's space physically encrypts the difference between something and nothing, between the human and the inhuman, between being and nonbeing, precisely because it is empty, because its permanent status is the empty nothing between appearances of something. While Peter Brook wrote of this empty space as something full of potential, his production of *Hamlet* in 2000 used theatre's emptiness as both an origin and a destination, which is to say a permanent feature of what shows in performance. A space of nothing where "nothing" happens, the acting area was set out on a large red carpet. A few pillows for interior scenes. Little else. The view of the nothingness behind the appearance of the performing actors is part of his debt to Asian theatre, particularly Noh and Kabuki, in which the concrete gestures of the actor incorporate all there is to know and see, yet still there is nothing; they mask death. This view on the emptiness of theatre renders the positive presence of the actor to a peculiarly vaulted space that encrypts the secrets of representation and death, the space of a riddle. The vault here is the disposition of three-dimensional space that functions like a body, which is to say as both a corpse and a living entity that enfold each other. The folding constitutes the space, both etymologically and physically. Inversely, then, the human body is also theaterlike: an inhabited space containing and exhibiting its own material and psychic history, ghosted by the continuing disappearance of its own present and presence, on a trajectory to and from nothingness, and encoded by family and cultural histories. Like the human body, the empty space of theatre is ghosted by its own history, by its family resemblances, by subjectivity and perception. Only the ghost light illuminates the fact that the space is haunted by an unknown past and by unknown others. The phenomenal appearance of the body, then, is also an encrypted space that, theaterlike, is haunted by the history of its own self-representation as well as the history of others who inhabit it. The body/theater is thus an exterior space that displays, like a hollow vessel or vaulted crypt, the surfaces of its own interiority. But such a space becomes most evident when it is cut, when its fragmented parts are severed from mundane contexts and show the sites of missing pieces. Those missing pieces become apparent in the paradox of theatrical claims that what happens in theatre is unreal. It is, in its materiality, at least as real as worldly matter. But because of its enfolded space, that reality is deniable, "untrue." Theatrical fiction is the deniability factor within theatre reality. The living presence of actors makes their ghostly status and the presence of nothingness, death, deniable. But the actors, as figures on a stage, are also cross-sections of the paradox and the fold. They cut across the fold at a fissure in the distinction between real and unreal, living and nonliving. At particular moments, and only briefly, they turn into ghost lights that illuminate the encrypted body and manufacture the haunted space.

As mentioned in chapter 1, the crypt is an image for a psychoanalytic notion of "incorporation." Abraham and Torok discuss incorporation as a topography in which a lost object, a rejected pleasure, is sealed off within the unconscious like a foreign body in order to preserve a moment of pleasure and at the same time to refuse to mourn for its loss. Distinct from "introjection," which involves the inclusion of a loved object and an expansion of the self toward the object, the crypt is a more radical and profound version of repression that seals off the lost loved object as a living dead. It is on the order of fantasy, says Derrida in "Foreword: *Fors:* The Anglish Words of Nicolas Abraham and Maria Torok," in their work on Freud's famous case of the Wolf Man, because

> fantasy *does not coerce,* it does not impose as Reality does (Reality as redefined in a metapsychological sense, but with an anasemic relation to the traditional philosophical, judicial, scientific, etc. uses of the word) from within or from without any topographical transformations. In contrast with Reality,

the fantasy tends to maintain the order of the *topoi*. All the clever tricks it can deploy obey a conservative, "narcissistic" finality. It is precisely this kind of resistance, refusal, disavowal, or denial that designates Reality as such: Reality is that which would require a change of place, a modification of the topography.[42]

Abraham and Torok elsewhere explain this sense of Reality specific to the "cryptophore" as the very thing that the patient denies. That is, by saying specifically "not that," the patient's denial situates the place within the psychic topography that supports the fantasy of incorporation. The denial of reality maintains the place and Reality of the living dead in the psychic structure. "Reality can then be defined as what is rejected, masked, denied, precisely as 'reality'; it is that which *is*, all the more so since it must not be known; in short Reality is defined as a *secret*. The metapsychological concept of Reality refers to the place, in the psychic apparatus, where the secret is buried."[43] This capitalized, metapsychological Reality is a secret location in the psychic structure and an internalized secret counterpart to the reality of the outside world.

Being secret, however, the Reality can also show itself in public, on the surfaces of speech and body, without fear of disclosure, not unlike Poe's famous purloined letter that hides in plain sight, in his short story of that title. It is secret even to those who incorporate the lost object, the "cryptophore." This encryption of the secret is entirely distinct from the conventions of repression. Repression is the consequence of a prohibition, and "only representations or desires are repressed." Repression belongs to a dynamic structure within the unconscious and the ego, like that of the hysteric. The cryptophore is a secret that shows but is obdurate against disclosure.

> The hysteric's desire and attendant representations are merely the offshoots of words that do not in fact voice desire or pleasure, but their prohibition. To call desire by the very name of its prohibition is the law of hysteria's transparent opacity. And that is fundamentally what we all do.
>
> Unless we also carry one—or many secrets. . . . What does it mean to be a cryptophore? How does such a condition occur? Just as desire is born along with prohibition, Reality too, at least in the metapsychological sense, is born of the necessity of remaining concealed, unspoken. This means that, at the moment of its birth, Reality is comparable to an offense, a crime. The

crime's name is not identical with prohibition, as is the case in the desire of the hysteric. Its name is genuinely affirmative, therefore unutterable, like the name of God or of orgasmic delight.[44]

Elsewhere Derrida describes the uncanny architecture of the space of incorporation that protects the secret of a "Word-Thing." It is the place-less place that breaks in between the dualism of conscious and unconscious to create an "artificial unconscious." It preserves the exclusion of an unspeak-able pleasure in an indecipherable word-object. The cryptic rift belongs neither to the discourses of language and texts nor to the spatiality of objects and therefore registers only as a nonsense, in both sensory and linguistic ways. It is subject neither to repetition nor to return, because it does not enter the unconscious in such a way that leads to return, because it is the effect of a "refused mourning." Its inside surfaces are its outside; it is a place of no-place that kills the object in order to preserve the object of desire and preserves it in order to kill it.

> The cryptic enclave, between "the dynamic unconscious" and the "Self of introjection," forms, inside the self, inside the general space of the self, a kind of pocket of resistance, the hard cyst of an "artificial unconscious." The interior is partitioned off from the interior. The most inward safe (the crypt as an artificial unconscious, as the Self's artifact) becomes the outcast . . . , the outside . . . with respect to the outer safe (the Self) that includes it with-out comprehending it, in order to comprehend *nothing* in it. The inner safe (the Self) has placed itself outside the crypt, or, if one prefers, has consti-tuted "within itself" the crypt as an outer safe. One might go on indefinitely switching the place names around in this dizzying topology (the inside as the outside of the outside, or of the inside; the outside as the inside of the inside, or of the outside, etc.), but total con-fusion is not possible. The parietal par-titions are *very* solid.[45]

The French have a word for this paradoxical image of inside/out. *Appareil* roughly translates into the word *apparatus,* signifying at once formal or organizational appearances—or conversely the appearance of formal orga-nization—as well as the machinery, paraphernalia, or appliances that con-stitute a structure. Rather than a "deep structure" that underlies external appearances, *l'appareil* is a display of structure, a visible form that shelters an emptiness or wound. In the context of surgery, it relates to the "dispo-sition" of the organs; in architecture, to the disposition or arrangement of stones, particularly in the form of vaults or domes. In other circumstances, it refers to the "dressing" that binds a wound. In psychoanalytic fields, Laplanche and Pontalis refer to the *appareil psychique* as having an interior. The word is a significant constellation of spatial ideas that link the external and visible elements of a structure to a very specific form, the vault. The apparatus shapes a hollow interior whose surfaces keep the secrets of the dead.

The architectural image of the "psychical apparatus" provides a sense of how the psyche may be not just an immaterial, mental, or emotional abstraction from the body but an organization for the body. More than a metaphor for similarities between psyche and soma, that is, this sense of the body and of theatre suggests that the organization of the body is an appearing structure for the organization of the psyche. The psyche, "spirit" or "soul," the haunting ghost, is not simply translated or manifested by the body; rather, it organizes the body and is visible on the surfaces that, like the form of the vault, are nonetheless hollow, empty. This means that the body, as the theater, is a site, like a crypt: an apparatus designed for both protection and preservation. This image refuses the psyche/soma split and the bar that divides either one in its function as Signifier. It further insists on the simultaneity and copresence, even fusion, of psyche and soma. It is also to say that the *appareil psychique* is not simply analogous to the body but *of* the body. The functioning of the body, then, directly correlates to the functioning of what we may call the psyche. By taking a place in three-dimensional space, the body is the organizational "equipment" whose very organization creates the spaces of preservation and protection. Language is the one thing that exceeds the psyche/soma and provides the ability to conceive of the difference by virtue of its own apparatus. Exceeding the body, however, does not mean that language fully escapes it. Those aspects of the psyche that exceed the physical body through language find them-selves in turn incorporated by language in its sonorous, rhythmic, poetic bodies. Pathological in the case of Freud's Wolf Man, the cryptophore none-theless takes its strange status from the same impossible mixture of words and space that constitute the "theatre of memory." "One could say that the cryptic forum is the general theater of all the maneuvers, of all the trans-actions made to prevent the contradiction from turning into a catastrophe,

into one of those two catastrophes between which one has but to choose. . . .
It must first be recognized that the crypt is itself the catastrophe, or rather
its monument."[46]

As a space intended for representation, a theater/body memorializes both
lack and loss as a condition of the positive and material aspects of representation. That conditioning of representation by lack/loss, whose ultimate
instance is death, is neither a matter of someone's personal death nor an
abstract concept. Rather, formal absences in the materiality of the representation locate the place of death that representation itself creates: the crypt,
the hollowed vault of a space of an exterior internality. Inhering to the
materiality of the representation, in this case the materiality of the space
of a theater building—or, in writing, to the differences between the sonorous and the graphic, the spatial and the verbal—the inevitable separation
between the inert material signifier and the signified leaves an empty space,
a shattered anatomy, haunted by spirits. These haunting spirits are the re-
mainders of human desire to attach life to the corpses, presence to absences,
and to bring the representational "thing" to a life inhabited by meaning.
That desire was perhaps best articulated by Artaud as theatre without representation. Derrida explains:

> For what his howls promise us, articulating themselves under the headings
> of *existence, flesh, life, theater, cruelty[,]* is the meaning of an art prior to mad-
> ness *and* the work, an art which no longer yields works, an artist's existence
> which is no longer a route or an experience that gives access to something
> other than itself, an ur-text or an ur-speech.[47]

As Derrida notes, that desire is impossible to realize in any actual performance, impossible to make more "real" than its presence as a lack in the
empty space of the theater. Artaud's claim to a sign that is free of representation outside itself, free of an object outside or beyond, free of repetition,
veils an idealism whose enactment in the formal materials of performance
is always only a potential. Its very lack of achievement, however, generates
the continuing efforts in both philosophy and theatre to bridge the aporia
of lack, of loss, of death. Dance often comes closer than the embodied
texts of drama to the presentation of the body as hieroglyph, as a graphic
sign made by the body, still breathing with life. Hence Artaud's injunction
against "masterpieces" of drama. "Artaud also desired the impossibility of

theater, wanted to erase the stage, no longer wanted to see what transpires in a locality always inhabited or haunted by the father and subjected to the repetition of murder."[48]

The threat of amnesia is, of course, the reason for building monuments and museums as well as for writing and documenting. But there are different sorts of memorials. Those made to be permanent are built or written to oppose forgetfulness. Those that are edifices keep a memory dedicated to the dead in a material structure. They are meant to keep memory safe from the decaying actions of time. The material space of the monument specifically incorporates the dynamic of remembering and forgetting. That is to say that in the monument both forgetting and remembering are materialized, in the stone, marble, or concrete. But the stasis of the monument, the stillness of the crypt, replaces active mourning, and its habitual presence also becomes a way of forgetting. Another kind of memorial is spontaneous, ephemeral, like those appearing after sudden shocks and catastrophic disasters. They appear on roadsides at the site of traffic accidents. They appeared after the death of Princess Diana; in New York City in Union Square after the World Trade Center destruction; at church doors; at the sides of city streets. Usually made of flowers or candles, scrawled messages or pictures, a toy, a flag, a stuffed animal, these memorials are not meant to last. They are, rather, performative gestures of grief. They are momentarily expressive or expressive of the moment. Not assembled to combat the forgetfulness over time, they speak in the present of an otherwise unutterable sorrow. They are a means of doing something with the grief, a means of acting it out ritually rather than containing and solidifying it. The placement of the flower, the candle, is the gesture of grief, not a substitute for it. Such memorials create a focal point or vortex around which the living lay their tributes to the dead.

The permanent memorial, by contrast, becomes a substitute for grief. The edifice stands in for the act of mourning. Though the act of building may be a performative gesture, permanence transmutes the act into an object that, like an idealized love, both refuses and replaces the act. It is the marker of a trauma that stands in place of what cannot be spoken of, and it presents to sight what cannot be seen or witnessed: death. The memorial object tries to escape time by being timeless but, over time, engenders forgetfulness. The memorial statue or edifice literally incorporates the phantoms of haunted memory and freezes them in matter, having no hollow. But as an edifice, it incorporates the impossibility of forgetting at the same time that it allows forgetting to occur. The tomb, the monument, is thus a cryptic substitution for the act of mourning.

Freud used the image of the monument to explain the fixations of hysterical patients in his lecture on psychoanalysis at Clark University in 1909. In that speech he made the famous declaration that "our hysterical patients suffer from reminiscences." The hysterical symptoms, identical to hysteria itself, he said, were the "residues and mnemic symbols of particular [traumatic] experiences." With a remarkable analogy that noted the public displays of the psychic apparatus, he said to look to "the monuments and memorials with which large cities are adorned."[49] He cited the thirteenth-century cross at Charing Cross in London (or, by 1909, a copy of the original cross, as Ernst Jones pointed out in a footnote), where Henry II marked the resting places of the cortege of Eleanor d'Aquitaine's coffin on its way to Westminister. That cross and the Monument of the Great Fire of 1666 are Freud's reference points to the public and material symbols for memory.

> These monuments resemble hysterical symptoms in being mnemic symbols; up to that point the comparison seems justifiable. But what should we think of a Londoner who paused today in deep melancholy before the memorial of Queen Eleanor's funeral instead of going about his business in the hurry that modern working conditions demand or again [of] a Londoner who shed tears before the Monument that commemorates the reduction of this beloved metropolis to ashes? . . . Yet every single hysteric and neurotic behaves like these two unpractical Londoners. Not only do they remember painful experiences of the remote past, but they still cling to them emotionally; they cannot get free of the past and for its sake they neglect what is real and immediate.[50]

The public monument is the vehicle for forgetting, for getting on with what Freud calls real and immediate. As the monument becomes subject to time, its presence is ever more evidently an inert relic, unable either to speak of that which it marks or to speak to those who remain. Having paid due respect to the dead by building it, the public is free to leave off its mourning and get on with the business of life.

Lacan, at one point in "The Field and Function of Language," aligns amnesia with the unconscious in an index that points to the signs of history preserved by encrypted material reality. He writes:

The unconscious is that chapter of my history that is marked by a blank or occupied by a falsehood: it is the censored chapter. But the truth can be re-discovered; usually it has already been written down elsewhere. Namely:

in monuments: this is my body; . . .

in archival documents: these are my childhood memories . . . as impen-etrable as . . . documents when I do not know their provenance; . . .

in semantic evolution: this corresponds to the stock of words and acceptations of my own particular vocabulary, as it does to my style of life and to my character;

in traditions, too, and even in the legends which, in a heroicized form, bear my history;

and, lastly, in the traces that are inevitably preserved by the distortions necessitated by the linking of the adulterated chapter to the chapters surrounding it.[51]

The cryptic sites, in other words, are in bodies, in documents with unknown provenance, in word choices, traditions, distortions: these symptomatically locate loss of memory or, in the case of trauma, what has never been recorded in consciousness. The "truth" of the blank in memory, as in his-tory, can never be recovered in any pristine form. If it returns, it returns already eroded by absences. The lost history returns neither as the original nor as a duplicate, for the lost history has not gone anywhere from which to return. It is already in place as a fault line or a fissure that shapes a psy-chic topography of history. Lacan's list is an index not of *what* to look for (the "truth") but of where to look for the losses that are hiding in the plain sight of physicality and all the sensory mechanisms, hearing, touch, taste, sight, and smell. Look, in other words, to the body, the corporeal mani-festation of its own past, where gestures, tics, rhythms, comportment tell of its losses. Take note of fragments, images, tunes that seem to have no source. Pay attention to the choices of words, sounds, their etymologies, the gaps in sense, the leaps over time; notice how word choices both for materiality and for abstraction manifest the unwritten and written history. Secrets are revealed in rhetorical and poetic forces. Pay attention to the heroic narrative of an idealized identity or the idealized clarity of right and wrong to discover the cover-up. And especially notice the sites of distor-tions that betray the presence of unseen bodies, like those invisible black holes that are found only by the warping of the space around them. Look, in other words, to the materiality, not the meaning. These locales hide the lost history on their surfaces, where the writing is sometimes so obvious it is invisible. This idea was present in the earliest days of Freud when he wrote of the case of Anna O., in which he and Breuer first found the effectiveness of a "talking cure." He said, "Wherever there is a symptom there is also an amnesia." That is, whatever is forgotten is being manifested even while it is unrecognized. Amnesia is in no way like a secret, which is something known and held back. It is the utter lack of the consciousness of a time that the body nonetheless has lived through, so it is the body that bears the traces.

What should we, indeed, think of a Londoner who pauses to weep at the resting place for the cortege of Eleanor d'Aquitaine, or, for that matter, at the gates of Kensington Palace, for Princess Diana? The mourning signaled by the flowers at Kensington Palace, however, was theatrical rather than memorial. It is now long gone. That is to say the placing of flowers established a monumental site, though not as a permanent structure but as temporary one, a theatrical one. That particular outpouring was a transitional, ephemeral, transformative process and as such aligned with the performative transformations of theatre. Similarly, the elemental aspects of Maya Lin's memorials, the running water at the Civil Rights Memorial or the granite scarred with names at the Vietnam Veterans Memorial, resist the encrypted space and give mourning back to the earth, as the water runs over the markers of time, as visitors descend and emerge along the wall. In other words, there is motion and meeting, not stasis and observation. The names on the Vietnam wall are listed in chronological order, "so," she is quoted as saying, "a veteran can find his time within the panels": a place, that is, where the living can find his or her *time* from among the dead. Rather than a means of forgetting, these more recent memorials, such as Lin's and Arad's, show a way of remembering and encountering loss without hysterical symptoms.

The deadly monument, by contrast, is intended to remain a permanent public object, like the hysterical symptom or the neurosis, each one resisting the intersubjective, transformative character of performance in the theatrical space. This is where the theater, cryptlike, stands apart from the solid monument: its hollowness both preserves and empties itself through performance, allows remembering and forgetting to be simultaneous instead of sequential, because they are what is "being done." In other words, its haunted space reflects the therapeutic space of exchange both between the encrypted past and the present intersubjective space and between living and dead.

Amnesia is a preservative, a sheltering crypt where the voices of the forgotten dead are mute. It is not even a space as much as an *appareil,* an ordering even within appearances, that passes the limits of consciousness in order to preserve a trauma against what filmmaker Claude Lanzmann has called, with reference to the Holocaust, "the obscenity of the very project of understanding" and what Blanchot has identified as the danger that a disaster will "acquire a meaning instead of a body."[52] Amnesia holds in abeyance what is too horrific, life-threatening, and dangerous to remember but is too fundamental to forget. It keeps time and thought from entering the traumatic space and turning the reality of the traumatic loss into fact and process, which are subject to change and challenge. Cryptic amnesia serves as a kind of sacred space for the psyche's unassimilated terror. If I cannot remember, I cannot falsify the testimony, though I risk others falsifying my past. Rather, I can hold it, literally incorporate it, as a structuring principle of my being in the sense that the amnesia itself preserves the reality of the traumatic loss that made me. As a preservative, however, amnesia also aligns itself with the repressed, which inevitably returns in fragments, dreams, and symptomatic behavior that reveal traumatic loss at the same time that they keep its secrets.

The writing of history, however, simply because it is writing, maintains the fiction of its historical truth. In writing, repetition is impossible. The performing of history, for all its manifestly fictional status, maintains instead the living and material reality of history. It repeats the catastrophe. One asserting truth, the other instantiating the real, writing and performing form an alliance within a theater. But the alliance is uneasy, because in many ways each desires the status of the other. In calling itself or being called "performative," historical writing seeks the status of the real; in referring itself to texts and records, theatrical performance cites its relation, however faulty, to the true. If they join each other, it is only by way of metaphor: writing performs, performance documents. Yet both written and embodied historical performances are, in these terms, rituals of a certain kind of recovery from historical amnesia. The inevitable faults of that recovery, its imperfections, occur through the processes of cryptic condensation that preserves the past either in the present of performance or of reading, either in the guise of truth or of real, but rarely both together. In spite of all that is lost in the condensation process, both reach toward points of contact between the past and the present, toward the "something to be done," or, at a minimum, toward remembrance and the "kernel of the real." Only when the signifiers of representation are left to "float," unattached to assertions of truth or reality exclusively, undetermined by certain meaning, do the truth and reality of historical ghosts have the affective power of the uncanny, to make the apparitions of history both familiar and strange.

The further question implied here is, How does a text, which is a cryptic version of its theatrical production, become an active agent in the reproduction of itself, of its own history, in a material register? This is more than an issue of how a text "serves" a production or vice versa. A text's cryptic element, the condensations and consequent losses of the real in writing, is already an incorporation that both preserves and conceals a kind of amnesia. It just happens to be an amnesia directed toward a future rather than a past. In an entirely straightforward way, the forgotten element, the impossible element of a written text is the body, the animated corpse and its three-dimensionality. Although a written text can have its own kind of corporeality in its graphic image on the page, in its puns, rhymes, sonority, all but the graphic element demands further incorporation, whether by human or by machine (since it is not exclusively a matter of "liveness"). Texts, too, serve as monuments of the past. In a psychoanalytic vocabulary, the play-text stands in the dimension of the Symbolic as a kind of veil that covers an absence of the real. It conceals the gap that is the lost, forgotten real within written history, like the curtain that covers an empty stage. As a veil with its own thematic and historical characteristics, the text allows the entry of historical apparitions from both past and future that suit those characteristics. It gives access to the phantoms deriving from the history of its own production as well as those that would make it relevant to its own future, which is our present.

A human body ghosts a text, and the ghost is encrypted there as a condensation of incorporation. Out of that invisible or transparent body, incorporated by textuality, an exchange takes place in the emptiness of the theater, in the hollowness of the visible, inside-out surfaces of three-dimensional space. There, words become acts, and objects become speech that whispers, like ashes, like leaves, in the voices of the dead, like the sound of falling water, reflecting absence.

chapter 3

Objects
Lost and Found

But O for the touch of a vanish'd hand
And the sound of a voice that is still!
—TENNYSON, "Break, break, break"

One of the distinguishing characteristics of theatre as opposed, say, to books or film is its use of real and tangible objects. As Bert States writes: "In reading the eye is an anesthetized organ, little more than a window to the waiting consciousness on which a world of signification imprints itself with only the barest trace of the signifiers that carry it. In the theater, however, the eye awakens and confiscates the image. What the text loses in significative power in the theater it gains in corporeal presence, in which there is extraordinary perceptual satisfaction."[1] The sources of corporeal presence onstage have only increased as sculptural, three-dimensional space has taken precedence over pictorial space and realism has introduced more and more objects to the stage. That is to say that in addition to the visual images on a stage, some aspect of the three-dimensional reality of the objects supplies a good deal of the perceptual satisfaction of an audience. As theatre fills its spaces with tangible objects—though it has not always been so—objects start to resonate not only with significance but also with usefulness and materiality.

A telling exercise (or useful exam question) for the significative use of objects would be to give a prop list from a play. Such a list would imply the time and place of the play or a performance; it would suggest differences among symbolic, iconic, and realistic elements. It would speak of a world. A prop, like a souvenir, can hold an entire play as well as a cultural milieu in potential, as Andrew Sofer has so well detailed in his book *The Stage Life of Props*. If I say "samovar," for example, one might well recognize that it belongs not only to Chekhov's historical moment and to the realism of his plays but also to the ways in which the samovar embodies and signifies the historical and existential anomie of the Chekhovian world, even while the samovar itself could be innocent of such significations. Or the multiple toasters in Sam Shepard's *True West* might not only signal a certain obsessive kleptomania but also come close to the horror of autonomous appliances running amok in a strange sort of hyperrealism of matter. The importation of real restaurant booths and equipment in the realism taken famously to an extreme by Belasco would not just refer to a world but be it. An object may expand into a symbol of other things, like Lovborg's manuscript in *Hedda Gabler* having all the implications of creativity, childbirth, and futurity; it may be iconic, like the tree in *Waiting for Godot*, which becomes, for some, the sign of a Christian cross, or like the hollow crown in *Richard II*, in which death keeps his court and whose "deep well" signifies the vacancy in the sign of power and kingship. An object may thus become larger than itself as it expands toward multiple associations and meanings, or it may contract toward mute materiality that refutes and escapes the habits of making meaning. In other words, stage props clearly participate in the signifying, narrative, and stylistic fictions of the drama as well as the culture, and they also supply the material, aesthetic, and tangible reality of things in themselves. Throughout the range of possible cases, some ratio is always at work, creating a tension between the tangible materiality of an object and its representational function.

Operating in the dynamics of that ratio, perceptible aspects of objects onstage give them a complexity and density that remain largely implicit. Some of these aspects are what I want to explore further here. First is the pleasure of tangibility and the objects' appeal to the sense of touch beyond any purely visual and imagistic import. Next is their function for memory and their status as memorial devices that, through touch, form an attachment to what has been lost. In this aspect objects suggest a model for historiography that to some extent depends on, at the same time that it confounds, the rift that de Certeau talks about as fundamental to the writing of history. An object onstage may or may not be authentic in the sense of something coming from the everyday culture. Once onstage, both authentic and fabricated items have a medial function as representations of representation. For the complex intersections between writing and material objects as representations of representation, I will look in some detail at *The*

America Play, by Suzan-Lori Parks. It is through the intersections of objects
and their narratives that history can be written, not in terms of authenticity or of recording what may or may not have happened, but in terms of
commentary, often ironic, about such recording of history. And finally, I
will consider how theatre brings objects into a phenomenological complexity that allows them to be "thought" not as objects but as what Heidegger
called "things."

Especially when they are simply sitting backstage or in the prop room
prior to their uses in a performance, bereft of both text and performance,
prop objects can seem suspended between both worldly and fictional uses.
Stored in a prop room, the objects constitute both an archive of past productions and a promise of possible ones. A prop room holds objects out
of context, neither fully in the world nor yet onstage, in representation.
Arrayed on a backstage table, ready to perform, objects also have a unique
status. Both room and table are virtually inert spaces in a zone between
the creation and the delivery of the objects into a public space where they
will ground the actors in a material reality and serve as messengers to an
audience, enacting and representing an era, a history, a place, or a character. Covered in paper, the table lays out all the objects that come and go
from the stage during a performance in the order of their appearance onstage. Each one is outlined and labeled, identifying what it is and when it
is used: crown, act 3, scene 4, or umbrella, act 1. The prop manager can
then account for anything that is missing before and after a show, track it
down, and replace it if necessary. The actor always knows where to take
and replace any prop. It is a mundane and efficient practice that keeps the
flow of objects going smoothly on- and offstage.

Like items in a lost and found, props backstage implicate a history without an obvious order: a disparate group of items that beg for a story, like
Pirandello's six characters in search of an author. They ask to be played with,
touched, recovered, and used. Precisely because they are in suspense between
instrumental usefulness and an imaginary field, there is a certain pleasure
in handling and discovering them. A telephone, a gun, a crown, the samovar, the umbrella, the carrots, an alarm clock: like lost toys, they elicit the
imagination, as fragments of one world lost and another yet to be played
out. Props enter the theater from an elsewhere and give themselves over to
the pleasures of touch paired with fantasy, like the games of acting classes
that transform an object into something else simply by alternative uses. That

is, the prop room is a storage place for objects that are essentially in transit: they arrive backstage from outside the theater, whether found at a junk store or built in a shop. Though they are destined for the stage, for use, and for reidentification by an audience, it is at the point of stillness that they contract into their material specificity, which is neither aesthetic nor representational, neither messengers nor message. The in-between space of the prop table breaks down the dualism between world and stage in what might be called an aspect of "readiness." If the prop room is primarily an archive, the prop table makes its objects ready to emerge from a static or suspended condition into use and activity.

Tadeusz Kantor's notation on the post office articulates the state of the object on the prop table:

> It is a very special place
> where the laws of
> u t i l i z a t i o n
> are suspended.
> Objects—letters, packages,
> packets, bags, envelopes,
> and all their content—
> exist for some time
> independently,
> without an addressee,
> without a place of destination,
> without a function,
> almost as if in a vacuum,
> in between a sender and a receiver
> where both are powerless,
> with no meaning,
> bereft of their authority.
> It is a rare moment when
> an object escapes its destiny.[2]

Once put into a stage space, an object is destined to travel. Traveling, it is subjected to the power and authority of users (performers) as well as "sender and receiver," with their often competing or contradictory investments of "content" within the object. But during its life on the prop table or in the prop room, that content is absent. A particularly haunting image on a prop table, however, is the outline that graphically marks the place where a prop belongs. It is like the contours that mark the position of a body at the scene of a crime. The outline announces not only where a prop belongs but also when it has gone missing or is in use. It follows the contours now bereft of touch. At rest on the table, filling in the absence the outline defines, avoiding the fluidity of uses, references, and meanings, a prop is fully itself, at home but inert. Once sent toward its "destiny" onstage, the prop leaves behind only the outline of its former self-identity, when it had no function. Not only does the outline mark the absence of the object; it remembers the placement of the self-identical object now lost to itself. The outline, in other words, is a nostalgic site that calls the body-object home.

What that outline is missing is the touch of the object. The perceptual pleasure of objects in the theater connects at least on some level to the sense of touch. Obviously audiences only rarely, if ever, touch the props of a performance. But in addition to their visual and significative information, props have the tangibility and availability that contribute to the perceptual density of the stage. That is, objects are perceived both in their three-dimensional reality and in their availability to touch and the human hand. However much imagination may take a prop to the scene and narrative of a play text, its sensory appeal exceeds significance in the same way that a material souvenir offers a pleasure and a memory different from snapshots of a vacation or a sight-seeing tour. Both will certainly register memory but with very different indices. A souvenir object is a fragment of a whole experience; it belongs to the time and place of its own origin as a souvenir. In other words, it is part of the experience it will later come to represent, whether that experience is shopping or shell collecting or rock climbing.

One of the stranger examples of just such a souvenir can be found on the exterior walls of the Chicago Tribune Tower. Embedded in the surfaces of the exterior is an odd assortment of rocks. They are spread around the front and sides of the building, some at street level, some at eye level, and they go on up past where one can see and reach. Each rock has a label beside it. These, it turns out, are "famous stones." There are stones from the Great Pyramid of Cheops and the Great Wall of China. There are stones from the Berlin Wall and Gettysburg, a Colorado cliff dwelling and Hans Christian Andersen's home in Denmark; from Corregidor in the Philippines and

Pearl Harbor; from northern California's petrified trees and Georgia's Andersonville Prison; from Tennessee's Cumberland Gap and the 1947 U.S. Navy expedition to Antarctica; from the dome of St. Peter's in Rome and John Brown's cabin; St. Lo's Town Hall, the White House, Pompeii, Londonderry, Fort Ticonderoga, the Little Bighorn, the Roman Colosseum, the Temple of Tears in Amsterdam, the Sibyl's cave in Naples, Mammoth Caves.

Robert McCormick, publisher of the *Chicago Tribune,* began the collection in the 1920s with stones he had picked up from historical sites around the world. Other reporters over the years added to the collection from their overseas assignments. What appealed to McCormick and his reporters that would make them want to gather these rocks and put them on display? A certain element of souvenir hunting and site saving seems implicit, with the same impulses that make one pick up shells or stones from the beach and bring them home. These stones bring some sort of irreducible proof from a historical site. But of what are they proof? That the place exists? That someone was there? Their tangibility is quite tangible, so to speak, but impenetrable except perhaps to geologists, the historians of the earth. Perhaps their appeal is simply that they set places already designated as historical or newsworthy in a sensory register. Perhaps they simply memorialize the elsewhere of their origins so that the *Tribune* can in some way own its own heritage. But the stones on the building require labels to testify to their sources, so they are already caught up in the writing that both identifies and tries to guarantee authenticity. The stones are called famous but surely cannot take any credit for their fame. That has to be supplied by human stories. They apparently appeal to a desire for copresence with a past that is tangible and material. However, because they have been lifted from their original context, any sense of copresence has to be taken with a certain amount of faith that the labels are true. According to the *Tribune's* literature, any addition to the collection now has to be authenticated, though by what process it does not say. A stone must then be stored for ten years to determine whether the site it came from remains significant for at least that long.

What makes this, as the *Tribune* says, "one of the world's most fascinating free outdoor historical exhibits" unless it is the cognitive dissonance between the impenetrable, tangible rocks and the stories that made them famous? Certainly, in part, the sheer fascination comes from the range of times and places brought to stud the sides of the building. While the sense of historical ordering is haphazard, one could easily say that it concretizes history as a collection of incidents, isolated from one another but held in the wide matrix of news. Most of the stones are from places one has heard of. But their appeal remains strange.

That strangeness, I'd suggest, rises from the jarring sense that they are inert matter that seems to serve as individual witnesses to distant places, far gone events. They are there, present, but they are also holding, in some sense, the absent sites they came from. They witness with a kind of relentless objectivity, an objectivity so severe that it cannot speak lest it falsify reality. The stones turn history into a kind of contagion, one's living body in contact with a witness that did not just see events but belonged in the materiality of events. The tangibility of the stony witnesses brings a distant and imaginary site into sensory presence, as survivors of history's losses, testifying to the reality of the event or site. They bridge the gap or rupture of written history's intelligibility. "This" stone is of "that" place, event, time. Furthermore, the stones carry a present touch (though many are beyond reach) back through time, extending from immediate moment toward another time when they rested in the earth or a building. They bear duration toward another, past time in their objective presence. But one gets strangely caught between the tangibility of the objects and the names of their origins. The stones ask one to reconcile a register of written information of an elsewhere with the immediate sense of touch. If one pursues that reconciliation very far, the result is a cognitive dissonance that borders the uncanny. What was the relation among the materiality of the rocks, the reality of the places from which they came, and an imaginary reconnection with those places through the rocks via the labels? Together the registers of touch, imagination, and writing raise a certain kind of doubt along with wonder. Is "this stone" "that place"? Is "there" now "here"? What information does touch add to the name and narrative of another place or time? Can one touch "history" or "elsewhere"? Or do history and elsewhere necessarily remain at a distance, across de Certeau's rift?

The historical, memorial, and nostalgic functions of objects are possible because objects already relate to humans through a paradox of intimacy and exclusion. On the one hand, objects, particularly in the form of possessions, are extensions of an individual self and the body: they define, enlarge, and extend individual corporeality beyond the limits of the body. The "object relations" of infancy, of course, enable both connection and autonomy. Through somatic, sensory bonding, an infant becomes part of the world and gradually learns to feel itself feeling and recognize its dependence on the object as well as its independence. In that process it learns to differentiate itself from other. The story of object relations is fundamental here because it imagines the first appearance of an object and a primary rift in the constitution of a subject, in the establishment of difference between self and other, of self as other. There are various and competing versions of the tale, from Freud to Melanie Klein to Heinz Kohut. Each one advances a distinct view on libidinal drives and psychic structures that have consequences both in the diagnosis of pathologies and therapeutic treatment. Despite their variations, they all provide a perspective on how material objects, which include other people, are relational, how attachments and losses form a psychic structure, a sense of self, and its affective connection to objects.

A simplified version of the various theories of object relations would say that, from the totality of a symbiotic, undifferentiated relationship between mother and child, the first object is not known until it is lost, until it goes into exile. Through sensory, somatic bonding with a mother object—who is not yet an object—an infant begins in symbiosis but gradually becomes part of the world through separation and the development of a sense of difference between self and (m)other, self and objects, self as object. What is not clear to the infant, at first, is whether it is self or other in exile. It is only felt as a breaking point, whose repetition gradually defines the contours of self and other. The establishment of the object according to Freud and Lacan comes with language and the so-called mirror stage in which language and the image come together to project both wholeness and difference upon the self in terms of the ego. In its preverbal and precognitive state, the infant cannot fully distinguish between the lost object and the affective and sensory experience of its loss, which is how and why objects have to be understood in both their material reality and their phantasmic, psychic force. In the "throwing out" of the material other, the subject as other is formed. The not-yet objects (mother and self) move into the realm of sight as they are separated from the somatic totality of touch. A subject nevertheless retains much of its imaginary connectedness through substitute objects and fantasy. For the subject, an object of attachment, however much it is material, is also an internalization of its loss in the somatic outline of a memory. That loss is internalized to the extent that, even in the presence of a fetish object, one can never really quite touch it *enough,* long enough, deeply enough, to complete the void created by the first loss, the first object. The outline of the loss is then often filled in by fantasy, which retains a sense of connection, a connection that is often later called meaning. That memory calls the object home to its "proper" place of self-identity, even while it retains an imaginary connection, in particular to a fetish object.

This amalgamation of object-relation stories is simply a way to imagine the moment when an object makes its appearance as an object, that is, to consider it phenomenologically and psychoanalytically as an emergence of otherness. And I am imagining that moment as one in which something is, as the word *object* suggests, "thrown ahead." Expulsion is at the literal core of the word *object.* Ob-ject: to throw before or against and therefore, elsewhere, to oppose. The word contains the act of expulsion that is also a presentation, a show or appearance, even a symptom (as in a "presenting symptom"). The event of expulsion produces subject and object as reciprocals of each other: it is a point at which a subject also begins to emerge as an object. In its exile the object begins to gather a history for itself, as does the subject; each begins to become a representative for its own past and future in relation to the other. As the ego dominates, objects tend to disappear into usefulness, as extensions of the body, or into meaning, as extensions of the psyche, or into fantasy and ideology, as functions of power and identity.

Objects also are, or at least can be, specific means of attachment or re-attachment, which is how we tend to love the possessions of loved ones: they are not metaphoric substitutes for the person but metonymic connections, attached by mutual touch. For a subject, the departure of the object of attachment leaves a somatic memory, a scar at the site of expulsion, supplemented by fantasy, and activated somatically by the senses. This is why some objects have more appeal, evoke more affect, are more desirable or more meaningful than others: they fill the somatic outline of a lost object. If the emergence of objects initially defines differences and distinctions as well as inaugurating the primacy of the ego, objects are also vehicles for re-connection to somatic pleasure through other senses. The immediacy of touch also makes contact not so much with the other but with an object shared with another. The touch of a shared object evokes intimacy, identification, and love.

Because one's possessions often endure longer than the body, it is possible to find in the objects left behind the ghosted identity of the owner, as though that owner had left an impression of her touch and her identity on the surface of the thing. The endurance of the object carries the memory of the touch and holds on to the intimacy cut off by death, which is how objects become sacred relics and memorials of the dead. Objects hold time still in material presence. Anyone who has gone through the possessions of a dead parent or absent loved one recognizes the traces of the person, the time of the person, and the touch that remains with the object. One's own possessions, recovered after a long time in an attic or closet, similarly become memorials to former, lost selves, to one's own otherness. The extension of the identity remains because the identification endures. At the same time, the object makes the absence of the person even more acute. In its obdurate materiality and inanimate otherness, it excludes attachment, presence, and identification. The lack of human touch is all the more evident because the object refuses its attachment to the person insofar as it stands alone, discrete.

The preservation of objects in museums, memorials, or collections, like the transmission of family heirlooms, turns history into an intimate relation for touching the past, marking as well the intimacy of loss. The tangibility of the witness brings a distant and imaginary site into an objective presence, as a survivor of history's losses testifying to the reality of the event or site. Objects also carry presence back through time or into the future, expanding by means of their "sameness" from immediate touch toward another time when they rested or will rest in the earth or the building or the closet of a loved one. In their sameness they sustain a duration that knows no temporal gap. They bear duration toward another time that both is and is not the same. The impulse of a tourist to collect objects from sites visited surely belongs to a desire to possess the durability of the past and future and to feel that other as the same. To own a remainder/reminder of some other thing or place or time extends oneself into that other by touch, expanding one's own time into the time of the other. But the longing or desire for such expansion implies the moment when one anticipates an end. The souvenir object anticipates the death of the present and memorializes it as a durable good. Whether it is specifically touch that supplies the connection is admittedly debatable, since so many souvenir objects end up either on display or tossed into junk piles. But at the very least, souvenir objects are things to have by means of holding. What are they, though, without the narratives that accompany them? Susan Stewart writes that the capacity to serve as traces of authentic experience is . . . exemplified by the souvenir. . . . Like the collection, it always displays the romance of contraband, for its scandal is its removal from its "natural" location. Yet it is only by means of its material relation to that location that it acquires its value. . . . The souvenir speaks to a context of origin through a language of longing, for it is not an object arising out of need or use value; it is an object arising out of the necessarily insatiable demands of nostalgia. The souvenir generates a narrative which reaches only "behind," spiraling in a continually inward movement rather than outward toward the future. Here we find the structure of Freud's description of the genesis of the fetish: a part of the body is substituted for the whole, or an object is substituted for the part, until finally, and inversely, the whole body can become object, substituting for the whole. Thus we have a systematic transformation of the object into its own impossibility, its loss and the simultaneous experience of a difference which Freud characterizes as the fetishist's both knowing and not knowing the anatomical difference between the sexes.[3]

What Stewart calls its impossibility I am calling its uncanniness, in order to suggest that the object is more than a trace of authentic experience and that the souvenir does not automatically incite a narrative of nostalgia, though it can certainly do both. The theatrical and performative dimension to the perception of objects exceeds the literary. The literary perspective begins in a derealization of the object, whereby it is always already within a narrative dynamic. Literarily, the object does belong to the issue of authenticity and authorship, which requires the kind of research and labeling that authenticates the *Tribune* stones. The subtle but important difference between the "real" and the "authentic" that the theatrical dimension supplies is in the specific tangibility of the object and theatre's capacity to collapse both significations and narratives into three dimensions and surface textures. In that dimensional space, the object certainly retains its possible function as a fetish, but even that function has the additional phenomenon of touch. Or, more precisely, its fetish power operates through the sense of touch, the originary bond of attachment. What makes the object uncanny is that it is contradictory in terms of distance and presence but not impossible. Authenticity is irrelevant in the context of the sensory real. Stewart says, "The possession of the metonymic object is a kind of dispossession in that the presence of the object all the more radically speaks to its status as a mere substitution and to its subsequent distance from the self. This distance is not simply experienced as a loss; it is also experienced as a surplus of signification. It is experienced, as is the loss of the dual relation with the other, as catastrophe and *jouissance* simultaneously."[4] Touch refutes dispossession of the object as a substitute: the stones of the *Tribune* building offer the passerby no guarantee that they are authentic or that one stone has not been substituted for another, yet they remain tangible and even ask to be touched in a way that the rest of the exterior does not. Touch binds the catastrophe of distance in time and place to the *jouissance* of surplus. One aspect of the surplus is certainly narrative. The performative surplus, however, is not one of narrative alone but one of the sensory reality that connects objects to bodies by touch.

Sensory perceptibility increases the information from an apparently lifeless object and connects its oscillations between meaning and matter to the nervous system. It complicates any simple duality between its expansion toward meaning and its contraction toward matter. Artifacts exceed the dualities of simple imitation and representation by means of touch in terms of not only object relations but also the kinds of information touch supplies. Object relations, in other words, are not exclusively phantasms but also phenomena. Real objects have texture, weight, temperature, shape, though certainly those sensory details, too, can be the objects of fantasy. As Eve Kosofsky Sedgwick writes in reference to work by Renu Bora on texture:

> I haven't perceived a texture until I've instantaneously hypothesized whether the object I'm perceiving was sedimented, extruded, laminated, granulated, polished, distressed, felted or fluffed up. Similarly, to perceive texture is to know or hypothesize whether a thing will be easy or hard, safe or dangerous to grasp, to stack, to fold, to shred, to climb on, to stretch, to slide, to soak. Even more immediately than other perceptual systems, it seems, the sense of touch makes nonsense out of any dualistic understanding of agency and passivity; to touch is always already to reach out, to fondle, to heft, to tap, or to enfold, and always also to understand other people or natural forces as having effectually done so before oneself.[5]

The sensory aspect of souvenirs offers an alternative view on objects suspended on a prop table between worldly uses and staged meanings. The prop table, in this view, becomes a tangible archive with a variable narrative.

The *collection* of props might then provide a model for historiography that does not include the rifts between past and present, nature and labor, discourse and the body, as de Certeau put it. The collection answers those dichotomies with sensory reality. A collection of fragments out of context, they are mute, disparate items; material metonyms for names and narratives, like the news or the mail, props accumulate without temporal order. At most, a formal order may put like objects with like: chairs with chairs, lamps with lanterns, swords with scepters, toasters with tea kettles. The temporal order is unimportant; the prop objects compose a disordered history, collected ad hoc, almost by chance. Arrayed there, the objects are fragments in isolation. As a historical archive, such a collection cannot clarify itself by designating an other. If anything, it multiplies the rifts. While pragmatically theatre props may be set out in an order of use in the narrative of a text, they are also always ready to be recontextualized by new or alternative narratives, new orders and uses. Other plays might be written from the same things.

The things collected in a prop room thus offer a model for materialist history. Isolated and adrift, they call out for use and significance but also make all the more evident the artifice of the narratives that would give them authenticity, order, and meaning. Materialist history, in now familiar terms, tends to defy the "grand recits" of the master historical narratives, to use Lyotard's terms, of progress and development or at the very least to denaturalize those narratives. In a state of suspended animation, the collection of the prop room divorces material objects from their labels and even their uses, such that a correlation between the objects and the truth of their labels is provisional at best. History in such a form, memorialized by tangible objects, takes on the design of an array, or arbitrary collection, that calls not for telling or naming but for retelling and renaming. No longer appropriating the past in order to tell about the present, no longer simply bridging the gap between past and present, an apparently arbitrary display of objects is available for commentary and response.

One of the best examples I can think of for using a collection of objects for commentary and the recontextualization of history occurs in Suzan-Lori Parks's *The America Play*. At a moment in that play, young Brazil, son of the Foundling Father, acts as a sort of museum docent or tour guide for a series of artifacts displayed in the Hall of Wonders. The Hall of Wonders is the equivalent of a history museum. It displays artifacts that have been dug up from "the Great Hole of History." The speech demonstrates Parks's knack for moving seamlessly between material objects and imaginary objectification, both of which constitute an inheritance from the past. It also underlines the irony of museums in the way that they reify and identify the past through their narrative selections.

> To our right A Jewel Box made of cherry wood, lined in velvet, letters "A.L." carved in gold on thuh lid: the jewels have long escaped. Over here one of Mr. Washington's bones, right pointer so they say; here is his likeness and here: his wooden teeth. Yes, uh top and bottom pair of nibblers, lookin for uh meal. Nibblin. I iduhnt your lunch. Quit nibblin. Quit that nibblin you. Quit that nibblin you nibblers you nibblin nibblers you.

The speech goes on and is worth quoting further for the move into ironic commentary:

> Over here out newest Wonder: uh bust of Mr. Lincoln carved of marble lookin like he looked in life. Right heress thuh bit from thuh mouth of thuh mount on which some great Someone rode tuh thuh rescue. This is all thats left. Uh glass tradin bead—one of thuh first. Here are thuh lick-ed boots. Here, uh dried scrap of whales blubber. Uh petrified scrap of uh great blubberer, servin to remind us that once this land was covered with sea. And blubberers were Kings. In this area here are several documents: peace pacts, writs, bills of sale, treaties, notices, handbills and circulars, freein papers, summonses, declarations of war, addresses title deeds, obits, long lists of dids. And thuh medals for bravery and honesty; for trustworthiness and for standing straight; for standing tall; for standing still. For advancing and retreating. For makin do. For skills in whittlin, for skills in painting and drawing, for uh knowledge of sewin, of handicrafts and building things, for leather tanin, blacksmithery, lacemakin, horseback riding, swimmin, croquet and badminton. Community Service. For cookin and for cleanin. For bowin and scrapin. Uh medal for fakin? Huh. This could uh been his. Zsis his? This is his! This is his!!![6]

The play is in part an exploration of the relationship of contemporary African-Americans to the lack of historical record and their absences in its narratives.[7] Focusing on the assassination of Abraham Lincoln, the play works through the performative repetitions of that lack and attempts at recovery. It enacts the production of history as an installation of objects that testify to lived experience. But the speech reminds one that such lived experience includes "thuh lick-ed boots," "cookin and cleanin," "bowin and scrapin." The objects are mute without the accompanying articulations or labels that identify with humor and horror the quality of the lived experience. Words and things need each other to generate a meaningful perception of the past, but the attachment of words to things is always mutable and variable, subject to changing names and labels. Just before the scene, Brazil has been digging in the stage floor, searching for the artifacts that will provide concrete evidence of a lost African-American history. Brazil searches, he says, for bones, the material signs that what is lost was once alive. The empty hole, replicating theatre's empty space, situates the loss of memory and a radical absence of history. The artifacts he recovers are placed in a museum space, the Hall of Wonders. They testify to the reality of a lost and unrecorded past. They are quite literally souvenirs: arrivals from below, coming from the emptiness, the hole, of the past into the presence of performance. Brazil's identifications give them ghostly authenticity.

The testimony of objects, in other words, brings into the present not just *what* was lost but the tangible presence of loss, loss in the form of a thing that nonetheless calls for a name and an identification. The recovery of history and its evidence is an imaginative and performative act of naming. This is a fact often lost in the empirical presumptions of museums. The objects are not whole ("This is all thats left.") and have lost the context in which they were used. Once named and staged—in the theater or the museum—they are no longer simply real but ghostly. Of course, in terms of a production, they never really *were* real because they are stage props; yet, they *are* real because they are stage props. Both representing the real and undermining it, those objects circulate between their materiality and the ghosts of representation. They do not disappear into the usefulness of ordinary objects but testify to the reality of the ordinary. Both real and alienated, they enter the museum as "wonders." That is to say, they are the objects of wonder in multiple senses of the word: enough to inspire awe, enough to provoke speculation, "I wonder if . . . , I wonder what . . . , I wonder how . . . ," enough to invoke the numinous aura of a ghostly past and an elsewhere. They are ghost objects that can still be felt. Tangible, they mark their own disappearance from time past as well as their persistence in the present. The objects that Brazil takes from the hole represent the souvenirs that serve, as Susan Stewart says, "as traces of authentic experience. . . . We do not need or desire souvenirs of events that are repeatable. Rather we need and desire souvenirs of events that are reportable, events whose materiality has escaped us, events that thereby exist only through the invention of narrative."[8]

In the case of African-American history, it is precisely the reportable events that have escaped, having conventionally been tied to the story of emancipation and the assassination of Lincoln. These souvenirs supplement the lost narrative and reconstitute history in matter. The supplement, however, is not a positivist history but an irony in relation to the received history. The objects are material, but the commentary identifies the ironic posture that speaks from alternative positions from within history. These objects may well have a certain fetishtic value as "part objects" of a lost origin that is missing from the performance of the present. That origin is not authentic—which is to say authorized by documents—but it is real, occurring in the present moment of performance. The events do not exist in narrative. Rather, the materiality of lived experience, which always escapes narrative, is recovered in performance. In the production of *The America Play*, African-American history repeats, not authentically in Stewart's sense, but materially.

The objects dug up from the Great Hole of History in *The America Play* nonetheless implicate the lost narrative and genealogy that haunts Brazil and Lucy, his mother. They seem connected to the "forefathers," which Parks also writes as "foe-fathers," but without the binding coherence of narrative. Unlike the private souvenir that Stewart discusses, they are public artifacts in performance. But as part of a collection, which she also discusses, these objects similarly represent a collapse of time: "In the collection, time is not something to be restored to an origin; rather, all time is made simultaneous or synchronous within the collection's world."[9] Unlike the public artifacts of a museum, the artifacts are multiplied by their theatrical status as representations of representations. In performance, that is, they are representations whose inauthentic status as props stands between the authenticity and artifact of museum objects. Yet it is not enough, therefore, to call them illusions or to relegate them to realms of fiction or pretense. For Parks uses their status as stage properties, as representations of representations, to align the loss of the real with the reality of the imaginary in the material terms of performance. She employs the slippage between material objects and their implied narrative to stage the profound absence in the center of historical reconstruction.

On the site of that absence the play stages the fantasies of history and its phantasmic recovery of a past. Objects onstage, like those in a museum, are distanced or alienated from everyday usefulness. Memorial objects are enduring in their materiality but variable in their availability to multiple and imaginary narratives. They require a narrative to maintain a connection with their past, yet it is through the narrative that they become alien to themselves. The narrative turns them into representations of themselves, and it is that act of historical transformation that Parks's play stages: it is a play of in-between actions. For at the same time, the play represents the persistence of materiality, of objective evidence, that suggests proof even if it is partial or ironic. The persistence of the object makes a claim to its sameness, resisting the narrative representation and variability and denying fantasy. Yet that materiality is also out of context, and thus the object is also alien to itself through its materiality.

These exchanges between the modes of alienation and connectedness render the uncanny sense of the object even in the midst of ironic commentary. It bears the traces of the unfamiliar familiarity by which Freud characterizes the uncanny. It is and is not itself: neither matter nor fantasy is determinate. As a representation of a representation, an object becomes its own ghost. The phantasm retains the connection to the past at the same time that it dematerializes the object. This is the very function and status of the memorial object as fetish: it retains a connection through the materiality of an imaginary vehicle. It is thus both more and less than what it materially is and was, creating the uncanniness of the living dead.

This is particularly true of objects that once belonged to someone, like the jewel box of Lincoln or the false teeth of Washington. Their attachment to living beings becomes an attachment to the past that denies any rupture or difference between the living and the dead. What once belonged to someone else, like an heirloom, now belongs to "me" or, in the case of the museum, to a public. It connects me at the same time that it reminds me of the loss. To "have" something that once belonged to another is concretely to feel the other. The object, however, becomes a possession in both senses of the word, in that to possess is also to be possessed. Ownership is founded in the fantasy of possession, but that is not to say that the fantasy is an unreal or a matter of pretending. It is, rather, what Žižek calls a mediation between a "formal symbolic structure and the positivity of objects we encounter in reality." He goes on to say that fantasy "provides a 'schema' according to which certain positive objects in reality can function as objects of desire, filling in the empty places opened up by the formal symbolic structure."[10] Fantasy also relies on a radical "intersubjectivity" (i.e., at its root) in which the object is the means by which a subject forms a connection (and thereby an identity) with an other. That is to say it is not necessarily the object itself but the object as it is identified with satisfying the desire of another that forms the character of fantasy. In the moment of Brazil's speech, the objects of Lincoln's jewel box and Washington's teeth are presented as historical fetish and historical fantasy; Brazil's desire to find "the bones," however, is an extension of personal fantasy into historical fantasy: to recover the material evidence that would bridge the gap between himself and his own forefather is itself a fantasy. The desire of the other, in this case, might be understood historically as the desire of the past for the future, the desire to persist into the future, to be known and recognized. Brazil's desire to find the bones, then, would be a desire to fulfill the desire of the past-other by touching the bones, making the connection.

Similarly, the petrified scrap of whale blubber is "out of context." No longer the living whale, it shares real material sameness with living and dead but is also self-alienated by the difference. Along with the materiality of its corpse, petrified over time as a scrap of blubber, comes the uncanny sense of the *touching* difference between living, sensate flesh and the dead object. In touching the object, one touches time in the register of the senses, time that is not separate from the object (as in the effects of time) but incorporated *as* the object in its present. It is the aura of possession in which one is increased or expanded by including the object that belonged to another in a material version of metonymy. The rhetorical trope of metonymy, that is, has a material, physical grounding in the phenomenon of touch. As a phenomenon it enters the dimension of fantasy that invests the object with a power that it would not otherwise have. It takes the sensate condition of a person who is alive to fantasy to give the object its aura and to "experience" the effects of the very aura she donates.

In the context of *The America Play*, Brazil actually takes the museum objects out of the realm of fantasy, which is based on the imaginary perception of the other's desire that asks, "What would you have of me?" When he addresses Washington's false teeth and (onstage) makes them "nibble," he is pointing to the object's own power, particularly in the context of American experience (as opposed to written history) to consume the present subject. But this is where Stewart's sense of the object's narrative does enter. The phantasmic subjectivity of African-Americans in this context is based on satisfying the desire of the "other" that is Anglo-American history to consume them, a fantasy too easily justified by the reality of having been "consumed." The intersubjective character of fantasy described by Žižek is thus related to the phantasmic identification of master and slave in Hegel's famous dialectic. It is the "plague" of the fantasy to constitute one's subjectivity by desiring to be consumed in order to fulfill the desire of the other to consume. Insofar as that fantasy constitutes an African-American subject as that which has-been-consumed, it locks the subject into a false identity and false identification with the "master." But Brazil articulates a refusal of the fantasy, refuses to constitute himself as the "subject to be consumed" that the teeth would seem to desire, according to fantasy. The move from the phantasmic to the symbolic requires such a denial: "I iduhnt your lunch. Quit nibblin. Quit that nibblin you. Quit that nibblin you nibblers you nibblin nibblers you."

Putting Washington's teeth on display in the museum—staging them— thus puts the phantasmic character of narrative history on display. Brazil's articulated refusal breaks the fantasy and moves the teeth and all they represent into the symbolic dimension. They are transformed by negation and are ready to be known in multiple, discontinuous dimensions: material, phantasmic, symbolic, historical, past, present. Even in the sameness of persistence, that is, they are not self-identical. Brazil's further speech then testifies to the reified attitudes that, like material objects, have belonged to the phantasmic creation (the creation in fantasy) of African-American stereotypes. The medals given—for "bravery and honesty; for trustworthiness and for standing straight; for standing tall; for standing still. For advancin and retreating. For makin do. For skills in whittlin, for skills in painting and drawing, for uh knowledge of sewin, of handicrafts and building things, for leather tanin, blacksmithery, lacemakin, horseback riding, swimmin, croquet and badminton. Community Service. For cookin and for cleanin. For bowin and scrapin"—correlate to lived activities. The medals are the symbolic difference from the lived reality that breaks the spell of phantasmic identification. Just as the material objects move into the space of representation, the museum, out of the great hole of history, so the immaterial objectifications move into public speech. Brazil's speech testifies to the reification of attitudes that have marked African-American history, but he refuses to be drawn into them. Rather, by means of speaking and identifying the medals, he marks the exit of phantasmic stereotypes and their entrance into symbolic irony. The medals he pulls out do not just "symbolize" the stereotypical behavior (bowin and scrapin). By identifying those phantasms in speech rather than letting the medals rest in the silence as objects, the speech marks the difference between the reification of a historical identity and lived experience. "Bowin and scrapin" belongs to both the reified stereotype and an experiential, or performed, gesture, but marked as a difference, "bowin and scrapin" is neither. It "floats" as a signifier of otherness in a space where the symbolic resides.

Parks indicates the radical nature of the loss of the real within history, which is the loss that trauma entails, but she also places it in the familial dynamics between husband and wife. As Brazil digs for the remains of his father, Lucy, his mother, gives account for all that she gave him.

> I could never deny him nothin. I gived intuh him on everything. Thuh moon. Thuh stars. . . . Thuh bees knees. Thuh cats pyjamas. . . . Thuh bees knees. Thuh cats pyjamas. The best cuts of meat. My baby teeth. . . . Thuh apron from uhround my waist. Thuh hair from off my head. . . . My mores and my folkways. . . . Thuh apron from uhround my waist. Thuh hair from off my head. . . . Thuh apron from uhround my waist. Thuh hair from off my head. My mores and my folkways. My rock and my foundation. . . . My rememberies—you know—thuh stuff out of my head. . . . My spare buttons in their envelopes. Thuh leftovers from all my unmade meals. Thuh letter R. Thuh key of G. . . . All my good jokes. All my jokes fell flat. Thuh way I walked, cause you liked it so much. All my winnin dance steps. My teeth when yours runned out. My smile.[11]

If the objects in the Hall of Wonders might be considered as a memorials to a lost narrative history, Lucy's list takes the play in another direction and places her relation to the past in terms of gifts of love. Neither fantasy nor fetish, these "items" are not objects but intersubjective, relational gifts. The speech records not objects but acts of love that dissolve obdurate materiality into images of quality (the bees knees, the cat's pajamas), of innocence (the baby teeth), of daily habit (the apron; the mores and the folkways), of spirit (my rock and my foundation), of thought and memory, of surplus (the spare buttons), of writing and music, of pleasure and self-sacrifice, and, for all that, of the body (the hair from off the head). This list makes clear that the artifacts of lived history make no distinction among material, affective, and imaginary objects. What is or has been felt is as real and historical as what is touched and imagined.

The historian's evidence for history in documents ("peace pacts, writs, bills of sale, treaties, notices, handbills and circulars") or history *as* documents is ghosted by what Derrida has called "archive fever"—a memorialization of a death drive. The ghost of the document appears out of the feverish investment of belief in the authenticity of artifact, an investment in a living death that produces a version of Benjamin's aura. In the case of the document, however, that aura emanates from the empirical, graphic facticity of writing that testifies to the once-upon-a-time presence of a human writer who is absent. The persistent presence of the paper corpse is ghosted by that loss of living presence in the paper corpse. The appearance of the ghost is thus a production of the investment of belief rather than any inherent truth contained in the writing. One of these ghosts makes an appearance as authenticity.

There was a report in the *New York Times* of a flag discovered in the "clutter" of the Connecticut Historical Society. Found in a box among "Civil War relics and about 76 years of dust," the flag was publicly presented "after three years of exhaustive research,"[12] which confirmed that it was the flag that hung at Lincoln's left in his box at Ford's Theatre the night he was assassinated. Those three years of research added to the flag object the real ghost of authenticity, the aura of belief, and the tangibility of that belief. Without the research, what? No imprimatur of authenticity to inform the touch. But of course the flag cannot be touched: it is too fragile to handle and, like any ancient relic, has to be preserved in an airless space, a vacuum that assures relative permanence but requires faith in the substance of documentation and trust in the endless potential for touchability even in the absence of it. A proper historian requires such faith and trust from a reader or a tourist. Documentation of the authentic invests the object with value, but it refuses the testimony of loss and doubt that would entail a double (theatrical) sense that suspends both belief and disbelief between the object and its label.

Tadeusz Kantor considered the nature of objects more thoroughly than most theatre practitioners and made some of the clearest attempts to "bridge the gap between representation and things-in-themselves," in Brigitte Peucker's phrase. A significant aspect of that bridge is the material effect of time on an object. She discusses the eighteenth-century picturesque genre's interest in "'the effects of age and decay' [which] explains the overwhelming fascination of the picturesque with ruins, structures upon which time has wrought its texture-creating effects."[13] The aesthetics of texture in the picturesque not only replicate the processes of time in the object of representation; they also make a direct appeal to the sense of tactility in the object. The tactility of an object, however, tends to deconstruct those significations by contracting history and its absences into the "thing itself" and tends to constitute a sensory dimension in which history is known. Kantor, in another context, similarly found ways to employ the effects of time on objects, not so much as "things-in-themselves" in any essential sense, but in terms of texture. In the surface textures of his objects he found a way to access a dimension that was neither realistic and utilitarian nor representational. He worked to erase the fictional contexts that stage the meaning of objects and instead to present them as autonomous phenomena that were nonetheless ghosted by use, history, and abuse. Explicitly rejecting the aesthetic movements of the early twenthieth-century avant-garde (constructivism, surrealism, cubism) and the progressive development of stage technology in the 1940s, he defined the "the poor object" as the "simplest, the most primitive, old, marked by time, worn out by the fact of being used."[14] He catalogs the objects in his 1944 production of *The Return of Odysseus* in a characteristically formal notation on the page:

A CARTWHEEL,
simple,
primitive,
smeared with mud.

> A BOARD,
> old
> rotten,
> with marks of
> nails and rust.

A CHAIR,
simple,
a kitchen chair,
well worn.

A GUN BARREL,
iron,
rust eaten,
big, thick,
not on wheels,
but resting on

A TRESTLE
smeared with mud,
cement,
lime.

A METAL ROPE,
thick and
rusty.

A LOUDSPEAKER,
military,
imperfect,
hanging on a metal rope.

PARCELS
covered with dust,
lime;
the audience "members"
sit on them.

WALLS
of the room
where the performance
takes place,
bombed
full of holes,
bare bricks,
coats of paint on the floor

A FLOOR
missing planks,
debris scattered all over.[15]

More than indexes or signs of time, the objects on Kantor's stage took on the affective sorrow of change and disintegration on their surfaces and textures. His objects were not props made for the stage, as Michal Kobialka points out, but real objects that might once have been useful and instrumental in the world but had lost that usefulness. Entering his stage world, those objects were ghosted by their former uses. They were witnesses to the losses and their own decay, but as such they enter the stage trailed by the reality of time that is not "stage time." They did not enter the hypothetical sphere of dramatic fiction but maintained the real time of mortality and corporeality. That real time itself became an aesthetic that was quite specifically tangible. His stage objects seem to beg to be touched specifically because of their textures. The texture of surfaces could be said to situate a "romantic" aesthetic that mourns the loss of beauty but has transformed that loss into another version of beauty tied to loss. Kantor's love of old objects spoke an aesthetic of loss as a tactile reality rather than an imaginary, romantic, or simply aesthetic condition, because the loss was also historical. The objects hold a tension between a former life and an ultimate death. Kantor's objects "throw out"—that is, present—the connection of corporeal, material life to death, such that death itself is made present.

If Kantor's use of worn and broken objects has since become a definable "look" for the stage, it was not initially as much to create an aesthetic as to *respond* to the reality of two world wars and to postwar conditions. As Kobialka writes:

> The object wrenched from war and from its technical and theatrical conventions was a "poor object"—for example, a rotten board, no longer able to perform its utilitarian function in life or theatre. This functionless object was, for Kantor, the source of his artistic inquiry into what Artaud called "nontheological space" and into the object's essence and existence. This rejection of the concepts of a traditional theatre space and of an "artistic object" controlled by imitation and representation had far-reaching consequences in Kantor's theatre, compelling him not only to eliminate the idea of a stage prop but also to redefine the role of stage design, costume, blocking, lighting, and, finally, stage action.[16]

The poor objects in *The Return of Odysseus* were not stage props in any conventional sense but, as Kobialka points out, means of creating a specific kind of "site that produced its own space and its own commentary."[17] History (recalling Parks's objects) is not being represented or imagined but being responded to. Nevertheless, those objects, like Kantor's later use of the old pews in *The Dead Class* or his repeating motifs of the bicycle wheel or the umbrella, come to constitute an aesthetic because they make an appeal to the senses, specifically to the sense of touch. In addition to the visual form of the umbrella or the bicycle, the tactility of the object gives its theatrical presence a sensory dimension that exceeds its visibility. The tactile excess, I suggest, is also the access to the alternative space that Kobialka argues cannot be designated by representational modes of signification. For in the early work with poor objects as well as that in the 1950s and '60s with "emballages," Kantor is able to isolate the phenomenon of surfaces: or more precisely, to bring surfaces to their phenomenological complexity. The surfaces of an old object carry the traces of its use and history, just as the human body does. But more important, the tactility of the objects separates the container from the thing contained, turning the container into an autonomous thing. "Emballage," meaning wrapping or packaging as well as the practice of wrapping, is an outside surface that both contains and conceals whatever object, or whatever lack of object, lies inside. In his "Emballage Manifesto," Kantor writes that it "actually exists beyond the boundaries of reality. . . . It could thus be discussed [and here he simply repeats: 'Emballage, Emballage, Emballage'—suggesting there is nothing further to be discussed] in terms of metaphysics. On the other hand, it performs a function that is so prosaic, so utilitarian and so basic."[18] The discarded and discardable wrapping of the object on display thus lies on the threshold "between eternity and garbage."

The theatricality inherent in this notion of emballage may need "unpacking." For implicit in this manifesto, as well as in Kantor's theatre practice, is the sense of theatre's spectacle as an explusion. Spectacle is the element that has been discounted, if not discarded, since Aristotle decided to list it and then ignore it in *The Poetics*. That theatre seems to be all surface, all spectacle, whose substance, if there is any, lies in dramatic action and character, is a long-time idea for devaluing theatre practice. From this view, spectacle—visible surface—is quite specifically something that is thrown out, expelled from the numinous core of essence, meaningful content, or invisible substrate. The degradation of theatrical spectacle to *mere* appearance follows an assumption that truth is located in an unseen or absent substance that ghosts the material presence: the Edenic realm of origins from which the object is thrown. What practitioners like Kantor demonstrate is that the seen and the unseen coincide, that there is nothing hiding inside or beyond appearances, and that the spectacle *is* the substance in which the unseen is present.

As spectacle, the material of theatre is also transient, discardable, and "one should remember, it is performed with a full awareness of the fatal end."[19] With the change of a vowel from *o* to *a,* the object becomes the abject: the thing that is not thrown before but thrown away, discarded; and the object always carries within its "thrownness" its potential as garbage, which is to say its own destruction and death. Surfaces carry the marks of time and of passage between coming and going. Those marks are, further-more, available not only to sight but also to touch. Kantor's use of old, worn objects increases the sensory dimensions of objects and thereby gives sense to history. That history is no less a matter of surfaces whose folds wrap themselves through time. His objects trace a history of expulsion from Edenic origins. Their material surfaces wrap, or "package," that history in such a way that the container and the thing contained are identical. It is the package that matters, because matter is the phenomenon. With a view on objects as folding time into their surfaces, we are able to see how objects then appear to shelter both past and future. They appear as dwelling places for objects between worldly use and representation. On Kantor's stage, objects are suspended but are not outside time, as though his stage were equivalent to a prop room.

In his notion of emballage, Kantor presents a sense of the stage object that echoes Heidegger's distinction between an object and a "thing." For the ritual of emballage—the creation of the wrapping—involves folding, tying up, and sealing. This mundane set of actions, common to any packaging, is a way of explaining how, as Heidegger tries to do, a thing (as opposed to an object) can be understood as an act. This is clearest in Kantor's nota-tion on the umbrella, which he "discovered" by placing one on a canvas:

> An umbrella is a particularly metaphoric Emballage; it is a "wrapping" over many human affairs; it shelters poetry, uselessness, helplessness, defenseless-ness, disinterestedness, hope, ridiculousness. . . . The actors in Mikulski's play *A Circus* [Cricot 2, January 13, 1957] used umbrellas as shields for their poor and deranged lives as well as for what was left of scraps of hope and poetry.[20]

The object as the dwelling place or shelter of poetry, uselessness, helpless-ness, hope, and ridiculousness is not an aesthetic nicety but a materializa-tion of an action, with historical, political, and social as well as personal and affective consequence and context. The sense in which objects shelter human coming and going becomes apparent most especially when the objects them-selves are in exile or lost. The departure of objects reciprocally exiles the humans to whom they are attached.

An especially acute example of objects in exile is the public work in San Francisco called "Defenestration," by Brian Goggin. It is a highly theatrical work. At the corner of Sixth and Howard streets, in a depressed, though increasingly lofty neighborhood, Goggin and a hundred volunteers took over an abandoned tenement building in 1997. Crawling along the sides of the building, hanging precariously from the roof, old furniture is sus-pended. Couch, chairs, tables, one with telephone, lamps, a grandfather clock, a bed, all emerge from the four-story building, seeming ready to fall. Calling up the sense of total eviction of people as well as the objects that constitute living space, the work is audacious, even ridiculous. It is a shel-tering space for the "scraps" of lives where hope and poetry are held sus-pended in the moment of expulsion. It is a site for the affect of loss and violence, at the same time exposing an audacious and ridiculous political and social system that throws out the poor while it builds expensive living spaces down the street. The objects are out of place, no longer, literally, at home; they no longer perform in an invisibly useful context. Furniture objects, especially sitting and lying places, are ghosted by the absent human bodies that have left their impressions on the surfaces. Having been turned into a work, the building becomes a poetic sheltering of the loss of shelter. Like the things laid out on the prop table, the objects are suspended between an origin and a destiny, between function and pure materiality: the between that characterizes the poetic object thrown out of the unmarked context of usefulness. There, at Sixth and Howard, the poetic object is acutely polit-ical. The objects are things in transit (and they periodically change), yet are held still with uncanny familiarity that makes one laugh even while recognizing the helplessness of the objects and their ghosts, unable either to fall or to retreat to the safety of a room. On the surfaces of the build-ing, "Defenestration" exhibits the helplessness of the people-objects who are all the more emphatically absent from the building, yet filling the streets below with hustle and heartache. This building is a public gift and a site of gathering of past and future. It is a still-life that puts the motion of the street in the foreground. Its objects, its monumentality, are a memorial to the losses being lived out below.

"Defenstration" is an installation that thus shows off objects in their multiple functions as attachments to otherness, as "things" quite literally thrown out into the world, as things in themselves as well as for others. It is at the point when things are thrown out that they show the relationship of objects to order and the ways in which objects help to maintain attachments to a world in the temporary illusions of control over that world. For in disorder they recall the way in which the placement of objects constitutes the ordering of the world. The disordering of objects thrown out of the context of everyday use, furthermore, is an act of both art and disaster, when objects and our attachments appear in their most vulnerable and transitory states. Alienated from usefulness, the objects "in themselves" become the site and sign of disaster.

Exactly one week before the destruction of the World Trade Center, a box of items entitled "Shattered Anatomies: Traces of the Body in Performance," assembled by Adrian Heathfield with Fiona Templeton and Andrew Quick, arrived in my mail, a gift, I found out later, from Peggy Phelan. It contained artifacts, images, documents, and drawings from more than twenty-five performance artists and critical writers. On top was a small, clear plastic box with an unidentifiable reddish substance inside, looking like a slug or some organic tissue. It was accompanied by a card with an image of a hammer shattering a mason jar full of something red. On the back of the card, a title, "Sharp Kisses," a name, Bobby Baker, a date, 13.04.1997, and a list of instructions beginning with "Take a glass storage jar full of strawberry jam . . ." Bobby Baker had (presumably) taken such a jar, put on protective goggles and gloves, hit the jar until it shattered and the jam oozed out, spooned the jam into a dish, removed the particles of glass, taken a spoonful of jam into her mouth, squeezed it out into the box, and spit out any remaining glass shards before "making the next kiss." It was impossible not to imagine the act, taste the jam, feel the glass, but also impossible not to recoil from the sensation, then wonder at Bobby Baker's commitment to the act as well as its transformation into artifact. The bottom of the box told me that this plastic box was number 388 out of 550, which hinted that Bobby Baker had kissed out 550 extrusions of strawberry jam. Then questions came up: Was the stuff in the box from the same jar of jam in the picture? Was the jar on the photograph the only one, the real one, or one of many, staged for the picture? Who took the photo? Who made the card? Where was it made? How many other pictures were there? Any? Was the jam in the box blood? (It looked more like a blood clot than jam.) Did Bobby Baker actually make all 550 kisses? Did anyone do exactly what the instructions said? Was it all an imaginary exercise in the first place, assembled to raise these questions?

My first response was amusement and pleasure in imagining the event and re-creating it through a kind of sense-memory projection. I took for granted that it really happened. But then the questions came up. The trajectory of my questions moved from those about material fact to those about abstract speculation. The initial questions took the evidence for granted and developed into doubt about the evidence itself, eventually turning doubt into the very principle of the encounter with the artifact. In spite of the questions and the doubt, however, the material objects were still present, tangible, pleasurable, admirably photographed and printed. Oddly, synchronistically, this artifact, along with others in the box, seemed particularly and aptly suited to the topic of fragmentation of objects in relation to the staging of history. Heathfield's project explicitly addressed the most abstract of my questions in his essay introducing the box: "What issues are at stake in the translation of live art into dead records? What forms of documentation and critical writing are appropriate to these ephemeral events?"

Such objects are thus fragments of a shattered whole and signs of a lost context, but they are also fast becoming indicative of an epistemology grounded in loss and mourning. What appears as a critical art project in "Shattered Anatomies" became a form of public knowledge and mourning one week after I received the box. Among the vivid images of the World Trade Center disaster broadcast on television were the fragments of everyday life. Scattered in the pulverized dust of collapse, the paperwork of ordinary business littered the streets everywhere. Details written, memos, postcards, letters, lists, accounts, notes, client files, computer printouts, pictures: the stuff of everyday business suddenly became signs of its own precarious existence as ordering objects. Signs of disaster—the disordering of those paper objects blowing in the wind, covering the streets, covered in dust—were ghosted by the people who moments before had been keeping those paper objects in place. On the front page of the *New York Times*, months after the World Trade disaster (July 14, 2002), a photo of a log from

the city morgue appeared. It recorded the body parts found at the site, list-
ing items in the fragmentary form of bureaucratic inventory: "unk. Fragment . . . tooth, . . . long bone . . . finger . . . lft. foot . . . right foot . . .
lft.leg. . . ." Even the written record, displaced to the front page of the *Times,*
became a testament to the power of the fragment to invoke horror and loss
measured against the wholeness of a human body. No longer a critical idea
or psychological habit, the fragmentary objects in that written record alone
provoked an excruciating confrontation with the reality of loss in an extraordinary event that occurred on an entirely ordinary Tuesday in September. Those parts invoke the fragility of wholeness itself. Like Kantor's work
with objects cut off from the context of wholeness, that written record
marks the fugitive dimension in things, against which the wholeness of
history is only a memory, and mourning, the appropriate mode: "without
an addressee, / without a place of destination, / without a function, / almost
as if in a vacuum, / in between a sender and a receiver / where both are
powerless." Like the interim space of the post office or the prop table, the
material fragments testify to destinies completed as they measure the difference between disappearance and remainder.

In his essay called "The Thing," in *Poetry, Language, Thought,* Heidegger
identifies objects as whatever interests the empirical habits of science, as
whatever is at a distance or can be called "objective" reality.[21] Objects in
the theater, however, take on new dimensions and other relations to "subjects," not simply because they are framed into significance, but because
they are in a sense suspended between themselves and aesthetic representation. At that point between the expansion into reference, history, and
signification and contraction into materiality, however, they can (again in
Heidegger's terms) "dwell poetically," and we might consider them in terms
of what he calls things. Distinct from history's record of losses over the gaps
of difference (between past and present, self and other, discourse and the
body), theatre objects can offer yet another possibility for history as a matter of intersections and interactions that do not avoid gaps of difference
but incorporate them in a chronic emergence. Consider for the moment
how the concrete and pragmatic action of a prop manager can be understood as acting out Heidegger's distinction between object and thing from
within the practices of theatre.

The prop manager is charged to find or create, gather, store, distribute, and place the objects to be used onstage. She prepares the appearances of the performance package: folding, tying up, and sealing the material forms that will produce the space of performance. Those objects will concretely "shelter" the performance and constitute its dwelling place. More specifically, she must make them ready for the actor at the right moment in performance. It is a job that is almost inevitably in service to the vision of a director and constrained by the aesthetics and economics of a production as well as by the pragmatics of actors who must handle the objects. By giving her story the terms *folding, tying up,* and *sealing,* which are taken from Kantor's work on emballage, the work of the property manager suddenly appears in alliance with terms in two of Heidegger's essays, "The Origin of Work of Art" and "The Thing": *making, gathering,* and *giving.* The prop, in these terms, is a gift, free of specific economic exchange and therefore free of commodification. It is an offering to the stage that from the stage is an offering to a public, harboring its meanings and its uses in the sensory specificity of texture and form, a poetry, pace Cocteau, *of* the stage, not on it. With meaning in reserve because of its liminality, the object is material, sensory, and historical, but also empty. This paradox makes it more available to perception. The emptiness through which it reveals itself is what turns the object into a thing.

Heidegger's own arguments hardly conclude with definitions. They rather force a reader to undergo a process of thinking toward an elusive thought in relation to the existing world. In his essay "The Thing," he aims the reader toward identifying the "thingness" of the thing: toward discovering what a thing is in itself in distinction to what a thing is as an "object," which is something "we place before us" either materially or mentally. He continually offers possibilities for isolating the factors that make a thing a thing rather than an object, then continues to undercut those possibilities by saying they are insufficient. Yet Heidegger cannot quite say just what the "thingness" of a thing would be as he proceeds through the essay. He defies common sense and common language and seems to be trying to lead the reader to some essence of material or mental objects, which at first glance would seem to be just what Plato was doing when he distinguished a material object from the idea (or mental representation) of the object, and both of those from the Form of the object *(Eidos).* For Plato, Heidegger seems to claim, "conceives of the presence [of a thing] . . . in terms of the outward appearance" and as an "object of making" that first requires an idea of the thing for the maker.

Instead of something that stands before, over, against, or opposite us (an ob-ject, thrown before), a thing, for Heidegger, is "what stands forth," which is not simply an outward appearance. The essay makes two claims about what standing forth might be. The first is the sense that the thing came from somewhere, which might be to say that it has a history, that it is the result of a process, either of self-making or of being made. The second is, more obscurely, that standing forth has the sense of coming "into the unconcealedness of what is already present" as the existential reality is revealed in its truth—the unforgetting, or *aletheia,* by which what *is* makes an appearance.[22] Standing forth is thus not a matter of showing some essential being but one of a relational presence; a thing stands forth *for* someone *as* always already having been there. The truth makes its appearance and becomes visible by unforgetting what is and has been present all along.

One problem in understanding this claim is that it seems to be identifying some essential nature of the thing, in the case of Heidegger's example, a "jug," which would be no different from Plato's Forms. But on a purely material basis, Heidegger points at the "holding nature" of the jug that becomes apparent when it is filled. Yet the sides and bottom of the jug are not what does the holding, even though they are "what is impermeable in the vessel" and allow it to stand. Rather, it is the empty space, the void, that does the holding; in shaping the clay, the potter who makes it is also shaping the void. "The vessel's thingness does not lie at all in the material of which it consists, but in the void that holds."[23] This characterization defies the commonsense version of the jug. Unlike a thing, an object is primarily a topic for science, suggesting it is something primarily created by empirical science in a quest for rational understanding and public agreement. Objective knowledge is the compelling mode for understanding and therefore for creating things that can be agreed upon as standing outside the production of an imaginary. While objective knowledge seeks on the one hand to recognize the independence of things in the world, on the other it creates the criteria for that recognition and can take in objects only from a materialist ground, defining the parameters of an object by the limits of its material body. The "thingness" of things, given the scientific experience of reality, has not yet "laid claim to thought . . . [has] never yet at all been able to appear to thinking as things."[24] With such a statement the difficulty remains: the thingness would seem be equivalent to either some essence or irreducible element that Heidegger wants to get to.

But the clue to an escape of the impasse comes with the possibility that the question is not just about the thingness of the thing—about some objective essence—but also about the mode of thinking that does not seek an objective essence and hence does not seek to dominate or subjugate the object to thought but to allow the object to enter thought as a thing in itself. In this mode, the thing is not a product of the mind but an otherness that is recognized as having its own life process, for lack of a better phrase. In the case of the jug, this life process is manifold, consisting of the void being made (or "gathered") both to hold and to pour out. Rather than reducing the jug to an essence, Heidegger expands its possibilities in terms of its giving out the gift of the liquid it was made to do. At this point in the essay, the jug becomes a site for a mythopoetic conception of its connection to origins and ends: its origins in the earth, through the clay that makes it; the wine that comes from earth, water, and sun; and its purpose, or gift, to humans, in giving out drink, and to the gods, in consecration. Unlike the object that memorializes loss, the thing is in some sense restorative of the material and tactile origins of somatic connection: a wholeness that is also always in constant change and flow, constantly different from itself, ever disappearing. Heidegger's image of an "outpouring" suggests this somatic unity and process that are an alternative to the story of object relations.

> In the gift of the outpouring that is drink, mortals stay in their own way. In the gift of the outpouring that is a libation, the divinities stay in their own way, they who receive back the gift of giving as the gift of the donation. In the gift of the outpouring, mortals and divinities each dwell in their different ways. Earth and sky dwell in the gift of the outpouring. In the gift of the outpouring earth and sky, divinities and mortals dwell *together all at once*. These four, at one because of what they themselves are, belong together. Preceding everything that is present, they are enfolded into a single fourfold.[25]

Heidegger then resorts to language that is characteristically opaque and tautological: "How does a thing presence? The thing things. Thinging gathers. Appropriating the fourfold, it gathers the fourfold's stay, its while, into something that stays for awhile: into this thing, that thing."[26]

In its opacity, this language points toward a thinking of a thing (as opposed to a concept) as that which stands outside the ordinary functioning of objects, as that which can be apprehended only poetically, which is to say by the *poiesis* that is a human way of world making that, on the one hand, is in excess of survival needs and, on the other, is a means of creating connections that are already present among the material earth and the human community and the mysteries of being. The thing harbors its past attachments at the same time that it foretells its future in exile, alienation, and decay by gathering the fourfold's stay.

The fourfold of being—earth, sky, mortals, and divinities—presents itself through the "thinging" of the thing. Suppose I translate: If "earth is the building bearer," it can also be called material sustainer of life, the home or ecosphere, "nourishing with its fruits, tending water and rock, plant and animal,"[27] which is never outside representation but also never identical to its representations. The "sky is the sun's path, the course of the moon, the glitter of the stars, the year's seasons," and this could also be called time, as measured by planetary motion, day and night, weather, which is to say change measured by matter. If the "divinities are the beckoning messengers of the godhead," they could also be called the dimension of the grace that calls for unconcealment in the gathering, giving, and receiving of the thing. And if mortals are those who are "capable of death as death," it needs little translation to say we are those who can die because we know we will die, which means we can represent to ourselves the unrepresentable.[28]

If the thing for Heidegger consists of bringing the fourfold being into presence, then the thing is that which gathers matter and time together and donates them as an offering of otherness that is beyond human power to know within the context of mortality. Stuff, change, mortality, the unknown: the crude translation for what every thing holds and gives out in its relatedness. Thingness is thus not an attribute of an object but something more like an event in its relation to an inseparable otherness: a moment when a material object is recognized as belonging to more than its representation, to more than is knowable, but not outside, for the thing also relates to thought via time and to mortality. These are also the gifts of the thing, as opposed to an object, which withholds or is lost. The *more than* means the thing is not exhausted by whatever it may signify. The unconcealing of the thing would be its appearance in its readiness or emergence, neither instrumentally useful nor signifying, though not without the possibilities for use and signification. It means the thing is not eternal but stands momentarily there, although within the temporality of representation—

the Da- of Da-sein—in the gift of outpouring of the fourfold unity. A thing stands independent of representation at the same time that it might be becoming and disappearing. It is historical but not intelligible in terms of the rift of written history. It is not, according to Heidegger, what Kant called a "thing-in-itself," which he claims would be only "the object of a representing that runs its course in the self-consciousness of the human ego . . . an object that is no object for us, because it is supposed to stand, to stay put, without a possible before: for the human representational act that encounters it."[29] The thing, rather, is a gathering in time and a moment of "unconcealing" of a manifold being that is not limited to representation and does not endure. As a gathering the thing does not refer to anything beyond itself; as a gathering, there is no elsewhere.[30] More unsettling is the sense that thingness, like the work of art, might not be generally or widely recognized, might not be shared between people, is not apparently subject to common knowledge, and most particularly cannot be argued for (only against). Because it is a gift, it may or may not be well received.

Using Heidegger risks misunderstanding. He continually threatens a nostalgic turn to some unknown ancients, or an unthinking metaphysics, or magical thinking. And yet, as I transfer his notion into the art of theatre and to the story of those who produce the objects of theatre, I wonder if the pragmatism of theatre and its objects aren't continually ghosted by the dimension of the sacred that has long been lost, like the outline of the object on the prop table. The sacred is not a matter of any religion or belief, nor is it in an object; it, rather, appears as a giving of attention toward the mysteries of the real and material world. The staging of things puts them in process, traveling between a gathering of objects from the world, showing them in the transit of performative present, and still allowing their embeddedness in signification to trail along. The sacred act is in the giving away of the object to misunderstanding and in maintaining faith in its sacrifice to the community gathering. The "thing" that is theatre allows for an emergence that is simultaneous with disappearance.

The history of theatre is a history of gatherings, regardless of any particular religious context. That is not to say that its history relating to Greek worship or to Christian mysteries is irrelevant. It is not just that theatre has turned "secular" or "profane" and lost some religious context that was there at a mythohistorical origin; it is also that the cause or source of community gathering itself has a sacred dimension in its chronically emergent condition in the face of loss and of death, which the living endure as a consequence of living. In the utter pragmatism of bringing together a community, in other words, the sacred appears not in some quality that is lost but *as* a losing gain in an unfolding of, in, and through time. Gathering is an action in time whose movement has a coming, a duration, and a departure. One meets a "thing" in mutual transit of coming and going, and with every departure there is an emergence of something else. Theatre gives power to this poetic formulation of the sacred by its utter pragmatism.

Pragmatic choices and actions in theatre characterize both the transformations among the mental, conceptual, and theoretical dimensions of ideas about theatre and theatre itself. That obvious fact, so often left in the general terms of "practical theatre," is rarely specified as the locus of theatrical transformation despite the decisiveness of such practical considerations. The importance of the choices of props is difficult to theorize, perhaps because they are so particular that their place in the transformational *process* to the "thinging" of theatre gets lost. That is, they seem to be static because they are objects. Understood in a thinging way, props are active; they belong to the temporal dimension of theatre, which includes immediacy and intimacy, duration and disappearance. This is of course a matter of perspective, but by including the prop manager in a broader theoretical story of theatre, I want to include a certain vulgarity in pragmatic actions as a decisive feature of theatre's ability to give flesh to the uncanny, and I want to see theatre itself as a "work of art" in Heidegger's sense of an unconcealing. That unconcealing is not of some latent Form belonging to objects, not some ontological category of essence. It is, rather, a revealing of the standing apart of Being, Da-sein, from within Being. Unconcealing in this sense is the self-revelation or self-representation of the object as coming into being both because of and distinct from human use or representation. In this sense unconcealing is a perceptual event of emergence in which something that is materially present is suddenly perceived as both new and always already there.

Giving flesh to the uncanny does not mean simply investing some object or body with a spirit, ghostly or otherwise; it means exploiting the temporalities of theatre as a temporal and material art, as an action and a process that invites a moment of meeting, which is an act that cannot be held, only given. The giving comes also in mundane terms, in the generosity of time and attention coming from actors, directors, technicians, and audiences.

If it becomes signified as an object, it is done so only in retrospect. The gift of time in the gathering collapses the felt (and generally lived) boundaries among past, present, and future, with the uncanny effect of perceiving something that has been there all along. In fact, the giving occurs only on the occasion of its perception, and only on its perception does it come into existence. No one can guarantee that perception will occur, and no two members of an audience may agree that it is occurring or has occurred. It is a fortuitous meeting and a rare experience, but when it happens that audience member has the sense of having been prepared for and of having been met and known. The gift of the artful thing is an event that might be thought of as a kind of reattachment of the lost object or at least a touching of the wound. It is brief because the gift appears only in the moment of giving; it thus also entails a memory of the first loss and a grieving. The artful thing is a gathering in motion that comes home just as it departs.

chapter 4

Empty Chairs
The Memorial Double

Do take this chair.
—IONESCO, *The Chairs*

Chairs are among those basic human objects that echo the human body. Inanimate reproductions of a human lap, with enveloping arms (or not), chairs duplicate the parental lap and the safety (or not) of its enclosure. Raising the body off the ground but unlike a stool or a bench, a chair traces anatomy, holds off the pull of gravity, and gives ease to muscle and bone. Its angles follow the skeletal joints of a body halfway to collapse, expecting the bending of the knees and the hinging of the hips. It supports the heavy weight of legs and torso, giving ease to the upright strain against gravity and imbalance. It furthermore stands midway between the creaturely need for rest and the symbolic, social configurations of order. The arms of a chair can at once embrace and discipline the body, welcoming it to rest or giving it the ease of authority.

Taken from the Greek, the word *chair* evolved, according to Eric Partridge, from *kata* (down/along) and *hedra* (seat), hence: *kathedra,* the four-legged, sometimes two-armed seat with a back, occupied by a bishop or perhaps a professor; hence the Latin cathedra, a bishop's or professor's chair.[1] Thus, speaking ex cathedra is speaking from the position of authority. Such an etymology suggests an archaic scene in which a figure of authority, granted by wisdom, dignity, or infirmity of age, takes a place of honor amid an attentive crowd. The failing/falling body, caught halfway to its reclining position in the grave, speaks to the listeners, who grant it the wisdom of experience and honor its proximity to death. That crowd gathers around to hear the words passed "down" from the chair. Organizing this crowd in space, the "chair" speaks from its place to the very social order it creates. The seat of power in this archaic scene maintains its privileges over those standing, particularly when it is set high, on a dais. Conversely, the chair is a place of vulnerability, and those standing figures may just as easily dominate the seated one, as though recognizing the body's fragility and its awkward position from which to stand and take action. The midway position, half up and half down, puts power and vulnerability in the same place, relying completely on context to determine whether the seated figure receives contempt or respect, whether it is on its way toward death or ready to return to life.

Chairs, closer to home, are also places for dreaming. Dreaming of a chair or in a chair, one dreams of repose, as Bachelard might say, at the midpoint between private thought and social order. Or, as Lacan might say, between perception and consciousness. A chair is an image for the body at rest without being asleep, only halfway to unconsciousness, a place for one's dignity. A place of singularity and of intimacy with oneself, "with one enormous chair," it's "loverly," as Eliza Doolittle says. The chair, like the parental lap, is a place to be longed for, returned to, to set off further dreaming of other places and possibilities, free from the demands for action. Depending on its shape and material, it embraces the body, sustains its weight, and touches it intimately. Chairs may be the site of one's identity, as in the familial distinctions of the fairy-tale bears, "Who's been sitting in my chair?" or in the human family dynamic, "Don't sit there, that's my chair." They are also places of sociability. One offers a chair to a guest as an invitation to remain, to be attentive to the present rather than gone in transit, to converse rather than to orate.

Chairs themselves are never abstract. They are, rather, readable objects of culture. A chair speaks of the kind of human that would occupy it, of social position and history, of class, of gender, of quality. A chair always has a character. Its materiality speaks of a technological era and practice, in wood or plastic, metal, canvas, cloth, or gold. Its shape may speak of whimsy, of authority, of intimacy; of modernism, tradition, naturalism, or invention. It identifies the person, the status, and the location of absent occupants in history, in social relations. Such variability suggests that in contrast to some ideal Platonic form, chairs are intimately and thoroughly imbued with the specificity of human action, occupation, power, and identity, character, history, and technology.

In addition to the particularities of history and culture, of status and quality, however, an empty chair speaks of a future arrival or a loss: it anticipates the person who will sit; it remembers the person who did sit. A body
leaves its imprint on the chair, which holds the memory of the body in
place. The pathos of an empty chair holds both memory of a loss and anticipation of return in all the particularity of a person, in character, in quality. It remembers both authority and vulnerability. A chair, in short, is also
a memorial device.

On a stage, chairs can trace dramatic history. Bert States, for example,
gives an acute reading of the difference between the chairs of Ibsen's world
and those of Chekhov's. Where Ibsen's characters will "sit on the edge of
it, bursting with news or curiosity," Chekhov's chairs "serve as the still
point against which we observe a dreadful passage of soul. . . . In a Chekhov silence . . . the tactile world, the visible world (which the talk is aimed
unconsciously at keeping at bay), this history-in-objects, quietly encroaches
on the human. . . . Suddenly you can hear the ticking of the objects and
the ceaseless flow of future into past: the world is no longer covered by conversation."[2] Ibsen's chairs disappear into what Roland Barthes calls the "effect
of the real." They are the familiar items of furniture that help to identify
that world as real, social, intelligible. Chekhov's chairs emerge from their
intelligibility as furniture and become strange objects that harbor the oppressive sameness of his characters' lives. "When they sit down to talk, as they
usually do, about life elsewhere, or two hundred years hence, or about the
need to work, furniture becomes the seat of discontent; to be in one world
and to dream of another is to confer on one's living space the status of a
prison."[3]

The stage consistently takes such worldly objects as chairs and converts
their phenomenological presence, their raw materiality, and their social particularity to its own purposes. That conversion, which turns the object into
a sign, effectively doubles the object. When the habit of seeing an imitative double or of reading meaning in the object becomes mere convention, as has happened in realism, a new re-forming or reseeing of an object
blocks conceptual habit and returns perception to the substance of materiality and form. Thus, Robert Wilson's custom of making chairs for his early
epics by suspending them in space *(The Life and Times of Sigmund Freud,
Deafman Glance, Einstein on the Beach)* or by loading them with materiality *(Overture, The Life and Time of Joseph Stalin, A Letter to Queen Victoria)*

"contradict the supporting role that furniture should play." As John Rockwell writes, "As the content becomes interchangeable with form, form itself gains density and becomes as Foreman says, impenetrable."[4] On viewing Wilson's stage and its objects, one has to fight against what might be called the will to signify, though the objects are not without intelligibility. The materiality and formalism, rather, have sensory effects that resonate with but do not necessarily create meaning, in the sense that meaning might belong to a cohesive world or coherent narrative. However, Rockwell reads the Stalin Chairs as intelligible objects: "Draped in lead they appear funereal. The lead reminds us that Wilson does not deal in theatrical trompe l'oeil. We are not being fooled by crafty imitation in sculpt-metal. This is cold, dense, and poisonous lead." And the Queen Victoria Chairs, he says, are "low seated, throne-like [and] resemble high backed machines of coercion." The Overture Chair "is removed from the world. Surrounded by a moat, its heavy oak timbers imply the power of an encastled king. A brass scepter attached topped with the flame of a jet of gas suggests not only the light but the power of sovereignty. . . . In another version, the chair is only a few inches high set on a large sheet of creased lead. The scale and the material more graphically emphasize its inaccessibility. . . . Similarly the Einstein Chair, eight feet tall [made of galvanized pipe] and requiring assistance to mount to its four-and-a-half foot seat, was used to raise Lucinda Childs as a witness in the trial scene in *Einstein on the Beach*."[5]

The acquisition of so many of Wilson's chairs as museum pieces emphasizes their singularity as objects that have no need for placement in dramatic or theatrical systems. Yet Rockwell's descriptions indicate that even outside such contexts, the chairs cannot utterly resist meaning. They cannot completely fail to signify, nor can they deny their own multiplicity or the capacity to hold historical memory. The resistance of those chairs to the imposition of meaning does not further signify the relativity of all significations or indicate meaninglessness. In Wilson's case, formalism is a tool that punctures the signifying habits of convention, not as a final signification, but as a step in an ongoing oscillation between habit—"the great deadener" for Beckett—and estrangement. A chair, in brief, is a multiple object: a material object and an abstracted, inanimate reproduction of a human body; a thing-in-itself and a social signifier. Each and every chair has a singular, phenomenal materiality but also holds a multiplicity of intimate and social significations. Every chair also carries an aspect of the uncanny insofar as it carries the trace of the parental lap (the familiar) in its inanimate form (the unfamiliar). These assertions are, of course, a matter of perspective and attention. But these variations of the multiple make chairs particularly theatrical objects in themselves, a theatricality that Wilson exploits. His chairs are theatrical even when they are installed as exhibits, because they invite attention to the uncanniness of the double.

What concerns me for the rest of this chapter is the way that theatrical doubling is both simply the province of theatre and the model for an epistemology by which perceptual experience is transformed into knowledge *of* experience. Before it is possible to name an experience as one's own, it is necessary to know that one is having or has had an experience. In other words, experience must first be differentiated *as* an experience in order to *be* one.⁶ This does not mean that something did or did not happen. Trauma studies make it clear that it is possible to undergo an event without any conscious register, but humans are also capable of creating the "as" experience—the reality of an imaginary form—out of any number of stimuli that may not correlate directly to some specific perceptual event. Thus Freud's proposal that trauma reappears symptomatically and repetitiously: the origin is a blank to the extent that it is undifferentiated, "unclaimed," in Cathy Caruth's word. The claim of an original trauma is countered by critics (and Freud's own disavowal of ubiquitous molestation) who refute the origin. Put another way, this means it is possible to be absent from events in one's own life, particularly when stimuli overwhelm the sensory or the cognitive systems. To paraphrase the House Subcommittee investigating Watergate, the issue is what do we know and when do we know it? In some sense, no experience is knowable until it is known that it is known, just as in *King Lear:* "the worst is not / so long as we can say, 'This is the worst'" (4.1.27–28). The unspeakable is just that, and tragedy belongs not to those who suffer it but to those who live to know it and speak it. Simply to call upon the touchstone of "experience" is to know that we know it. But it is quite evident that I have "had" any number of experiences that I do not and cannot know. Even at the level of a parasympathetic nervous system, much less of trauma, I live them out before I "know" them. Consciousness tends to lag behind events or to anticipate them; it is rarely, if ever, on time, in the present. Such an apparent tautology—that the unknown is unknown until it is known—has wide-ranging consequences in its paradoxical demand that the unknowable and the unspeakable be recognized.

The inevitable blind spot in consciousness demands to be accounted for, but precisely because it is a blind spot, that account can be done only through the double in the mirror, just as Horatio is Hamlet's double whose designation of the ghost of Hamlet's father as a "mote . . . to trouble the mind's eye" (1.1.112) is an anticipatory reflection of Hamlet's later statement, that he has seen his father in his mind's eye (1.2.185). The blind spot becomes visible *as* a blind spot through its reflection in Horatio's speech.

The privileging of the double onstage is simply a reiteration of the fact that all forms of representation, whether in words, images, or actions, objects or ideas, present the paradox of the double (consciousness) that is a singularity (event), and a singularity (event, thing) that is multiplied by memory, consciousness, language, and history. And in the constitution of that paradox, or, rather, in the oscillation between its extremes of singular and multiple, is a site that is neither one nor the other. It is a "theatrical site" that is productive of both, in that it is constantly transforming multiplicity—the echoes of meaning as well as resonances and references, memory, metaphor, and metonymy—into the singularity of "an" experience. Held in the provisional space of "theatre," an object is never not itself, yet it is rarely wholly itself. This double negative—not not itself, yet also other than itself—is the fundamentally theatrical element of an epistemological stance.[7] Such a stance takes into account the projections of meaning on an object that are not merely subjective projections but derive from a social and/or psychic relation to the object, and therefore both belong to and differ from the object. The double negative views the positive aspects of materiality in terms of a chronic departure into fractured multiplicity that nonetheless returns to the object. The provisional status of that theatrical site replicates the provisional status of one's life story whose material singularity—its objective/object character—is sanctioned by death and found in the corpse, which is the otherness of the living body, the future in the instant. In the meantime, the living body produces in the world the multiplicity of its thoughts, memories, and dreams, its analogies, metaphors, and languages, its departures. Chairs onstage offer occasions for exploring the effects of the theatrical double, by which a material artifact serves as a screen for the projection of meaning (as in Ionesco's play *The Chairs*), a memorial site (as in the Oklahoma City National Memorial), and an object that carries history and memory (as in Kantor's piece *Today Is My Birthday*), but is also the very vehicle by which an unknowable event, such as death, can be perceived.

The power of a chair to invoke both loss and return was not lost on the designers of the Oklahoma City memorial. At the site of the Murrah Federal Building in Oklahoma City, which was bombed in 1995, the Butzner Design Partnership created a grid of chairs set out on a grassy expanse. The chair seats and backs are made of bronze, each one supported by square translucent bases. In nine symmetrical rows, one for each floor of the building on which people were killed, in lines that correspond to the number of people killed on each floor, each of the memorial chairs is engraved with a name. The names contribute human particularity and individuality to the visual image of the expanse of chairs that measure the loss by a formal and numerical order on a grid. The order of the grid and the uniformity of the chairs subtract their particularity and situate the scope and range of the loss. The memorial dematerializes the particularity of lives lost and rematerializes them by measurement and number, creating a symbolic order. That order and uniformity give an uncanny stillness to the site, as though the chairs hold time itself in suspense.

Clearly the designers meant to do just that, since the site is flanked by monumental portals, the entrance reading 9:01 and the exit reading 9:03. The chairs sit on a grassy plane between the two portals, each marked by the sign of a minute. Set within a measure of time, the plane holds the elapse of those two minutes as everlasting, converting impossible marks of time into space. Impossible because the almost instantaneous transformation from ordinary life in a bureaucratic institution to a scene of massive death is impossible to grasp as a moment in time. The event is, rather, a puncture in the fabric of time that continues to unfold, creating a before and after, with its present only in memory. As trauma studies make clear, the moment of death of the other is always a moment that is missed.[8] Time, the measure of passage, never has a stop; yet time as a measure of consciousness is always at odds with the timelessness of the unconscious, in which all times are copresent. In the unconscious, Freud pointed out, there is no time. The trauma of the Oklahoma City bombing required a space to mark what was missed in time, a place to re-present the moment of loss that time swept away in survival.

The trauma of survival is, in fact, the trauma, for survivors suffer with a self-canceling kind of knowledge, both knowing and not knowing. For the radical loss that is death occurs at a moment in time that is not experienced. The contradiction between what one knows and what, simultaneously, cannot be known drains the survivor of selfhood, and a memorial site at the very least marks that contradiction as real and material and gives mourning a place to return to and, in returning, to grieve for the unknown. The Oklahoma City site indicates the impossibility of knowing that moment as anything other than an abstract point of information, giving it the most abstracted designation of time: 9:01. On the other hand, people enter the portal and, by their own physical action, pass through the abstract designation. The inscription remains a wholly abstract, yet physical, sign that is both accurate and inscrutable. The piece of information is powerful by virtue of its strangeness. It has no temporal content of its own. As a reference it points elsewhere. As a physical presence it seems almost like a betrayal, for the information is an insufficient account of the loss. Yet precisely because of its insufficiency and its inscrutability, it repeats the unmet moment of the death of others as it marks off the memorial space.

The site thus becomes a designated ritual space that doubles a nonexperience. The initial lack re-forms into an experience that constitutes a kind of knowledge that has nothing to do with information or, rather, has to do with the nothing that sheer information conceals. The portal marks the neither-nor space for memory and mourning. The ritual of entering a portal and exiting through another marked 9:03 brings about "having" an experience of a nonexperience, regardless of any degree of consciousness on the part of the mourner, the survivor, the tourist, the consumer. The efficacy of ritual, in other words, is less a matter of belief or understanding of symbolic dimensions than a matter of the facticity of the ritual, its performance, if you prefer, in the fact that it is done and that the experience is undeniable, regardless of meaning. The undeniability of ritual supplants the deniability and unconsciousness of traumatic loss, and the inscriptions on the gates repeat in informational effigy the missed encounter.

The abstract shapes of the chairs reiterate visually a similar ritual passage between kinds of time. The chairs have portal-like, rectangular openings in their backs, creating a frame, a space of passage. Shaping an empty space in the visible field, the chairs allow one to see through them. There is both no difference between one side and the other, and all the difference, which is made by the framing. The apertures make a continuum in space at the same time that the chairs, having a front and back, mark a difference. The cognitive dissonance between the initial event, the bombing of the building, and survival is represented by a reiteration of that dissonance in empty space. The temporal passage becomes spatial, and the blank in space becomes the means by which one sees an invisible reality in terms of the visible.

In a more literal way, those memorial chairs also enforce a recollection of the death of so many people while sitting at their desks, performing ordinary tasks. In the daylight, the chairs have the entirely mundane appearance of chairs. The proportions of the backs, however, make them appear also as tombstones in a uniform graveyard. This, too, is an aspect of their uncanny ability to invoke the double of death in the midst of life. For they are not chairs that tempt anyone to sit in them: hard, rectilinear, and made of bronze, they do not invite the body or invoke its shape. No human body would sit there. At night, they transform as the translucent glass bases glow against the dark, like ghost lights. Then, the failure of vision in the dim light suggests shapes and shadows that take the chairs out of their daytime features into a more manifestly haunted space. Like candles held in the dark, they more emphatically emphasize what cannot be seen, what is behind them. The lights hold off the dark at the same time that they measure it, inviting night thoughts of death and ghostly presences. The official Web site of the memorial says these lights make the chairs seem to float above their bases and are "beacons of hope." But whatever the official word, whatever the specific emotions the chairs evoke, the visual field of the graveyard then appears strangely alive in contrast to the inert objects of daylight. The lights dematerialize the chairs and in some sense release them from the gravity of the earth. But again it is precisely because they are chairs that their ghostly occupants also seem released, even while they are present. The designers seem to have insight into the double duty of chairs to invoke a presence and an absence for a specific body and therefore to serve as a site of both farewell and return.

In his play *The Chairs*, Ionesco was able to take the memorial phenomenon of chairs and turn it to critical purposes without losing the force of the object within psychic economies. What is a public, ritual function in Oklahoma City becomes an analytic tool in the play. The analysis combines an allegory of a psychical dynamics with an implicit critique of their place in bourgeois mentality and ideology. The invisible guests in *The Chairs* do not come from just anywhere. These ghosts appear from the specific conditions of the play, which are at the same time personal, social, and mythic.

The ghosts' invisibility against the phenomenon of the chairs enacts the concrete power of the imaginary within the material world and thus formally transforms a memorial function into an identifiable performance, a work of "art." Theatrically, in other words, these invisible figures elicit both phenomenological and signifying forces that the imaginary itself creates. Rather than two distinct modes, the visible chairs and their invisible occupants are indivisible. They belong to, come from, and are imbued with a deep sense of the theatrical double by which material objects take on the force and effect of the imaginary. The double aspect of the chairs, however, is brought up against their material singularity and apparent autonomy, through which they begin to dominate the stage and the humans, taking on a life of their own.

In the play, Old Man and Old Woman frantically fill the stage with chairs for unseen visitors. They are preparing for the entrance of the Orator, who will bring Old Man's message to the world. First comes the Lady, a person of dignity, of "class." Then comes the Colonel, followed by Old Man's former lover (Belle); then a Photo-Engraver, followed by newspaper men, a crowd of ladies and gentlemen, children (though "one doesn't bring children to a scientific lecture").[9] An ever-growing number of invisible people enter the increasingly claustrophobic space, indicated only by the growing number of chairs. The frenzied desperation with which the couple bring on the chairs sends the play to the borderline of farce and horror. Though nominally meant for the invisible humans, the chairs fill the space as though replicating themselves and driving the two old people into frantic action to answer their demands. The stage is gradually populated with chairs occupied by ghostly figures, signaling the oppressive character of both material reality and the social field. When the two old people are eventually trapped, unable to move freely in the claustrophobic space, which they themselves have created, they find the only exit is out through the windows to a suicidal leap to the water below.

In production, of course, it matters what kind of chairs are brought on. They need to be light enough to lift and carry quickly onstage, just as the actors need speed and agility to enter and exit through the eight doors Ionesco calls for. Like the horror movies whose monsters seem to be always replicating themselves, *The Chairs* socializes that horror through the proliferation of this entirely normal item of furniture, in a kind of farcical horror at the banal itself. Certainly the limits on a budget might mean that

the chairs are an eclectic collection of haphazard styles that indicate a certain kind of social diversity among the imaginary occupants. Wealthier
productions have made the chairs identical, in a mass display of fascist mentality and conformity. The chairs create the ghostly presence of their unseen
occupants and at the same time give them specificity and character. The
play of the material presence of the chairs against the invisible people gives
Ionesco the chance to signify the "nothingness" that inhabits the social reality of the two characters. That signification becomes Ionesco's indictment
of the theatrical dimension of bourgeois life that cannot identify the power
of its Imaginary to fill reality.

The nonrealistic scene that became familiar through those authors whom
Martin Esslin identified as contributing to the theatre of the absurd provided a new context for social critique that had become familiar in the
devices of realism. In *The Chairs,* that context is explicitly a matter of isolation. Both the scene of the play and its dramatic form cut ties with the
mundane social world and the habits of realistic representation. Realism
and the social world it represents are instead rerepresented by the ghosts
of the bourgeois realm of mid-twentieth-century Europe, ghosts that occupy
the chairs. Kenneth Tynan famously complained that, theatrically speaking, such an "escape from realism [is] an escape into what? A blind alley,
perhaps, adorned with *tachiste* murals. Or a self-imposed vacuum, wherein
the author ominously bids us observe the absence of air. Or, best of all, a
funfair ride on a ghost train, all skulls and hooting waxworks, from which
we emerge into the far more intimidating clamours of diurnal reality."[10]
Ionesco responded by saying:

> This "reality" seems to me much vaster and more complex than the one to
> which Mr Tynan and many others want to limit themselves. The problem
> is to get to the source of our malady, to find the non-conventional language
> of this anguish, perhaps by breaking down this "social" language which is
> nothing but clichés, empty formulas, and slogans. The "robot" characters
> Mr Tynan disapproves of seem to me to be precisely those who belong solely
> to this or that milieu or social "reality," who are prisoners of it, and who—
> being no more than social, seeking a solution to their problems only by so-
> called social means—have become impoverished, alienated, empty. It is pre-
> cisely the conformist, the petit-bourgeois, the ideologist of every society who
> is lost and dehumanized.[11]

The first image of isolation is that of Old Man and Old Woman becoming enisled. That isolation perhaps characterizes the existential human condition less than the petit-bourgeois "sensibility" to which the couple belongs. For Ionesco, the platitudes they recite, like those in *The Bald Soprano*, betray the dehumanization of a conformist society. Yet in addition to the indictment of conformity, Ionesco provides the links between his social critique and a more fundamental fear, which he confesses is his own and which he attributes to "all mankind." "I must ask myself what my fundamental problem is, what my most ineradicable fear is," and he later confesses it is fear of death. Surrounded by water, the first exchange in the play concerns the danger of Old Man leaning too far out the window, lest he fall in. "Water all around us . . . water under the windows, stretching as far as the horizon." But they are also surrounded by darkness: "There's no sunlight, it's nighttime, my darling." Reminiscing about the time: "It's six o'clock in the evening . . . it is dark already. It wasn't like this before. Surely you remember, there was still daylight at nine o'clock in the evening, at ten o'clock, at midnight."[12] Perhaps this is simply a matter of wintertime. But the darkness that surrounds them at least verbally, if not scenically on the stage, implicates a second image that becomes a source for the ghosts to come, an image made through the associated links among darkness, unconsciousness, and death. Designated emphatically as "old," these two characters are quite literally, and therefore quite symbolically, on the verge of death. This particular dark winter is enlarged to reinforce the isolation not only of the scene but also of old age and its fears of impending death. Such fear is a great creator of frightful ghosts, because it is a further dimension of the isolation of the individual. Without the corrective realities of a material, social context, such isolation generates the kind of subjectivity in which the imaginary dominates actuality or, rather, begins to constitute the doubling of reality as a subjective one.

That such subjectivity is Ionesco's own is something he confesses in his last response to Tynan, in which he uses the image of the "immense ocean of the infinite." Such subjectivity becomes a universalizing assumption of the play, by which the singularity of the individual can be read as a generality for all individuals. The chairs materialize their individual occupants, even as the play acts out the isolation of subjectivity vis-à-vis a social world. The allegory contains Ionesco's own blind spot toward the ways in which a sense of the universality in individual experience also belongs to a bourgeois ideology. In spite of himself, that is, the play mirrors Ionesco's position that such a condition is universal, even while it indicts the consequences. Writing about his alienation from his lieutenant during his military service and later from his boss when he worked as a clerk, Ionesco says:

> When my lieutenant and my boss are back in their homes, alone in their rooms, they could, for example, just like me, being outside the social order, be afraid of death as I am, have the same dreams and nightmares, and having stripped off their social personality, suddenly find themselves naked, like a body stretched out on the sand, amazed to be there and amazed at their own amazement, amazed at their own awareness as they are confronted with the immense ocean of the infinite, alone in the brilliant, inconceivable and indisputable sunlight of existence. And it is then that my general [sic] or my boss can be identified with me. It is in our solitude that we can all be reunited.[13]

Within the isolation of the island, of the subject, of the dread of death, and then of memory, Old Man and Old Woman begin to fret over history, memory, and change. Old Man, as he has done every night for the seventy-five years of their marriage, tells the story, the same story, of his life, of their life together, of the trip to Paris, a Paris of both memory and possibility, which, Old Woman claims, "never existed." The "absurdity" of a Paris that never existed is, in fact, the reality of an event that exists only in memory and therefore only in imagination, in dreams. When Martin Esslin designated such preposterous conditions as "absurd," he was not abrogating the accuracy of their representation and fully recognized that Ionesco was also telling his own story of exile and trip to Paris. For this scene manifests the way in which actual, material conditions migrate to symbolic conditions within the field of the imaginary, and the remarkable consistency with which certain kinds of images reiterate mythic or personal histories. For with "water all around," the stage room turns into a fortification against engulfment: it becomes a sign for the emplacement of consciousness against the overwhelming encroachment the unconscious, where memory, imagination, and dreams are all of the same character. At the same time, it works as the representational double of Ionesco's own confessed fear in the face of the "immense ocean of infinity" and reflects his own sense of the universality of such fear. The play itself thus ghosts the psychic life of its author and his blind spot, part "absurdity," part biographical reflection. Though such a formulation clearly reflects the habits of "Western culture" to universalize the experiences of subjectivity, it also allows for a critique of those habits by identifying the specific conditions that foster the myths of universality and by locating the rifts within mimesis that point to the imaginary dimension that orders the material world.

From a psychoanalytic perspective, a subject arrives in the world as it severs a creaturely symbiosis with a mother and gains language. Loss inaugurates the subject and the symbiotic attachment recedes into myth, into unconscious longing, but also into unconscious fear. Simultaneous with the fear of death comes a longing for reattachment, to the past, to youth, to others, to the mother. Freud's notion of the "oceanic" sense of infinity, related to the death drive and its association with the mother, echoes in Ionesco's statement quoted above but also in the exchange of Old Man and Old Woman in *The Chairs*. Old Man lapses into an infantile nostalgia, a return to the maternal "oceanic" desire for death, and Old Woman cooperates in that desire.

> OLD MAN: [sobbing] Hi, hi, hi! My mamma! Where is my mamma? I don't have a mamma anymore.
> OLD WOMAN: I am your wife. I'm the one who is your mamma now.
> . . .
> OLD WOMAN: My pet, my orphan, dworfan, morphan, orphan.[14]

This image of the self as an orphaned child in need of his mother articulates how the child's desires inhabit the imaginary of the adult Old Man. Through his babbling tears, the child appears as the ghost of a former self who dominates Old Man in his old age. The regression, so blatant in expression, seems absurd only in comparison to the ideal of a rational subjectivity. In the opening moments of the play, in other words, Ionesco lays a groundwork of memory, nostalgia, loss, fear, and longing. Infantalized by old age and the fear of death, surrounded by water that disconnects them from a social context, rehearsing the story night after night of their arrival in a village (Paris) that never existed, the old couple is set up to invite ghosts into their home. Their isolation in this room, fortified against abandonment, against loss, against the undifferentiated space of the unconscious, constitutes the initial condition out of which phantoms of social reality will soon appear, the phantoms that Marx called ideology. That isolation in the subjective space of individuality, in short, dematerializes the world on the one hand and reconstitutes the material world according to its needs on the other. The frantic activity of Old Man and Old Woman to fill the space with chairs for their invisible guests implicates the way in which the imaginary supplements the material world. The social and political world that Tynan could take for granted is here shown to be a construction of the world in terms of the imaginary. That imaginary is real and constructive in precisely the same way that theatre is an arena for the in-between, the both/ and, neither/nor double of the world: phenomenologically concrete, visible, performative, and real as well as immaterial, abstract, ideational. That imaginary compels its characters to act and brings the material world into conformity with its needs.

One of the first ghostly figures or blind spots in the space of the imaginary does not occupy a chair. It is, rather, the articulation by Old Man of a subjectivity related to isolation, which is found in childhood narcissism: that sense of an exclusive and special self, of uniqueness, of infinite possibility, of a total and totalizing self that dominates reality. In articulating that sense, Old Man equally implicates a characteristically bourgeois narcissism. In his allegorical representation of a psychic condition, in other words, Ionesco is also able to implicate a social terrain that indicts bourgeois habits: "I'm not like other people. I have an ideal in life. I am perhaps gifted. . . . I have some talent, but things aren't easy for me. I've served well in my capacity of general factotum" (119). Old Man, who "could have been anything," could, by the same token, have been everything: head admiral, head cabinetmaker, head orchestra leader. The all and nothing version of a self is the infantile ghost that haunts his old age. The idealization of an infantile self is characteristically isolated from a social self that integrates within a real community. Old Woman reassures him: "You're not like other people, you are much greater, and moreover you'd have done much better if you had gotten along with other people, like other people do. You've quarreled with all your friends, with all the directors, with all the generals, with your own brother" (119).

That imaginary, however, is not simply a projection of an ideal but an ideal that seems locked into a loss, represented by failing memory, fragmented stories, half thoughts, the sense of being orphaned in the world. "It's too far away, I can no longer . . . recall it. . . . Where was this?" At the same time, Old Man feels compelled to "tell it all" (120), to give his unique message to the world. From within their lost origin, Old Man and Old Woman memorialize that loss by speaking a world into existence. "It's in speaking that ideas come to us, words, and then we, in our own words, we find perhaps everything, the city too, the garden, and then we are orphans no longer" (120–21). A playwright obsessed by the difficulties of language and its limits of meaning, Ionesco here, as he does even more absurdly in *The Bald Soprano,* sets out the emptiness of speech. *The Chairs* situates the difficulties of language more specifically in a circumstance of loss than in the indictment of meaningless conversations of the middle-class couples of *The Bald Soprano.* More clearly here, language has a memorializing function through which it substitutes for loss. By speaking a world into existence, the old couple supplement the material world of chairs with words and actions. They speak their ghosts into reality; they invite the world into their otherwise isolated space by the placements of the chair objects.

The litany of guests are social objects more than humans. In an encyclopedic list, they identify the categories of social occupations that will appear: the property owners, the intellectuals, the janitors, the bishops, the chemists, the tinsmiths, the violinists, the delegates, the presidents, the police, the merchants, the buildings, the pen holders, the chromosomes, the post-office employees, the innkeepers, the artists, the bankers, the proletarians, the functionaries, the militaries, the revolutionaries, the reactionaries, the alienists, the papacy, the papayas, the paupers. These objects traverse the linguistic world by alliteration, becoming word objects that substitute for the human. They are the linguistic markers that stand in the place of loss that Ionesco makes particular as the loss of parents, the loss of origins, the source of their orphanage: "It's true then, they're going to come, this evening? You won't feel like crying any more, the intellectuals and the proprietors will take the place of papas and mamas?" (122). This version of the function of the imaginary thus most specifically objectifies human figures, suggesting that the very sense of what an object is, is the substitution of a loss by the imaginary. Such an act of substitution then begs the question, Which are the ghosts: the parents ghosted by their social substitutes, or the social substitutes ghosted by the parents? The invisible occupants of the chairs are doubly representative of the process by which the longing for attachment transfers loss and absence into memorial objects. Through the course of the play Old Man and Old Woman take the word objects of that encyclopedia and move them into real chairs.

The first two figures, the Lady and the Colonel, who seem to show up to Old Man and Old Woman, elicit the old couple's obsequious deference to social class. In an embarrassment of social form, the scene with the imaginary Lady and the Colonel introduces the convention of conversation with invisible characters. They also implicitly render the questions common to all forms of polite social conversation: Who is speaking? To whom are we speaking? Is anyone there? Is anyone speaking? Language has become separate from embodiment and hangs in the absence of a body. A further indictment of social trivia, these invisible figures concretize the absence of a living being within such social niceties.

The next figures who appear to Old Man and Old Woman seem to arrive from a far more personal history, which is to say a far more personal imaginary. "You're still the same, in spite of everything. . . . I've loved you, a hundred years ago. . . . But there's been such a change. . . . No, you haven't changed a bit. . . . I loved you, I love you" (131). "We could have been so happy, I'm sure of it" (133). Belle, it becomes clear, is Old Man's lost love who remains ever different and ever same. She has been and is always lost, even in her return. In a parallel way, the Photo-Engraver elicits Old Woman's sexuality as she lifts her skirts and exposes her breasts, spreads her legs and "laughs like an old prostitute" (132). Those ghosts, elicited through language and behavior, display the chronic presence of loss and abandonment that constitute the appearance of an invisible psychic life in the material world: an invisible and imaginary reality that appears precisely in language and behavior not so much in the content of speech or action as in their encryption in formal, material, and symbolic echoes. Belle and the Photo-Engraver are the ghostly icons of former loves that haunt the old couple and return in speech. The opening of the play, with its explicit marking of failed memory, abandonment, and delusion, provides the foundation for the return of the illusory lovers. It sets out not only the associational chain of abandonment, romantic idealization, and sexuality but also the retention of obsessions as well as the one-sidedness of obsession. The chairs that hold these psychic dynamics become the memorial sites to their loss and their return.

Once the door has been opened to these personal ghosts, there is no stopping the entry of a mass of ghosts, who include reporters, children, a general public, eventually an emperor, all of whom are presumably there to hear the word of the Orator. Once the functional reality of the invisible is accepted, the couple is overwhelmed, and their enclosure becomes a circus. The ghosts take on a life of their own. Sound takes over the stage, as the bell rings continuously, as the motors of arriving boats bring in more people. The couple start selling programs and Eskimo pies as uninvited guests fill the room. The physical responses of the two visible characters turn farcical as they desperately try to maneuver around the chairs and the invisible people. An audience sees them trying to accommodate the invisible, adjusting themselves to suit the imaginary rather then ever questioning the basis of the imaginary.

There is also, of course, the question of the "message" that Old Man must tell. "I have so much difficulty expressing myself . . . but I must tell it all" (120). For this particular evening, however, Old Man has hired a professional orator, someone who will "speak in [Old Man's] name." He has ceded this language to an imaginary other, conceded that meaning belongs to another. The Orator and the message are promised to the invisible crowd that enters but also to the living audience of the play. The promise promotes anticipation of a revelation and a conclusion. If not now in the middle of the play, surely soon, the answer, the message, the verbal equivalent to Godot, will arrive. What is more, the entrance of the Emperor, who appears as a powerful light coming in through the door, seems to guarantee an ultimate auditor for the message. The notion of an emperor who hears is precisely an idea of validation. An audience with the Emperor, that is, authorizes the message. But this Emperor, like the other guests, is also invisible and imaginary, a projection of authorization onto a figure who is partly manifest by a blinding stage light, partly mythical, partly historical. The Emperor takes the best chair in the best position near the dais, and his empty throne is an emphatic image for the way in which the presumption of authority and authorization is a central and organizing principle of both personal and public space, mental and physical life. Old Man has conceded both language and the capacity for meaning to the imaginary other that takes up the central place in the room. And, of course, when the Orator finally arrives in the figure of a "flesh and blood" ("this is not a dream!" [154]), real, material person, a real audience might just equally concede meaning to that figure, since, finally, another real person has entered the stage.

Yet this real Orator is only real. As flesh and blood, he/it is stripped of the imaginary but embodies the absence hidden by the signifier, for he

cannot speak. He is the void of the linguistic signifier. Deaf and dumb, a
poser ("he waves off requests for autographs"), the Orator is immobile as
Old Man and Old Woman leap from their window, ceding for the last time
their meaning to the other: "You will tell all . . . bequeath my message" (159).
Even death is no guarantee of meaning: there is no narrative closure here
to make sense of their lives. With an exit line, "Long live the Emperor!"
Old Man leaves behind only the imaginary projection that his meaning will
be heard and authorized. As the speechless Orator gurgles and writes on
the chalkboard ADIEU APA, the farewell of the old couple is a farewell to
"pa" the father figure, god, who would promise meaning. The real human
can provide no message, and the now absent couple are, as he writes on the
board, perhaps only "ANGELFOOD"—which is to say eaten up by the void
that *is* the messenger or signifier without a signified. Like the play itself,
they may only be the stuff that would feed on and be fed to angels, the
messengers of god. But they too have been messengers without a message,
sending signs, available for interpretation but empty.

If all this is what the play is up to in some sense, the empty chairs are
the stage props that situate the reality of the emptiness. Like Robert Wilson's many chairs, they have sensory effects that provoke but cannot guarantee even this allegorical reading of the play. They accept but refuse to be
fully consumed by possible meanings, symbolic displacements, or imaginary projections. On the other hand, the play text gives enough context
to say that these chairs concretely situate the losses that inhere to the acquisition of language and the inaugural loss in the formation of a subject. In
a psychoanalytic framework, language is idealized to the extent that we
would make it a substitute for parental attachment; that is, to imagine that
language has an attachment to and guarantee of meaning is to imagine
and to re-create the very attachment that is lost at the moment that language is acquired and specifically the "I" is born.

The "nothingness" that Ionesco stages in *The Chairs* and in the chairs,
specifically, if elliptically, makes the connections between the orphaned
state of the old couple, their longings for attachment to father, to mother,
to meaning, to validation, and to the acting out of those longings as they
arrange their world according to an imaginary that is predicated on loss.
The emplacement of an ideal at the site of a loss is more fully a substitution for the loss. The ghosts in the chairs are in a sense aftereffects of
that substitution. Conscious of being an orphan, Old Man in particular is

haunted as much by longings for attachments to the body of the absent parent as for its parental substitute in the body of language, which is absent of message. The absent parent, like the absent message, creates the void out of which the world is re-created in and by the imaginary.

The least interesting thing about *The Chairs* is an imputed message that "it's all meaningless" or "there's nothing but nothingness" or some such sign of existential despair or absurdity. Such a message quickly becomes a trivial cliché unless it is accompanied by the affective roots of the ghosting process. It is at the point of the substitution for loss that the stage representation most closely touches on the reality and the affect of the ghosts that arise between language and the material world. In *The Chairs,* that affect is something close to hysteria, the emotional substrate of farce. What this play stages, in short, is the act of substitution that constitutes not only an essential element of theatricality but also its centrality both to the representation of the world and to the consequent behavior that orders the world. It is the very capacity to substitute one thing for another, to reconstitute a lost object in a present object, to transform the material objects of the world into imaginary objects, and the imaginary into the material, that characterizes the foundation of mimesis. This sense of mimesis is not a matter of visible reflection or mirroring, nor is it the exclusive province of theatre, painting, or other representational "arts." It is, rather, the point in a psychic topography where the experience of loss generates a demand for a substitute.

The mimetic double in this sense is predicated on a lost attachment and reclaims the object through its substitute. Whether that substitute is in the field of the Symbolic or of the Imaginary depends on whether its attachment is to the unconscious or whether it is distinguished as a substitute, an acknowledged replacement. In a real psyche, such a demand and its continued attachments to the lost object dwell in the form of melancholy. In a theatrical psyche, that demand is elaborated in the affective force of performative style, here the hysteria of farce. The inability or refusal to mourn the break in attachment is the source of endless mourning in its pathological form; the seeking of attachment is the source of desire in its more benign form, as in comedy.

In its representational aspect, which is to say in "art" like *The Chairs,* the mimetic habit is separated from the individual psyche and becomes observable and distinct, yet rooted in individuals. One can mourn in public given the public face of the object. In its most effective conditions, the mimetic reconstitution of "nothingness" in the play can echo the personal experiences of loss as well as the possibilities and the limitations of substitutes. At issue here is not so much the meaning of the work or its general "appeal" to experience as it is the points of contact with a reality for which the stage and staging are an inevitable and necessary practice. This is a matter of theatre as a dimension of the reality in which doubling is a province not simply of artful representation but of the internal division of self-representation. The mimetic act itself generates the space of an in-between, drawing from but not simply reflecting a reality.[15] The double is not simply a copy that stands in a relationship of otherness to the true, nor can it be stated in positive terms. It is between the lines, in the syntax and performativity of a text, of an act, of a work.

At its affective best, *The Chairs* reiterates the emotional conditions that call for acts of substitution, displacement, and mimesis: conditions of the orphan, the fearful, the bereft, the forgetful and forgotten. That an empty chair can do this relates phenomenologically to the conformity of chairs to the human body and the easy metonymy between the object and the human figure. A chair is not only metonymically connected to the body; it is also analogically related, so between the perception of contiguity and/or similarity, a chair makes even an absent body present, and, as Freud outlined and Lacan took up, it is through such processes that we constitute the imaginary of the world, substituting one thing for another, exchanging people for objects. One of the most powerful instances of this exchange, as well as the highly conscious use of substitution and doubling and the intimate connection among personal psychic topography, public performance, and work, was the production of Kantor's work *Today Is My Birthday*, presented on January 24, 1991, the month after he died.

As Michal Kobialka writes, anyone "who had the opportunity to see any production of the company [Cricot 2] will remember Kantor, who, like a ghost, hovered within and without a performance space." In almost all of his Cricot 2 theatre pieces, that is, Kantor had the habit of remaining on-stage throughout the performance. "He gave the actors the sign to enter the performance space at the beginning, put the actors in motion, corrected their movements, and closed the production at the end. The stage was filled with his presence, his gestures of scorn and praise, and his creative energy."[16]

As Kobialka describes *Today Is My Birthday,* there were three large picture frames, center, right, and left stage. In the stage right frame was a substitute Kantor wearing a white shirt, black suit, and black scarf. Kantor's own recorded voice started a monologue that had been recorded during the preparations for the production. At a certain point the voice stopped, and the substitute Kantor ("the Self-portrait") fell out of his frame, took up a paper, and began to read. The recorded voice then interrupted, and the double went back to his frame but then finished the monologue. The stage was dominated, however, by the chair Kantor would have occupied during the performance. It remained empty as the Kantor double went in and out of his frame. If Kantor, while alive, always prowled the stage as a ghost, this production of *Today Is My Birthday* after Kantor's death brought him back as a living presence in which the chair gave a palpable place for memory to seat him. With a substitute Kantor prowling there, his body also kept its image and ghostly presence onstage, making the absence of the real Kantor tolerable to a point. The intolerable point came when the Kantor double was taken out of his frame by three people dressed as Russian soldiers and into the dark through the central frame. As Kobialka describes it:

> In Act V, three Russian soldiers pulled the Self-portrait from the frame of his "painting," his space of art, and into the death chamber (the central frame). The floor between the frame and the backdrop was raised in such a manner as to resemble the gates leading to an open grave. . . . When the Self-portrait left the stage, the vortex created by his absence was overwhelming. The chair within his frame, the chair at the table, and the central frame were empty. A split second was needed to recognize the image, but the emotion raised by it stayed much longer . . . in memory.[17]

Kantor's empty chair onstage is poignant in itself. The actor, Self-portrait of Kantor, however, while manifestly false, provided a sufficient substitute to keep the reality of death in abeyance and the empty chair simply a sign of his absence through the course of the performance. Kantor's recorded voice, doubled by the voice of the actor, also allowed the substitute versions of Kantor to give him presence onstage. That presence was imaginary to the extent that the substitutions prevent a full acknowledgment of his death and absence, even in the midst of knowing it was true. While the double is present, the reality of the loss is affectively inaccessible. The deniability of what is real is a primary function of the imaginary, which is capable of sustaining contradictions and accepting the manifestly false in order to maintain the solace of attachment. The desire to keep others alive, even while knowing they are gone, gives substitutes—the mimetic doubles made by metonymy, displacement, and metaphor—their power to preserve the imaginary attachment. The double provides the site of a return, a site for memory as well as a site of denial, a site to which ghosts return again and again. The knowledge of his death and the experience of the loss are separate even when the empty chair marks Kantor's former place. It is not until the substitute is removed from the stage that the chair becomes fully empty, when the knowledge and the experience coincide. It is through the mimetic double that the imaginary attachment is maintained. Even the ceremony of his removal is not complete until the double absence binds the true and the real in the image of multiple empty chairs and empty frames. The "vortex" of the event is the vertigo of a fall into the reality of absence, from which there is no return.

Kantor's work makes unique points of connection between the real and its doubles. His customary appearance onstage was a ghosting of the theatrical by the real. His particular and inevitable absence from the stage that signified his real death became complete only when the theatrical ghost, his double, also disappeared from the stage. More than a well-defined dichotomy or uncanny pairing of life and art, *Today Is My Birthday* followed the logic of his entire career that was consistently concerned with the presence of death in life. The logic of *Birthday* fulfilled the potential reality of death that had been present all along. In bringing together the intentionality of work with the accident or unintentionality of death, that production completed his use of representational devices that organize practices within both fields, art and life, devices of memory, dream, doubling substitutions of the true for the real, the real for the true, the objects of life, and the life of objects. The intentionality that goes into fashioning works of art made from the stuff of life inevitably kills the life of the stuff. Even before his death, Kantor's work brought the deathly double of the living into view with his mannequins, his bodies wrapped in burlap, his clothes hanging in closets. His empty chair in *Birthday* simply reiterated what he had done all along. The vortex of the event might easily be attributed to the reality of his death, but in performance that reality moved from a datum of knowledge (i.e., a fact devoid of feeling), which is to say a denial of death, to an acknowledged experience (i.e., a traumatic loss felt and thereby acknowledged) only when its derivative, its representation, its substitute, the second Kantor, was taken from the stage.

An empty chair is always available for a ghost. The difference between Kantor's empty chairs and those of the Oklahoma City National Memorial is vast, however, because the former occurred as a performance that has now passed and the other remains an emplacement and a memorial site. That difference is crucial, certainly. The chairs at the Oklahoma memorial site transfer the temporality of loss and grief to a material space and thereby hold it still. Those chairs not only give a locus to memory; by doing so they also replace memory and in some sense take it into their very materiality. Mourners can "get on" to whatever extent they allow those chairs to hold their grief and the ghosts of their loved ones; they can revisit them without carrying them. By contrast, the chair in Kantor's piece provided the experience of loss and grief as a perceptible trauma, because it occurred in the conditions of an event. It was not simply a representation of loss; neither was it not not a representation. The double negative is vital in a literal sense, which is to say it lives in the simultaneity of experience and knowing. The real absence of Kantor onstage that was also not not a representation of the real was the divided double that reflects trauma as both present and other. The passage of an event in time, whether onstage or in a real explosion, gives no place for the duration of grief. The event is specifically a vortex. An event within representation is also a representation within an event, which theatre is. This version of mimesis is what Derrida has called the "hymen," the "antra," or "entre" in the sense that it is a function rather than an object, a portal that occurs at an intersection constituted by the double negative of mimesis. It is that space between the demarcations of difference through which slips the real, not as a state of being, but as a passage in which difference and sameness intersect and exchange places. The survivor knows only the undecidability of the sameness on the two sides of another's death—before and after: a sameness that is nevertheless wholly different. The point at which everything is irrevocably and totally changed, yet horrifyingly stays the same, situates the affective response for the survivor, the viewer.

The hymen, the confusion between the present and the nonpresent, along with all the indifferences it entails within the whole series of opposites

(perception/nonperception, memory/image, memory/desire, etc.), produces
the effect of a medium (a medium as element enveloping both terms at once;
a medium located between the two terms). It is an operation that both sows
confusion between opposites and stands between the opposites "at once."
What counts here is the between, the in-between-ness of the hymen. The
hymen "takes place" in the "inter-," in the spacing between desire and fulfillment, between perpetration and its recollection. But this medium of the
entre has nothing to do with a center.[18]

This "between space" is one that cannot be taken as a premise for further
argument or further understanding of being. It is, rather, a space that must
be achieved every time, won through working through the reality of survival. This necessary effort is part of the reason Derrida continues to be
difficult to read and why he also always seems to be writing the same thing.
That same thing is not propositional, nor is it precisely descriptive; beyond
paradox, it belongs as much to ordinary mourning as to philosophical history. Real events inaugurate a perception and conception of the ghosts that
haunt the undecidable conditions that are both historical and personal,
ghosts that pass through the impossible space of a facticity absent of experience. The memorial stands in the place of the absence, giving it materiality. The event initiates the undecidable, giving it affect.[19]

The Platonic sense of mimesis presumes a difference between the true
and the false, the original and the copy. The theatrical double resists their
differences. In logic, this theatrical version of the two can be stated this way:
"The following statement is true. The previous statement is false." The situation between those statements, yet constituted by their relation, reflects
the doubleness of the real and the surrogate that Kantor's work consistently
performed. Both real and representational, not real and not not representational, his ghostly presence onstage issued the fundamentally theatrical
status of undecidability, in which the manifest material reality and living
actors both contradict and underline the absences and the dead they invoke.
In his criticism of the various avant-gardes—Dadaism, ready-mades, Symbolism, Conceptualism, Happenings—as they became general and hence
conventional aesthetic movements, Kantor insisted on his conviction that
"it is possible to express life in art only through the absence of life, through
an appeal to DEATH, through APPEARANCES, through EMPTINESS and the lack
of a MESSAGE."[20] Even more particularly, he writes of an earlier production,

The Chair (Oslo, 1970), in which "the object became empty, deprived of expression, connections, references, characteristics or programmed communication, its 'message'; directed 'nowhere,' it changed into a dummy."[21] His own empty chair in *Today Is My Birthday* could not help but represent, could not help but fill the space with his absence, could not help but deliver the message that he was dead, and thereby could not help but turn against the anti-representational practices of his Theatre of Death. Nevertheless, precisely in that turn, precisely because it was his, the empty chair reinforced practices in his life's work, which harbored death and absence in the present, which were obsessed with the materialization of thought, memory, and time, yet always refused a message. The empty chair held his double death as one thing. *Today Is My Birthday* called the past into the present in an uncanny mimetic double that became the work. The undecidability of the difference and the sameness between past and future, passing through the present—the hymen—of performance, gave an occasion for mourning, with Kantor doubly gone.

The text of that piece, like the text of Ionesco's *The Chairs,* gives the frame for the double, a frame that Derrida calls the "palisades," which mark a boundary through which pass the both/and, the neither/nor of presence and absence in performance. Like the empty message of the Orator, the ghosts in the chairs are signs without a signified, messages without a meaning. The ghosts are embedded in the text, produced in performance, in theatre. The literariness of the text offers the signifying materiality that surrounds the absences that inhabit the stage and the performance.

In a similar way, the material elements of the Oklahoma City National Memorial enclose and frame the impossible. The memorial creates a stage on which the performance of every visitor may reperceive loss through its objects. The absences memorialized there occur not in the material substances of the objects but in their abstract, numerical order and, more emphatically, in the empty rectangles in the backs of the chairs. Those apertures concretize the sameness of the space on either side of the chair backs, a space that nevertheless shows the absolute difference between one side and another. Time flows through those spaces in the present, situating the difference between the ghosts that sit there and survival, the other side of the trauma, between the past explosion and its future in grief, between loss and memory. The sameness and difference of the view between the spaces are passages through the "hymen" of the chair backs, representing the trauma and yet refusing to represent, being concrete and symbolic yet pointing beyond the material to the limits of the symbolic in the uniformity of space. The chairs individualize each loss with a name and a place, making no claim on universality, only on the rift that separates and connects the living and the dead. The chairs remain there, as onstage, as the sites of death's power and life's vulnerability.

chapter 5

Double or Nothing
Ghosts behind the Curtains

> Somewhere between
> Dressing room and stage:
> An actor leaves his room
> A king enters the play,
> And at this I've seen the stage hands
> Laugh out loud with their bottles of beer.
> —BRECHT, "On the Everyday Theatre"

Brecht was notoriously insistent that "die Wahrheit ist konkret," the phrase inscribed on the lintel of the doorway to his Danish home in exile. Anyone entering that house may well have had such truth confirmed by a hard knock on the head. In the above excerpt from Brecht's poem, the laughter of the stagehands suggests they know the difference between an actor, the concretely living person, and a king, the ghostly stage illusion. Or perhaps laughter is their way of knowing that the difference between the actor and the king is a false dichotomy that only supposes that king and actor are two different persons, one living, one a ghostly double. Laughter explodes the dichotomy like a knock on the head, or, rather, the explosion of the dichotomy produces laughter. In his encomium of the "everyday theatre," Brecht praises the concrete truth of theatre. His practices, so dedicated to making visible the apparatus of theatre as a material and social reality, situate his theatre in a fundamentally comic scene, which is where the realities of the world come to the fore, set off a dialectic with the imaginary double, and release an audience from the mystifications of mimesis. The comic scene, of course, does not imply simply a jolly farce full of good jokes or the troubles of young lovers aiming at social union, but the distinction between comedy and tragedy as one between an idealized and a worldly set of conditions. Brecht's stagehands' view of the actor and the king, the off-stage person and the onstage (and idealized) character, puts them in a position to see both the contradictions between and the identity of the two. They can take the stance of the ironic figure, who has a perspective on both. Their laughter arises from the space "somewhere between" as the two collide. The position of the stagehands is also comic in a broader sense in that, unlike the representation of a tragic hero, their function is not to complete themselves in an aesthetic act but to keep the act going, to make sure it repeats itself, with an ironic view on everyone's mortality. They keep renewing the world, which is the very renewal that comic form draws on. Professional ties keep them tethered to repetition and representation, to both actor and king, but their position effectively mocks the apparitions of the stage.

Touchstones for materialist reality in Brecht's view, stagehands connect the spectacle of representation to the reality of practice that leads out the backstage door to the world. But that practice is not in view. The work of the stage crew does not as a rule register in the performance unless it is specifically designed to introduce theatrical reality to the stage, for aesthetic, political, or economic reasons. That real work is on the inside of the spectacle but outside the rules of public display. This position gives the technicians double privilege and dual perspective, for they are fully responsible for the execution of a performance on the one hand and free from the constraints of public decorum on the other. From the inside of the performance, they are free of the signifying dimensions and emotional tenor of texts and performances that, for audiences and the interpretive practices of critics, make the performance what it *is*. The designated space of representation excludes the technicians and keeps them out of sight and mind, yet it is utterly contingent upon their presence and their work.

One could say that Brecht approached the "theatre and its double" in almost direct opposition to Artaud, the former finding the potential for thought in the comic contradictions of the double, the latter trying to erase them. Their opposite approaches to the doubles that theatrical mimesis implies might be seen most easily in the difference in their uses of curtains. Whereas Artaud would eliminate the division between performance and audience in his aim for a single, "holy" space for his practices, Brecht emphasized the function of the curtain by cutting it in half. These opposite approaches to curtains are my way into exploring the way theatre manifests the double, first by creating two spaces, then by dissolving them. In other words, curtains are a phenomenal means for theatre to generate the ghostly doubles of representation known as mimesis or imitation but also ultimately to dispel them. At a most basic level, theatre curtains delineate a space of difference, which is simply to say that curtains make two spaces out of one. They create divisions between play and audience as well as between onstage and offstage. Curtains mark a boundary line and delineate the differences that count as actor and king and allow real beer for the technicians while the king must drink imaginary champagne.

Historically in Western theatre, curtains go back at least as far as the Hellenistic stages, where archaeological evidence shows the trench and holes assumed to be used for posts that held a curtain. Marguerite Bieber's classic book on the history of Greek and Roman theatre shows the trench in front of the *scaenae frons* and stage at the theater in Pompeii, where, she writes, the *aulaeum* was lowered. That stagewide curtain was distinct from the *siparia,* which were hung above the *scaenae frons* and could be lowered or pulled aside. The *siparia* would apparently be hung in front of a city view in comic plays, and one example is found on a vase painting from Naples.[1] It shows an actor, possibly Aristophanes (ca. 380 B.C.), "dancing as Perseus" in front of what appears to be a curtain.[2] A marble relief from Naples shows a curtain behind an actor contemplating a tragic mask and another a scene from New Comedy with a curtain covering what looks like a scene building.[3] Some curtains are painted to illustrate a scene and at the same time make it possible to reveal a scene behind the scene. That is, the function of the curtain can be to show a scene and to hide one simultaneously. In proscenium theaters, curtains block the audience's view of the stage and mark the boundaries between on- and offstage.

My point is not simply to make a historical gesture toward some origin of curtains but to suggest that in the history of Western theatre the curtain's division of space offers to the phenomenology of perception a double perspective that both displays and hides, conceals and reveals. That dual function alone might be enough to undermine confidence in appearances, but as boundary markers curtains further create a spatial division that correlates to concepts of true and false, real and unreal, practical and imaginary.

Whatever willing suspension of disbelief occurs in the face of a dramatic fiction onstage, the curtain locates a social, aesthetic, and ultimately ideological contract between the audience and the stage. The curtain's boundary indicates what may and may not count as a performance and in this way acts as a kind of material legislator. From the audience we agree not to count the backstage life that includes stage manager, light and sound operators, dressers, property managers, curtain pullers, or makeup crews: the technicians and stagehands of theatrical production. The prohibition belongs admittedly to a historically determined social contract that is reinforced by those spatial configurations of stage design that hide the crews. An audience agrees to ignore the presence of technicians and to accept instead that only the visible or auditory results of the onstage work will be counted as performance. That agreement discounts any naive ignorance on the part of an audience, for, if asked, surely anyone would acknowledge that what occurs onstage is contingent on the work and the workers offstage. Blocking out that knowledge simply involves following the rules of the game and accepting the conventions of framing that announce what does and does not call for attention. When a stage crew comes on during an intermission to change scenery or props in full view of an audience, it announces in effect, "We are here and not here, doing real things that you see, but do not see as representational because they are actual. We are here working, but we are not signifying." Through such an agreement we submit to a law that distinguishes between the real performance and the other reality of the backstage work in almost the same terms by which evidence may or may not be admissible in court. That law of theatre gets complicated, however, because it implies two different criteria for real, or at least for what is admissible as real. The backstage work belongs to the real world because it is not a signifying, representational action but a productive one. At the same time, a production in front of or outside the curtain line is the only admissible reality, yet is governed by laws of pretense or imitation and of signification. The obviously necessary work of the backstage space is thus deniable and publicly inadmissible to the laws that govern divided space of theatrical representation. The history of theatre could be written in the stories of both lawbreakers who bring backstage crews and technicians onstage or eliminate the curtain to make one space and conformists who keep in place the law of differences between inside and outside, imaginary and real.

The law of the conventional boundary between the visible stage and the invisible stage crew actually establishes different degrees of, rather than different kinds of, material reality. Yet how many people love to take tours to see what *really* goes on backstage? How many feel that in going backstage they have a sense of privileged access to the secrets of the "real thing"? Consider the interest in the backstage tours of regional theaters. Those tours offer a sense of privileged access while they give tourists contact with the inside spaces of theater. That contact with the real scene fulfills a certain kind of desire to see what is normally invisible and to be part of the scene of the real thing. There is a sense of gaining secret knowledge about the truth behind the illusion of the stage space, though in practice that secret knowledge is banal, perhaps vaguely disappointing, certainly mundane. It is something like being in the kitchen while the meal is prepared instead of waiting in the formal dining room to be served. Not only is there the access to secrets; there is also a shared community bond that goes into participation in the work.

The sense of access to secret and invisible spaces backstage is contingent on the idea that any public performance, even a musical concert or one-person show, is merely an appearance, a contrived construction of a scene, a persona or identity. Performers backstage are imagined to drop character or persona and to be on a par with the ordinary reality of carpenters and cutters. The public face of the performer turns to private concerns backstage. Workers, in other words, supposedly have no imaginary persona, no mask; put more simply, people onstage have different concerns, not different realities, from those off. Visiting the costume shop where clothes are being made, or seeing the prop storage where objects once seen on stage are in full view, holds its own kind of appeal that arises not because the objects and people backstage are actually more real than the objects and people onstage in performance but because the spatial model of inside and outside creates a geometry of difference. The spatial image not only incites the desire to see more or to see the truth but also reinforces the conviction that what is conventionally hidden and then revealed is truer and more real than any fabrication. This sense of the real, which is felt as privilege, thus actually requires a hidden space, an invisible practice, in which desire might find its object. And that desire is powerful enough to find reinforcement in the social contract within theatre. It further suggests that the perception of the difference is founded on a desire for ever more reality or, rather, that desire is founded on a perception of difference or, in psychoanalytic terms, lack. That desire requires the instituting of otherness, which is supported by the spatial images of inside and outside.

The proscenium curtain, in other words, reproduces a structure of desire.

Regardless of what may or may not be behind the curtain, its use inaugurates an elsewhere and the possibility for further revelation. It materializes a desire to see more, to see truth, to see the real. Likewise, the curtains that mark the boundary between on- and offstage redouble the space. The backstage world is theatre's other, internal double. If the edge of the stage, as Herbert Blau has often said, is the point of contact between the hallucinations of the theatrical spectacle and the viewing world, then the backstage constitutes an internal boundary of another real that is both concrete and functional.[4] That backstage world is in some sense doubly hidden. Not simply concealed beyond the stage scene, it hides also in its obvious necessity in the creation of that scene. Its pragmatic functions make it seem transparently real when compared with the hallucinations of the onstage world. Yet the purpose and function of the backstage activity is contingent on and justified by those hallucinations.

The social and affective contract that differentiates kinds rather than degrees of reality in theatrical space signals not just the acceptance of convention but also the contingency of desire on prohibition and invisibility and the willful refusal of contradictions to that desire. "I know, but all the same . . ." is the effective inner monologue that can at once acknowledge an objective character to reality and still discount it. Related by Freud to the attachment to a fetish and not unrelated to Marx's version of the commodity fetish, the expression "I know, but all the same . . ." captures our capacity to deny even what is most obvious—or rather, to deny especially what is most obvious. In the psychoanalytic framework, the fetish preserves a belief in the existence of a maternal phallus. But as Mannoni points out, it is not merely that the fetish represents a denial of reality, even with the fetishist having "seen" the contrary (i.e., that the mother has no phallus). The fetishist has repudiated the proof that she has no phallus but does not then simply hold to the belief that she does—a simple substitution of one belief for another. Rather, the fetish preserves belief *because* she has none; the experience of her lack is thus not erased but kept as an "indelible stigma" that marks the fetishist.[5]

If we translate the sexual foundation of Freud's fetish into the epistemology of theatre, we might say that the curtain is the fetish object that allows us to forget that there is "nothing" behind it. We know in some way that what is behind the curtain is only more of the world. But the curtain materially holds our belief that there is something more, some further signification that does not lack the significance of the world. It holds our belief that there is an answer to our desire. We know that "it's only theatre," and at the same time we hold the curtain to the promises we want it to make. We can dismiss the experience of lack in the world by saying "it's only theatre." To say "it's only theatre" is a way to deny the obviousness of appearances, as though both truth and reality were somewhere else. The mundane reality of the backstage throws us back to the hallucinations of the stage and catches us in a cycle of denial, "I know, but all the same. . . ."

The structure of desire for a reality that is always further off, always elsewhere, implies that it is necessary to exclude what is obvious and mark it as *merely* real. The fetish maintains the desire by looking through theatre's material and objective character and using it as a lure for an imaginary real, the more obscure object of desire. At the same time, the fetish gives the imaginary a concrete presence and brings desire to a here and now. Through the fetish of the stage double, it is possible to ignore, dismiss, or discount the internal reality of stagehands and the backstage world and, at the same time, to remain fascinated by the possibility that backstage the reality might coincide with the elusive real. Conversely, a strictly empirical view accepts only the concrete world as real and takes that real as the truth that is apart from the imaginative, the constructed, the ideological formations of desire, when they are in fact working together to create what *is*.

The curtain, like a boundary and barrier to visibility, thus seems to hold instinctive pleasures in its folds but is also fundamental to our metaphors and images of representation. It creates an experiential geometry of space that situates abstract ideas and to some extent shapes those ideas in a structure of opposition and difference, particularly in terms of inside and outside. Gaston Bachelard writes of how the experience of inside and outside becomes a metaphor that supplies sense to many kinds of abstract and dualistic thought. He summarizes the point here:

> Outside and inside form a dialectic of division, the obvious geometry of which blinds us as soon as we bring it into play in metaphorical domains. It has the sharpness of the dialectic of *yes* and *no,* which decides everything. Unless one is careful, it is made into a basis of images that govern thoughts of positive and negative. Logicians draw circles that overlap or exclude each other, and all their rules immediately become clear. Philosophers, when confronted with outside and inside, think in terms of being and non-being. Thus

profound metaphysics is rooted in an implicit geometry which—whether
we will or no—confers spatiality upon thought; if a metaphysician could
not draw, what would he think? . . . In a lecture given by Jean Hypolite on
the subtle structure of denegation . . . he added: "you feel the full significance of this myth of outside and inside in alienation, which is founded on
these two terms. Beyond what is expressed in their formal opposition lie
alienation and hostility between the two." And so, simple geometrical opposition becomes tinged with agressivity.[6]

The stage curtain and its spatial divisions are clearly part of the artifice
of staging. What do we find when the curtain is removed? One of the most
enjoyable, and for my purposes allegorical, moments for the removal of a
curtain comes in the 1939 film version of *The Wizard of Oz*. The film, in
fact, compresses many of the more theatrical details in L. Frank Baum's
book. In the written version, each of the four heroes approaches the Wizard alone, and to each he appears in a different disguise: to Dorothy, he is
a giant head with rolling eyes sitting on a throne; to the Scarecrow, he
appears as a beautiful, winged, green-haired woman dressed in green silk
gauze and wearing a crown of jewels; to the Tin Woodman there appears
an elephantine, woolly haired beast with the head of a rhinoceros, five eyes,
five arms, and five long legs; and to the Cowardly Lion, Oz is a great ball
of fire. Upon their return to Oz after killing the Wicked Witch, the Wizard is only the Voice who greets them. His command to wait another day
before fulfilling his promises (a return home, a brain, a heart, courage) sets
off a chain reaction: the Lion roars, Toto jumps, a screen falls, and out comes
a little old man with a bald head and wrinkled face who admits he is a humbug with only the skills of a humbug: a ventriloquist with costumes, props,
and special effects. The film version, of course, renders the scene with Toto
pulling aside a curtain and exposing the Wizard manipulating the dials and
levers of a great machine and sputtering the now famous and oft-quoted
line, "Pay no attention to that man behind the curtain."
   If the pleasure of that moment is the exposure of Oz's theatrical humbug, it is the curtain that makes it possible. In classical terms it is a moment
of anagnorisis, the moment of recognition of what has been going on all
along behind the veil of appearances. For Aristotle, anagnorisis is part of
the temporal structure of plot, as when Oedipus finally recognizes who he
has been. *The Wizard of Oz* exemplifies all those moments in theatre that

materialize a moment of recognition. It seems likely that the mere exposure of the truth is at least as satisfying as what is revealed, though one does not want to correlate the recognition scene in *Oedipus Rex* too often with that in *The Wizard of Oz*. But what exactly is the connection between the truth of what is revealed—that wizardry is only humbug—and the mechanism by which it is revealed? Is it the contents of the revelation of the crime, or the mistake, or the error in judgment, or the classical hamartia, or the act of revelation itself that gives pleasure? These elements may never be fully separable. The point, however, is that the truth alone, as a piece of data informing us that the Wizard is a humbug (as is Oedipus in his way), is insufficient and inseparable from the mechanism and the moment at which that truth is revealed. It matters, in other words, not just what is revealed but when and by what means.

To put it another way, timing makes all the difference. When true and false, real and unreal, are notions held by the spatial images of inside and outside, they remain fundamentally inert or static concepts, partaking, as Bachelard says above, in the metaphysics of being. Similarly, when theatre is identified via the curtains in the strictly spatial images of inside and outside, we can play indefinitely with the inert concepts of real and unreal, true and false, pragmatic and illusory, world and imitation. But when those spatial elements join the temporality of theatrical performance, theatre undermines the implicit ontology of spatial concepts such that true and false lose the force of their distinction. What becomes of the theatrical double, however, when theatrical space joins the time of performance and the timing and plotting of revelation? What becomes of the distinctions between the world of the stagehands and the world of the play?

One of the characteristics of modernism in twentieth-century theatre has been the elimination of the curtain and the confounding of the boundaries between theatre and the world. Most notably by Piscator and Brecht, attempts to demonstrate the reality of the theatrical apparatus and to make visible all the elements of the mode of production have produced a distinctive set of theatrical practices. Allowing a set change to occur in full view of an audience and opening that reality to public view, theaters have reinforced the Brechtian aim for the theatricality of theatre to be obvious, without the mystique of illusionistic secrets. Piscator and Brecht helped to create an aesthetic and political legacy to make the apparatus of theatre visible with their onstage lighting instruments, half curtains, and stage machinery.

Such practices belong to a trajectory toward the postmodern refusal to distinguish the real as that which is always further back, behind the curtain and hidden from view: a refusal to defer desire or to turn desired reality into a fetish object. The inclusion of the stage crew in the total event has erased not only much of the mystique of the hidden stage world but also many of the pieties about mimesis as a double. In a sense, the playfulness that characterizes postmodernism is the comic play of inclusiveness and delight as opposed to desire. Pirandello broke the division between on- and offstage realities in *Six Characters in Search of an Author,* or at least inverted the duality to suggest that all the world is a theatrical sham or a hall of mirrors. Having his actors build the scaffolding/crematorium in *Akropolis,* Grotowski made sure that the labor involved in making a set was visible. And Kantor's presence in his theatre pieces, showing himself as director and author, broke down the conventions of representation as a double or imitation, created by an absent writer or director. In various ways and with varying intentions, all this work would appear to break down the implicit division in representation and to exercise the material reality of the theatre event.

All such work to bring in more and more reality confirms an appetite for a real that is present and belonging to what is represented but not part of dualistic, spatialized thought. A curtainless context persistently puts a focus on the reality or the "eventness" of the representation. The deconstruction of inside/outside and the elimination of a concealing curtain suggest a move to an "outside" beyond boundaries but also a move to an infinite inside and an indefinite overlap between the phantoms of signification with production and labor. Yet in spite of such self-conscious efforts to dissolve the boundaries between the working real and the imaginary, as soon as some worldly actuality becomes included in either the space or the moment that is framed as significant or representational, the idea of a real again tends to go into hiding elsewhere, into another space of difference, still further off. That is, coming out of the specific practices of theatre, a general principle of "theatricality" inhabits many different kinds of events involving spectacle, such that theatricality itself implies a difference between a field of action in the world and a field of action onstage. In this sense, theatricality is what makes things show themselves, what puts them on display. To put it even more basically, it is virtually impossible to escape dualistic thought entirely.

Perhaps this is why the discoveries on a backstage tour or in the appearance of technicians onstage are often disappointing. In a sense that world is not quite real enough. The desire to possess the real is an impossible one even in the real world, for it is almost impossible to have a perception without a prior framework for that perception. A difference always remains. For the space between the real of worldly, material objects and the real of representational objects is a space of difference, characterized by a neither/nor, both/and relation between actuality and representation. The idealized Real escapes them both, yet it is to the idealization that they both owe a debt. Neither identical to nor excluding the present, the ideal Real is both a lure and a sustaining presence, access to which, like the backstage reality, seems closed, occulted, and always available, mundane. Reality is always there, present, but with its failure to signify or find representation in a conceptual framework (or what Lacan might call the Imaginary or the Symbolic), there is no apparent access, and the lure remains. This is the point of Kafka's famous parable of the Law, the door to which a man waits at all his life, only to be told at the end of his life, when he asks the gatekeeper why no others have entered there, that the door was made only for him.[7] Without its designation or signifying phantom, the door is only a door, a material presence bereft of both meaning and, for the man, usefulness. In fact, however, that access is always available as a practical reality. Only the prohibitions created by the idealized Real—the Law of difference between reality and illusion—keep him from using it.

The hidden backstage and the visible onstage worlds belong to the same world not because there "is" ultimately only one world. Rather, the theatrical division between external and internal, visible and invisible, duplicates and is an instance of the ec-static sense of Heidegger's Da-sein: the being of Being whose being is to stand apart from itself. Being-there on either side of the curtain is constituted by a being apart that continually turns toward a being-here. Audience, stage performance, stagehands, world, and representation, all belong to the total theatre for which there is no outside yet which sustains a standing-apart from within itself. The curtain plays into and materializes such paradoxes. It materializes a sense of an idealized Real that is always further off. But its own status has a differential function. The curtain itself is neither an object of desire nor a thing that is either in or out of representation. Does anybody ask: What does that curtain mean? What does it signify or represent? One is more likely to ask: What does that curtain hide? What is behind it? The curtain is not a space one can enter, yet it creates such a space as a gathering place that makes visible the fact that what is there is also here. It materializes a function and, like Heidegger's Da-sein, is impossible to contain in representation, because it is the presence of a difference that belongs to and emerges from the very field that it differentiates. Whether between the audience and the stage or the stage and the backstage, a curtain sets off what are loosely called worlds, but it is nonetheless a worldly object. It announces a certain theatricality but conceals only more of the same world, which it brings forth.

Likewise, *Da-sein,* for Heidegger, is not a generic or universal term that simply covers all instances of being, for such a term would require a "higher" concept from which a definition could derive. He posits Da-sein, rather, as the existential ground out of which the questioning of being emerges and which the question addresses. "This being which we ourselves in each case are and which includes inquiry among the possibilities of its being we formulate terminologically as Da-sein."[8] The question of being is open from within being: a standing apart from a place within, not over and above. "To work out the question of being means to make a being—one who questions—transparent in its being."[9] In his later work "The Origin of the Work of Art," Heidegger formulates the idea of making transparent the being of the one who questions as an "unconcealing." But it is never an object or a content that is unconcealed, as though the truth were finally out and apparent, except insofar as that revealed truth is the humbuggery of the human endeavors to manipulate images and power.

Where does this leave the ghosts of theatre? Are they still simply the imaginary, invisible, or immaterial double that representation and repetition imply? They may well be identified as the insubstantial doubles, the obscure objects of desire for the real, or the commodity fetishes of Marx, which he described as ghosts. To try to identify a ghost this way turns it into a thing, even it if is a "thing without phenomenon," as Derrida writes.[10] If ghosts are no more than the disembodied and immaterial doubles of the material world, it seems to me they are not really ghosts but metaphors that perpetuate the dualities of real and unreal, true and false, material and immaterial. It is certainly possible to say meaningfully that the theatrical spectacle "haunts" reality or that the backstage workers "haunt" the scene, as the past haunts the present or the present haunts the future. If haunting is a useful way to describe the strange double aspects of theatre through metaphor, ghosts themselves are better found in the aspect of transparency that curtains also provide. Let me start with a concrete example.

Angelo Ingegnieri, quoted in the Introduction, used the semitransparency of a veil to create what he considered a more realistic ghost effect. Ingegneiri produced *Oedipus Rex* for the opening of the Teatro Olimpico in 1585 and wrote extensively on techniques for the most realistic production of ghosts onstage, for, he says, "I have never yet seen a ghost on the stage that did not appear ridiculous."

> The front of this perspective set, diminishing in size and finally becoming very small, may be the more conveniently covered (and also when the proper time comes, uncovered) with a dark veil. This I deem necessary for two reasons. The first is that behind it—and particularly if it be moderately thick—one sees somewhat indistinctly all that happens in the rear of the stage; the second is that it provides greater realistic effect to the appearance of the ghost, which as an infernal thing, ought to darken the air around it. . . . This veil, then, ought to be placed so far from the front of the set that the ghost may appear and move easily in the open space beyond. The ghost should be all draped, rather than dressed, in black silk or some similar light material. Its hands and feet should not show: it ought to look like some shapeless thing, moving rather on small wheels than taking formal steps and walking like a human being.[11]

Ingegnieri found in the veil a means to make appearances uncertain. More specifically, he found a way to make the living actor take on the appearance of the dead by making the figure uncannily inhuman with drapery. Along with its capacity to create a boundary, to conceal and reveal, to generate desire, the curtain derives power from its flexibility to be both movable and permeable. Depending on its actual material, it can be either opaque or transparent. Whereas the opaque allows the actions of concealing and revealing, transparency gives us a double vision that makes the objects in view both concrete and strange. The ghost is not hiding behind the veil, nor is it the veil itself. It is, rather, the product of the veil and the consequence of concealing.

Reading Ingegnieri's treatise now, I cannot quite imagine the horror his techniques were meant to produce. There is a certain charm or wonder or amusement in imagining the effects of the veil and the shapeless thing wheeling about the stage. There is also a certain sense of revelation in the treatise as it describes the techniques by which the ghosts were created. The document opens a view on another time and place, another cultural mentality, another system for making theatre. This is simply a way to say that the sense of revelation seems to count at least as much as what precisely is revealed. The pleasure of historical research, in other words, is something like the pleasure of the backstage tour. They both assume that a real is what we are finding there. One finds out how they—those others, from a different time and place—"really" did things. But whether it is the reality or the sense of discovery of a previously hidden secret that gives pleasure remains an open question. What reality is discovered: the difference or the sameness between then and now? the continuity between times? The document itself is a kind of veil that appears to reveal something but also conceals the past like a temptress and opens a host of further questions and desires to see the ghosts of the past. Ingegnieri's treatise is moderately useful for pointing to the uses of a veil to create ghosts, but it creates ghosts of its own that try to speak across time. Something appears from behind the veil, but what is it?

What exactly is so alternatively charming and unsettling about seeing an actor peer through the proscenium curtain to check out the audience? In part, we see her human curiosity, which comes from that "other" world of characters and representation and focuses on our world. The alien is like us, or we are like the alien. But the permeability of the membrane is what makes it possible to confound the two. What is the appeal of backstage plays like the Duke of Buckingham's *The Rehearsal* and Ronald Harwood's *The Dresser* and Michael Frayn's *Noises Off*? One element of that appeal is certainly the play within the play that exploits the difference and the overlap between the on- and offstage farces. We see the first act of *Noises Off* as the rehearsal of a play, which is a conventional marriage/adultery farce. But then in the second act we see that the characters of that farce have their counterparts among the actor-characters who replicate the interpersonal dynamics of the play. Between acts one and two, the set changes from the exterior stage scene to the interior stage scene, where the jealousies, rivalries, and egos of the actor-characters affect the performance of the play whose rehearsal we have just seen. That is, we see the two worlds simultaneously through the aperture of the door. Our laughter, I suggest, is not simply at the doubling of farce upon farce but also at the intersection or collision of the two farces at the boundary between supposed pretense and supposed real, which is itself a pretense. The aperture effectively unmoors the differ-ence between real and imaginary, on- and offstage, and shows them inter-penetrating. That interpenetration involves what Arthur Koestler called the "bisociation of conflicting codes," which in this case are the codes of act-ing or pretense and the codes of genuine or real feelings and situations. But those supposedly real feelings and situations are themselves encompassed by the play and performance. Our laugher comes not just from a collision between real and unreal, true and false, but also from a recognition that the dichotomies are true *and* false, like the laugher of the stagehands.

Bert States put the case of Molière acting as himself in *The Impromptu of Versailles* as an instance of theatre "positing an exception to the aesthetic rule that the image is not the thing." He goes on: "Of course, at bottom it is a false exception because Molière is *still* not Molière; or rather he is Molière *plus* a Molière text, or Molière *minus* the freedom to 'be himself.'"[12] The "acting *as*" is what the theatre curtain materializes in its dual capacity to sep-arate and bind together. The plus or minus Molière both veils and reveals the real person, who is acting like himself when image and thing coincide.

A similar, classic example of the permeability of the boundary between real and its representation is Shakespeare's *A Midsummer Night's Dream*. In the rude mechanicals' performance of Pyramus and Thisbe for the court, Snout (or Flute, in the Folio) acts as Wall. "And such a wall, as I would have you think, / as had in it a crannied hole or chink, / Through which the lovers, Pyramus and Thisby, / Did whisper often very secretly" (5.1.157–60). From one point of view, the play arranges its characters in a hierarchy and dualities: Titania and Oberon as king and queen of the fairies; Theseus and Hippolyta as the mythical king and queen; the young lovers; the rude mechanicals. There is the court/real world and the forest/magical world. Both the hierarchy and the dualities are confounded, however, when, as often happens, the same actors play Titania/Hippolyta and Oberon/The-seus; when the rustics enter the magical space of the forest; and when Puck returns to the stage to enfold the audience within the artifice of a dream that is the reality of the performance. All this is well enough known. I point to the chink in Wall, however, to suggest that what seems initially to be a simple system of alternation between court and forest, which belongs to the pastoral convention, is a more complicated system of interpenetration be-tween multiple worlds, complications made possible by a chink in the wall.

The hole, the permeable place in the boundary, is no-thing. It is the meeting place of the lovers, to be sure, and more than one production has turned it into a bawdy joke as the mechanicals playing Pyramus and Thisbe speak and kiss at the crotch of the lime-encrusted Snout. Nothing in itself, the chink in Wall not only makes communication between the opposing sides possible; it also allows us to see that the two worlds are arbitrarily divided into opposition and that they are part of one world. No-thing, as the Buddhists would say, is not simply the opposite of something or non-being as distinct from being. Wall, like a curtain, creates the image of duality. But the court and an audience see the oneness or simultaneity that extends beyond and outside the limits of Wall. The duality or division it represents is a momentary, useful, and aesthetic framework, but like all the duos of *A Midsummer Night's Dream,* court and forest, play and audience, dream and waking, the two parts interpenetrate.

No-thing, the chink in the division of space, is thus more akin to time than to space in its intangible but real presence. Invisible but always material and acting on the visible, time is nothing. The spatial formation made by the dividing Wall or by the theater curtain is permeated by that nothing. Like Bottom's dream, it is a bottomless nothing, because the material and immaterial, the imaginary and factual, belong to a dynamic system that the self-consciousness of the artifice generates. Artifice breaks the unity or sameness of the real and imaginary worlds, yet also shows them folding into each other. We lurch between the totality of the play and its internal divisions that show the playing of a play. But the difference is not unlike Bottom's transformation into the Ass that he already is. Like a dream image that shows another kind of truth to reality, the turn of Bottom into an ass gives an image for who and what he already is, just as the play gives an image to the event of the marriage for which it was performed and suggests that the real event too can be seen from another perspective, as though it were a dream—that is, suggests that the waking world is always further off.

Puck's return at the end of the play offers the audience a perspective that would be sub specie aeternitatis were it not coming from within the play. The perspective he offers is not a view from some transcendent site above or outside but from within the dream that is the play. "If we shadows have offended, / think but this, and all is mended, / That you have but slumb'red here / While these vision did appear. / And this weak and idle theme, / No more yielding but a dream" (5.1.423–28). Puck returns the audience to its waking world with the belief of having dreamed a world that is as concrete, material, and present as the waking one. Yet that return takes us to Vladimir's question in *Waiting for Godot:* "Was I sleeping while the others suffered? Am I sleeping now? Tomorrow, when I wake, what shall I say of today?"[13] From Vladimir's temporal perspective the "shadows" of the *Dream* are not merely the imaginary characters whom the actors portray, or even the selves of yesterday who have disappeared, but the selves of today, seeing themselves from tomorrow. In this sense Brecht's actor and king are both shadows, because they both appear through the veil of theatre. They are both ghosts because they are both apparitions. The performance itself works like a permeable curtain through which waking and dreaming exchange their aspects. Just as dreams come out of the image system of a real if sleeping being, the division between imagination and material facticity is shown as a permeable and temporal barrier.[14] Puck is thus a figure of the classical *eiron,* who is both inside and outside the fiction, actor and character, body and artifice. In his speech we find both the performer and the character, who serve to include the duplicity of representation as the real and productive act and to turn reality into a shadow of itself. Which one, actor or character, dream or waking, is the ghost of the other? Each one is haunted by the other, because the curtain, or veil, of theatricality that lies between allows them to interpenetrate.

The spatial division between inside and outside thus becomes a phenomenon without a correlate spatial epistemology. Or rather, the epistemology in which true and false, real and unreal, have spatial correlates turns into an epistemology of time, because time permeates the space but is without substance. We become suspicious of appearances, not because they are unreal or untrue, but because they are temporary and temporal. Time unconceals more. This means not only that appearances, like performances, pass away in time but also that time returns in appearances and performances. The visible world is not only itself; it also is inhabited by the past, and what appears is more than it appears to be, as Dorothy learned about the Wizard's chimera, as Bottom failed to learn about being an ass. Appearances, thus permeated by time, are ghosts, which are the unresolved or unrevealed elements of the past inhabiting present appearances. Heidegger illustrated the principle by noting that the inside of a piece of chalk is just the outside further back.[15] There is nothing more behind the curtain but other appearances further back, appearances whose sources are present in time but also derived from time, whether past or future. The unconcealing of the phenomenon further back takes time and disappears in time, just as the chalk eventually crumbles into dust, just as the ghosts of the past eventually disappear, replaced by other ghosts in need of working through.

The work of theater is the working of the double, and through the rift of doubleness difference makes its appearance in the unity of the world, with its internal divisions, its imaginary representations, its materiality, and its significations. The imaginary and the material make a double thing, which theatre works into the artful form of an event. In the disappearance of performance, duality is revealed as a constituent condition of perception and thought but is not the "thing" itself. But precisely because it is different from material objects, pragmatic actions, or identifying ideas alone, the working of the art, like an act, is both visible and invisible, doubtful and real. We give that working the name "theater": an embodied uncertainty subject to further construction and debate but in itself no-thing. From this perspective, the *work* of theatre is just what haunts all its creations and returns, like Hamlet's father, to demand that further work be undertaken for all the work yet undone. Like a mathematical function, the work/difference is a function that produces both ideas and practices, illusions and materialities. The constitutive difference is as much a part of the world as it is of theatre, but it is only in theatre that the difference itself is put on view and called pretense or illusion. The collision between the signs called pretense and the materialities produced by the rude mechanicals creates a laughter that exceeds our forms of thought as well as our ability to control time. Theatre allows us to think of the world in terms of true and false, allows us to imagine there is something more real behind the curtain, and at the same time knocks us on the head with its concrete truths. It shows us the humbug of appearances created by other humans in mundane practices. At the same time, it prevents us from holding on to the illusion of a final truth and a reality elsewhere and forces us to face our own disappearance in time. Theatre withholds permanence through performance. Forcing us to give way to the unfolding of appearances in time, theatre shows us to be more like the Wizard than Dorothy. We are unable to return to the comforts of Kansas and to imagine that we can wake up to reality, for the dream is endless. Rather, we take off in the balloon of time, shouting back, "I can't come back. I don't know how it works." The technicians backstage, however, do know how it works. They build the balloon in which the Wizard takes off and tell us that comedy is the mode of being and time.

chapter 6

Ghosts Onscreen
The Drama of Misrecognition

Rosen———?
Guil———?
(He gathers himself)
Well, we'll know better next time. Now you see me, now you———
(And disappears)
　　　　—STOPPARD, *Rosencrantz and Guildenstern Are Dead*

The character designated as Guildenstern in Tom Stoppard's play has just finished complaining about the Player's overzealous enactments of death, death portrayed tragically, romantically, death "for all ages and occasions," death by suspension, convulsion, consumption, by incision, execution, asphyxiation, and malnutrition, death by poison and steel, double deaths by duel. Death, Guildenstern wearily protests, "is not like that. . . . Death is not anything . . . death is not . . . death is the absence of presence."[1] Death, he insists, cannot be shown. In performance, pin spotlights focus on the faces of Rosencrantz and Guildenstern. The spotlights go out, first on Rosencrantz, then on Guildenstern, and each actor disappears. By contrast to the Player's histrionics, those disappearances are by far more convincing and appalling, drawing an emotional contrast between the pretenses of acting and the fact of disappearance. In that moment Stoppard captures the grain of death in the art of theatre. Death, like the encounter between analyst and analysand, can be known only in effigy, so it is the difference between the Player's histrionic pretense and the actual disappearance that takes the measure of the encounter. The difference between the Tragedians' fake death on the stage and the disappearance of Rosencrantz and Guildenstern from the stage pulls its emotional or affective force from the interplay between the visible and the invisible. The effigy in this case is blindness in the face of disappearance, the absence of visibility in the context of the visible. Equal to its capacity to make things visible, that is, the seeing-place that is theatre also makes things disappear in what might be called simply a more efficient and effective effigy of death.

Cut off in the middle of the expression "now you see me, now you don't," Guildenstern dies in effigy and promises a reappearance: "we'll know better next time" than to get on the boat for England, than to disappear from the play. It is the privilege of a dramatic character to reappear the next time the play is performed. But with that reappearance comes the ghostly aspect of dramatic characters in general. Stoppard exploits that aspect when, a moment after the spotlight goes out on Guildenstern and plunges the stage into darkness, the whole stage lights up and presents a tableau from the last scene of *Hamlet*. Those figures from *Hamlet* then appear more fully as ghosts who have reappeared full of life. As the Player has said, "light goes with life," punning that light accompanies life and also goes out with life. What appears with the light also goes off with the light.

This example from Stoppard is simply a way to approach the phenomenon of light in the theater insofar as it experientially correlates visibility with consciousness and life. But beyond that customary correlation, it opens onto the interplay between light and darkness that exposes the ghostly theatricality of visual evidence as a complex choreography between projections onto images and projections from images. Such projections lead out of theatre and into film, where images are made of light. Film is a mirror in which we see our own images and desires as reflected ghosts and play out a drama of misrecognition. Appearing, disappearing, and reappearing, disembodied by technology, those filmic images made of light circumvent the tests of mortality but lead to a confrontation with our own deaths in effigy. Such is the insubstantial truth of representation.

If candlelight and curtains were among the earliest means of conjuring ghosts in theatre, surely the most contemporary means are in film, where it is all the more evident there is nothing behind the veil and that ghosts are products of veiling. The screen is a curtain that hides nothing, for there is nothing behind it. Light projected onto a two-dimensional screen transforms candlelight and curtains into a technological apparatus that realizes an uncanny familiarity in visible images that are no more than disembodied hallucinations. Recording events that happened elsewhere and at another time and place, if they happened at all, transferring material mass into a spectrum of light and shadow, and projecting a two-dimensional image through an optical path to the psyche, film and its digital progeny bring ghosts into appearances as no previous medium has done. If no audience faints in horror at ghostly appearances on the screen, it is all the more taken in by the screen's images. Technology has provided the means to make ghosts an ordinary part of consumer culture but in doing so has familiarized and inured the culture against the absences and losses that the medium projects. To put it another way, it is difficult to be surprised or to experience the uncanny aspect that film entails. Audiences after the mid-twentieth century have grown up with disembodied images onscreen and have become so accustomed to disembodiment that the ghosts of the filmic apparatus hardly seem imaginary. At the same time, however, the filmic apparatus supplies a concrete source for an apprehension that there really is nothing behind the screen, that one's view of the world really is produced by projected images making an appearance from elsewhere.

In the previous chapter, I suggested that theatre both sets out and breaks down epistemological dualities of inside and outside, real and imitated, through the devices of the curtain. The curtain veils appearances at the same time that it frames attention and makes the invisible visible. In its aspects of pretense and illusion, theatre separates itself from the world; in its material aspects, it is made of worldly things. But there is a third aspect, which is generative and productive. The aspect of productivity keeps conceptual dualities in motion, resists a static ontology, and undermines efforts to let the mind rest either in concepts or in strictly materialist formations. Through performance, theatre provides a paradigm for a chronically emergent phenomenon that inherits the past and the legacies of the dead, both repeating and transforming those legacies into new appearances. That paradigm materializes in technologies of light. But it is the alternation between light and dark that models an epistemology of production and the ways in which the seen and unseen inaugurate a drama of misrecognition between an audience and images. If the pleasure of revelation belongs to the opening of a theatre curtain behind which are only more appearances (a chronic unveiling or unconcealing), then the technologies of light complicate such revelation in their capacity to create the dark. In other words, just as vital as its ability to create appearances is theatre's ability to make things disappear, to make an audience lose sight of things, and to incorporate blanks in visibility. The most extreme instance is the blackout. In every case the blackout is both an experiential event and a structuring device. That is, the vertigo of disorientation in a blackout is an effect that may well be also a plot point. It is as though what we most need to see in Guy Debord's "society of the spectacle" are the blank spaces on our field of vision, in our thoughts and experiences. Becoming conscious of our own habits of misrecognition is a productive movement of thought by which we return to ourselves.

The blackout, of course, has a history that ties it to both theatre technology and its status as a metaphor for a loss of vision, memory, or consciousness. Both material event and metaphor, the blackout became a staple of theatrical practice only in the twentieth century, when it served both to heighten tension in melodramatic realism and to designate transitions in episodic forms of theatre. Most notably in the quick comic sketch of vaudeville, the blackout is used to punch a punch line. In many ways, the blackout is simply light's way of replacing a curtain. The effectiveness of the blackout, however, as both metaphor and event, relies upon its suddenness, on the sense of shock and disorienting plunge into darkness. The coups de théâtre that were so much a part of Diderot's dramatic ideas suggest that the particular appeal of such a blow to the senses best suits an interior scene, the scene of family, or of individualism, or of love.

Diderot's bourgeois drama of the eighteenth century, closely connected to the acting style of David Garrick in England or the dramaturgy of Lessing in Germany and generally identified with Diderot's play *Le père du famille,* gave attention to an interior scene of bourgeois life and sentiment. It structured events around an affective blow to the audience, summoning concealed information to the light, anticipating further dangers, and suspending action in a frozen tableau, closed over by the act curtain. Like the later forms of melodrama and the well-made plays of Scribe and Sardou that grew from that structure of suspense, the realism introduced throughout Europe in the eighteenth century began a trend toward more and more minute explorations of interiority. From the line drawn between public and private life and the impact of economic, political, and social forces on the behavior of individuals, to the outlines of the unconscious, drama's interest in its emotional effect on its audiences became at least as great as its interest in a representation of a world. More accurately, perhaps, representation in drama took its formal properties from affective possibilities, which is to say from its capacity to move to tears, then to astonish, overwhelm, or stun its audiences.

Diderot, of course, knew that such power required careful thought and manipulation, through techniques that divided conscious forethought from emotional immediacy. Hence, his famous treatise *Paradoxe sur le comédien* defined the rift in consciousness required by an actor, the cool head and the warm heart, the calculation of an affect. His sense of the bourgeois drama reflected the technique of the actor in terms of that internal division, the divided consciousness. But beyond that, the stillness in the tableau images at acts' ends, followed by the closing of the curtain, helped eventually to define the modern subject not simply as an actor with a persona such as Hamlet ("I have that within that passeth show") but also as a structure that includes a suspension of consciousness, an absent center. "In the new drama," writes Lukács,

> . . . character becomes much more important and at the same time much less important. . . . Character becomes everything, since the conflict is entirely for the sake of character's vital centre; for it alone and for nothing peripheral, because the force disposed of by this vital centre alone determines the dialectic, that is, the dramatic quality of drama. Conversely, character becomes nothing, since the conflict is merely *around* and *about* the vital centre, solely for the *principle* of individuality. . . . Thus—and the essence of the stylistic problem is here—character is led back to more rational causes than ever before, and becomes at the same time ever more hopelessly irrational. . . . The drama comes to be built upon mathematics, a complicated web of abstractions, and in this perspective character achieves significance merely as an intersection . . . equivalent to a contrapuntal necessity.[2]

The vital center for Lukács is an empty center in terms of the drama, for it is a principle that is an intersection of forces, a product of milieu, having no independently "human" substance. This vital center is therefore a technology more than a form of humanism. Though Lukács distinguishes this modern character from that of the eighteenth century's "doctrinaire individualism," he is identifying the decentered subject that can be traced, if not to eighteenth-century doctrine, then at least to eighteenth-century technical practice that left a nonhuman absence between the technical calculation and the emotive presence of the actor. As Diderot explored the technology of Garrick's acting style, that is, and emphasized the importance of the formal, act-ending tableau, he introduced a certain kind of nonnatural, technical, even nonhuman element to the perception of individual consciousness, as a harbinger of Freud's introduction of the mechanistic elements of the unconscious. Through the nineteenth and well into the twentieth century, the suspended consciousness of both character-object and audience-subject became the locus of dramatic action and theatrical embodiment, aided not only by the work of Freud but also by the formal innovations of the symbolists, surrealists, existentialism, and, later absurdity. The stage blackout in those forms multiplied in its possibilities: as transition, as end point, as an intermediary space between presence and absence, but also as a sign of the unknown and unknowable part of the subject's construction. The mysteries of interiority that seemed so avant-garde, experimental, or pathological in modernist movements, however, can thus trace at least one aspect of their lineage to the codes of bourgeois and popular entertainments.

Theatre technology took a little longer to catch up with the dramatic concern with the coup de théâtre and the suspended animation that made an audience breathless with anticipation. In particular, the technology of electric lighting, specifically the blackout, brought with it the possibility of duplicating the actor's representation of a divided consciousness in the affect of the blackout for an audience, concretely turning the object of representation into a subjective experience. Though through the nineteenth century there had been a certain degree of control over gas lamps, which had replaced oil, the blackout was not fully effective until electricity became the primary technology for lighting, beginning late in the nineteenth century. As part of an increasing appetite for more and more realistic effects in the theatrical scene, electricity created special effects as early as 1846, when the Paris Opéra used electric arc lamps for a rising sun in Rossini's *Mosè in Egitto*.[3] Charles Wheatleigh experimented with electricity at San Francisco's Metropolitan Theatre about 1865 and gave it up as an experimental novelty that would never catch on. Though electric light was commonly used outside theater buildings, in halls and foyers, according to Frederick Penzel, until the 1880s gaslight still dominated the stage with its nasty smell, air pollution, and intense heat. As Richard D'Oyly Carte said, the gas jets consumed "as much oxygen as many people."[4] In 1880 the Teatro Paynet in Havana installed electric lights to create an imitation sunlight that shone through the stage windows in Miguel Ulloa's *El fruto de la deshonra*. The light could move across the stage tracing the time of day,[5] an effect that later astonished David Belasco's New York audiences in his famous twenty-minute sunrise. D'Oyly Carte happily, though still relying on gas as a backup system, fully converted his theater from gaslight in 1881, still having to supply his own power source, since municipal systems had yet to exist. A writer in the *Builder* of January 1882 said it would take another generation of artists before electric lights did not "disturb the memory" of splendid scenery of the past and, presumably, the softening effects of flame lighting. That writer apparently felt that theatre lighting needed the painter's eye. Electric light was simply too bright, showing up all the "poverty of ill-executed," painted scenery, taking out "contrast . . . shadow . . . the value of relative tones . . . proper relief in backgrounds, . . . and many other pictorial secrets."[6]

Electricity, however, gave new power and control over the realism of scenography to managers like Belasco. In accepting a tribute from the Dramatists and Composers Society of New York, Belasco said, "To copy faithfully the light of the sun and moon and stars that God Almighty has made for us may well exercise our greatest skill."[7] Though realism dominated the Western stage at the turn of the century, experimenters such as Adolphe Appia quickly learned to use electric light along with his geometric forms for abstracting the stage scene into temperaments. Through its technological apparatus, scenes took on moods: the stage could display a private mentality in public displays. Though there is no clear record of the first use of a total blackout onstage, the effect of the blackout through the use of electricity meant that it could induce sudden blindness. The blackout not only signifies a nothingness; it is a nothingness set in a visual register.

Insofar as any image of trauma is an image of darkness, which is to say an image without a picture, the blackout performs a traumatic loss. Onstage, the blackout is also an excellent way for the dead to enter the room. From the stylish entry of wife number 1 in Noel Coward's *Blithe Spirit* to the uncanny power of old Hamlet's spirit or Kantor's disappearance in *Today Is My Birthday*, the dark is a portal to and from an unseen space. Yet practically speaking, given the exit signs that safety codes require in modern theatre, no blackout is complete. It is therefore at best a representational blackout rather than a fully experiential one for an audience. Though it exploits the phenonemon of visibility, theatre's representational blackout is largely a point within the structure of a drama. It marks a point of leave-taking and a return of visibility that, in returning, takes on the idea of the uncanny, the return of the repressed. This uncanny, at least from a psychoanalytic perspective, occurs in some sense because the visibility that returns is familiar, "friendly" in Freudian terms, and strange. The period of dark, however, puts in question everything that returns to visibility: What happened in the interim? And what, exactly, has returned?

In many ways, the significance of the filmic cut or the blackout belongs to the inheritances of bourgeois drama and its trajectory toward ever greater depths of interiority, which paradoxically rely on a radical break between technology and human presence. Film technology began to incorporate the blackout not only as a moment in its narrative and dramatic structures but as an inherent part of its technical method. Techniques of cutting and editing around a blackout become narrative conventions that conceal the interior absences that constitute the medium itself. But those very absences situate a point of identification—a placeless place—between the unconscious of the film and that of an individual. Though the form of suspense has a long history, even (perhaps especially) the popular murder or mystery film is able to explore interiority and subjectivity on its surfaces. Any number of films explore and exploit the absence of visibility and the traumatic blow to consciousness not only as part of a structure of anticipation and suspense but also as constitutive of subjectivity in relation to the absence of light, vision, memory, and consciousness and thereby in relation to death. Perhaps what is most uncanny, however, is not simply the representation of that absence but the way in which film technology constitutes a space out of which ghosts emerge to be projected as visible images onscreen. These ghostly images, long separated from the embodied world, are then misrecognized insofar as filmic realism provides a fetish image that substitutes for and replaces the real. That is, film technology, incorporated into narrative and embodied as image materializes the site that Lacan designated as "between perception and consciousness": the dream. Film's technology includes both perception and consciousness, is identical to neither, and incorporates the unrecognized force of the unconscious in the form of the cut, the blackout, the editing process. An individual viewer can both see and not see those cuts.

By failing to recognize the force of the technological apparatus, even though knowing it is formative, we are more easily seduced by the power of the image that has none of the distractions or limitations of a real body. Film technology severs the continuity of a body in space to render a more purely imagistic continuity that elides the breaks between images. As a result,

an audience can grant the film image a kind of authority that escapes theatre, making film less of a mirror, which in live theatre reflects back a double in the form of an other, and more of an extension of the seeing eye, the
individual interiority. Put in these terms, film turns into a projection of
self that can absorb the differences between human psyche and nonhuman
apparatus, whereas theatre with its embodied community maintains difference and otherness because of bodies. Film is thus an almost ideal medium
for projection, misrecognition, and transference, particularly those films that
wear the guise of realism. The film is supposed to be complete and therefore to "know" what it is doing, what it means. It appears before our eyes
as an object. But a film is not simply an object insofar as it projects outward a subjectivity—a "subject-supposed-to know"—onto which an audience can project its own subjectivity as though it were other. In other words
there is a kind of mutual misrecognition of who is doing what to whom,
which is a version of the analytic transference and countertransference.

Film invites us to believe what we see, then often turns that invitation
into a trick that undermines belief. Merleau-Ponty called the willingness
to believe or the credulity in the visible "perceptual faith." "The certitude
I have of being connected up with the world by my look already promises
me a pseudo-world of phantasms if I let it wander. . . . It is our experience,
prior to every opinion, of inhabiting the world by our body, of inhabiting
the truth by our whole selves, without there being need to choose nor even
to distinguish between the assurance of seeing and the assurance of seeing
the true, because in principle they are one and the same thing—faith, therefore, and not knowledge, since the world here is not separated from our hold
on it, since, rather than affirmed, it is taken for granted, rather than dis-
closed, it is non-dissimulated, non-refuted."[8] Inhabiting the world through
the senses, particularly through sight, we believe, he suggests, because we
see, dividing into subjects and objects, true and false. Thought is a product of sense. The task, in Merleau-Ponty's terms, is to exchange the faith,
or what is taken for granted, for "knowledge" through the disclosure of the
world. One of film's tasks, in these terms, is to disclose the errors in thought
that come from such faith and to recognize (i.e., rethink) what the world
discloses.

The attribution of full consciousness to an other inaugurates the drama
of misrecognition: the drama of a failure to recognize and take into account
the inevitable partiality and failure of the other to know, a failure like one's

own. Symptomatically, among individual people, this misrecognition can be manifest as a recurrent fascination with a person or a topic, through certain themes in a person's conversations; it is especially noticeable in strong positive or negative feelings, even in supposedly disinterested or scientific interest. It may show affectively in enthusiasm or lust, irritation or anger, self-loathing or grandiosity. A total absence of feeling may be just as likely as an overvaluation of love or hate to indicate the presence of the dynamic. In this dynamic one experiences the unknowns of another person or "subject matter" through an imaginary belief that that other person knows what I do not (the subject-supposed-to-know). I ascribe knowledge and authenticity to that person or that subject matter that she or it, as a limited being like myself, cannot possibly have. A fetish comes about from the impulse to transform that unknown, as Peggy Phelan points out, into something one *does* know, an object, a definable emotion that one "can see, and securely own" in spite of knowing that the fetish object is not the same as that unknown.[9] The fascination, the thematizing, the interest, the lust, the irritations or the anger are the affective results of misrecognition that "also promises the threat and joy of self-dissolution." Phelan's succinct summary is this:

> Part of what motivates the misrecognition of the other is the real knowledge that one cannot see or recognize oneself. The failure to recognize one's internal other(s) is rehearsed and projected externally as the misrecognition of the external other. Thus psychic mimesis, an adequate reflection of the failure to see oneself, must be an integral part of "realistic" representation—in ethnography, in literature, in love.[10]

I was once discussing this passage in an office when someone walking in said, "Yes, but is all this true? Do people really do this? Is this real?" My only answer then was to say "Yes, but it depends on where you are looking for 'true,' and what you count as 'real.'" My suspicion was that, for that person, if any of this were true, it would somehow displace or even annihilate the real world as he understood it. If misrecognition were somehow the ground for relations, his own understanding of his place in the world would be threatened, and he therefore needed to dismiss the idea as an elaborate fiction that undermines action. A psychoanalytic account for misrecognition does not necessarily displace or dismantle other ways of understanding the world, does not present a universal truth, does not preclude action. Like Nelson Goodman's idea that the question is not *What* is art? but rather *When* is art? psychoanalytic accounts are occasions of perception on the limits of self-knowledge. The more general issue here is not whether a psychoanalytic account, or any theoretical stance, for that matter, is "true" or "real" so much as it is a matter of what it takes to recognize what it accounts for. Related to the problem of "finding a voice," the matter of belief—what to believe, how to be believed, how to believe oneself in the midst of self-deceptions, and how to encounter and deal with deception—is a foundational problem, as much for philosophy as for psychoanalysis, as much for fiction as for culture.

If film technology provides the apparatus that embodies the misrecognition of projection—that there is nothing real behind the screen—then film history provides plenty of examples that thematize misrecognition in narrative. It is surely not entirely coincidental that, however old that theme, the filmic apparatus comes to the fore about the same time as psychoanalysis. Between them, they raise unresolved questions about the reality and truth of visible images, the reality and truth of the unconscious. All appearances become suspect when the premises of psychoanalysis become realized in a technology. That is, the mundane world subsequently takes on those aspects of ghosts that are open to doubt, particularly as the individual psyche, rather than communal or social identifications, dominates the standard for experience. How does one trust one's own experience?

Stanley Cavell unpacks the issue of belief in the true and the real in his analysis of the remake of the film *Gaslight*, directed by George Cukor and starring Ingrid Bergman, Charles Boyer, and Joseph Cotten. Adapted from the play *Angel Street*, by Patrick Hamilton, this 1944 film tells the story of Paula Alquist, whose opera-star aunt was murdered years before. Returning to live in her aunt's house with her new husband, Paula (Bergman) is gradually convinced by him (Boyer) that she is going mad. She complains of seeing the lights in the house dim and of hearing sounds in the attic; she loses things; he finds things she claims to have lost; she fears the taunts of the young maid, played by the young Angela Lansbury. Not until a detective (Cotten), who knew her aunt, takes an interest does she find out that her perceptions are real, that her husband has been making those sounds in the attic in search of her aunt's jewels, and that he is the murderer of her aunt.

Cavell correlates the systematic torture of Paula, in "being deprived of words, of her right to words, of her own voice,"[11] to the philosophical and political implications in such denial, one that includes self-denial and skepticism but has been most sharply expressed in terms of gender. How can one believe the woman if it is impossible to believe she is real; especially, how is it possible for her to believe her own thoughts, given the terms in which she is told believe? "This denial of voice is not the loss of speech, a form of aphasia, but a loss of reason, of mind, as such—say of the capacity to count, to make a difference."[12] The film provides an occasion for Cavell to show the conjunction of "madness, skepticism and the *cogito,* together with the issues of discipleship and of the finding of one's voice."[13] He presents a way of understanding the dynamic of the ghost image with both its psychoanalytic symbolism and a philosophical rationale. Though the film was originally produced in England as *Murder in Thornton Square,* already a remake of the 1940 film *A Strange Case of Murder,* Cavell finds the sign of a particularly American struggle with self-doubt and belief in the issues of both voice and visibility. Referring to Emerson's idea that Americans are especially "afraid of exposure to the consciousness of others (say of otherness, so of exposure to ourselves)," he writes that "Emerson draws the conclusion that we mostly do not exist, but haunt the world, ghosts of ourselves." If this quality is indeed part of American culture, it may well be related further to the triumphs of American technology and American film, which serve as screens for the refusal of public exposure:

> When the detective first sees Paula, he says he thought he saw a ghost. . . . But the detective is surely also responding to a quality of Paula's own bearing—of, let us say, her being bound but unclaimed. The price of Descartes' proof of human existence, of the mind's inability, as it were, to doubt itself, to doubt that it doubts, is that our relation to our bodies is attenuated: the price of Emerson's proof of human existence, our exposure to the consciousness of otherness (say our subjection to surveillance), is that our relation to ourselves is theatricalized, publicized. It is no wonder that it is in melodrama, and in movies, that such matters are worked out.[14]

The willingness of Paula finally to expose her madness to the detective proves she is finally inhabiting herself, not being inhabited by her husband. Relating the fictional situation of Paula to Freud's famous discovery of transference and countertransference and to his failure of analysis in the case of Dora, Cavell says, "I begin to speculate about why it is that women play this originating role in both these developments by way of continuing to think about the history of skepticism in Western culture, particularly about its inception or representation in Shakespeare and Descartes, especially with respect to philosophical doubts about the existence of what philosophy calls other minds—as though both psychoanalysis and film testify that by the turn of the twentieth century psychic reality, the fact of the existence of the mind, had become believable primarily in its feminine (one may say passive) aspect."[15]

The visual register of the film is indeed apt for identifying the psychological somnambulism or trance behavior that manifests the self-doubt of the woman trying to adjust her sense of reality to that defined by her husband. Trance is not just the symptom but also the condition of being possessed. Paula follows Gregory's commands as well as his beliefs. And she doubts herself legitimately, because the source of those beliefs is her negative other, which inhabits her, which tells her she loses things, forgets herself, misplaces, steals, and otherwise fails to distinguish the material from the imaginary. The detective, contrarily, identifies as real the very things she doubts. Objectivity comes in the form of a material relic from the past: the detective affirms his provenance by giving Paula the mate to her aunt's glove, which, as Paula relates, the aunt had given to an "ardent admirer"—a boy of twelve, who now, as a man, returns it to materialize the truth of that past in the symbolic and material dimensions of the glove. The self-deception consists, in part, of her commitment to the other who inhabits her and her readiness to be committed to an asylum by her misrecognition of Gregory as the subject-supposed-to-know. The material signs of the truth of the past are also the focal points for misrecognition in the present: the glove, the jewels from her aunt's dress, the letter that identifies Gregory as, in fact, "Sergius," the murderer. Eventually in the climactic scene, Paula uses against Gregory the very doubt that he created in her: she holds a real knife and claims that because she is "mad," the knife is imaginary. Each of the material items works initially as a memorial of the past that is recovered in its truth when it is exposed as a memorial.

And here is where the question of the crypt, discussed by Abraham and Torok, again becomes relevant to understanding how, as Cavell points out, the film also traces a therapeutic process. For the commitment to Gregory masks a more primary loss. Abraham and Torok point at the form of loss that becomes an "incorporation" of the lost object, related to melancholia as opposed to mourning. As discussed in "All the Dead Voices: Memory and History," incorporation involves an encryption. Abraham and Torok refined Freud's ideas in "Mourning and Melancholy," in which he distinguishes melancholy not only by a loss that is unknown but also by a symptomatic display of self-loathing and self-reproach. Freud initially connects the level of self-hatred in melancholy to the displacement of hatred for an object of love that has been withdrawn. Instead of finding a new object, the withdrawal of libido into the ego creates an identification of the ego with the abandoned (or abandoning) object. Identification with the lost object then requires a lost ego.

Maria Torok, however, differentiates more specifically between mourning and melancholy on the basis of the terms *introjection* and *incorporation,* focusing on the "opposition (both internal *and* external) between the process of introjective inclusion and the fantasy of incorporation."[16] Introjection, developed from the term introduced by Ferenczi in 1909, is an extension of the "autoerotic cathexes" (libidinal attachments to the self, i.e., self-love) to include love of the other as the self and, for Torok, "not only the object but the instincts and desires attached to it" (xvi). The process of introjection of a lost love object, equivalent to mourning, is "gradual, slow, laborious, mediated, effective" (xvii) in reorganizing libidinal energies. Introjection here expands self-love to include the other. Incorporation, by contrast, marks a "refusal to mourn." It contracts into unconscious possession of the other and therefore possession by the other through the denial of loss. The unconscious refusal puts the lost object in a *place,* as though it were actually kept "in" the body, that is, sealed off from even the unconscious libidinal processes: as though it were a monument and memorial that preexisted every corporeal memory. "I pretend to keep the dead alive, intact, *safe (save) inside me,*" says Derrida, "but it is only in order to refuse, in a necessarily equivocal way, to love the dead as a living part of me" (xvi).

The concept of incorporation is further a form of magic: "fantasmic, unmediated, instantaneous, magical, sometimes hallucinatory" (xvii). In this process, desire (libido) is both maintained and excluded from consciousness, sealed off against any kind of knowledge other than the phantasmic, magical, and hallucinatory.

Incorporation is a kind of theft to reappropriate the pleasure object. But that reappropriation is simultaneously rejected: which leads to the paradox of a foreign body preserved as foreign body but by the same token excluded from a self that thenceforth deals not with the other, but only with the itself. The more the self keeps the foreign element as a foreigner inside itself, the more it excludes it. The self *mimes* introjection. But this mimicry with its re-doubtable logic depends on clandestinity. . . . "Secrecy is essential," whence the crypt, a hidden place, a disguise hiding the traces of the act of disguis-ing, a place of silence. . . . Introjection speaks: "denomination" is its "privi-leged" medium. Incorporation keeps still, speaks only to silence or to ward off intruders from its secret place. What the crypt commemorates, as the incorporated object's "monument" or "tomb," is not the object itself, but its exclusion, the exclusion of a specific desire from the introjection process: A door is silently sealed off like a condemned passageway inside the Self, becom-ing the outcast safe: "A commemorative monument, the incorporated object marks the place, the date, the circumstances in which such-and-such a desire was barred from introjection: like so many tombs in the life of the Self" (Torok, "Maladie du deuil"). (xvii)

Incorporation is an unconscious refusal to mourn. The subject thus em-bodies not a secret object of love but a secret exclusion that forecloses the acknowledgment of desire and loss as an absence, secret even from oneself. Self-denial and complacency are symptoms that make the subject a living tomb, susceptible not only to the projections of others but also to the pro-jection on others as subjects-supposed-to-know.

As *Gaslight* progresses, Paula's somnambulism increases under the influ-ence of Gregory, but her trance in fact appears at the very beginning of the film when she emerges from her aunt's house after the murder. From the beginning, then, Paula appears as one of the living dead. In that trance she follows the order of the man who leads her away from her murdered aunt's house, saying, "You've got to forget everything that's happened here. . . . You must think of the future, dear, not the past." She is going, he suggests, to study with Signore Guardi, her aunt's best friend, who might turn her into a great singer, like her aunt. So the young Paula embarks on an identi-fication with her aunt, to take on her aunt's voice. Such identification with the murder victim is a form of being possessed by the lost object, and as Cavell points out in his theme of the "unknown woman," the aunt herself substitutes for Paula's mother, who died at her birth. In other words, the aunt is already a displacement, signaling a foreclosure of the loss of a mother. It is not the aunt but the nonexistent mother who is incorporated. The film fades to black. Ten years later, the "incompleteness" or "refusal" to mourn is apparent. The film cuts to a point where the voice teacher, Signore Guardi, tells Paula that though she looks like her aunt, her "heart is not in" her singing anymore. "Each time you come here you look happier and you sing worse." She has fallen in love with Gregory, but here love is a sign of a failure of her own voice. If her image has improved ("you look happier"), her self-expression has diminished in love. "Suddenly it's as if nothing has existed." Even her music means nothing.

What sounds like a radical overstatement is more precisely accurate: the crypt is a radical absence of self: semantic as well as material reality as well as self. The film has incorporated that absence structurally in the cut between Paula's departure from her aunt's house and her appearance in Guardi's studio. She is "too happy," which is why the maestro said tragedy is something she could never understand. Then the maestro says to her, "But now there is a chance to free yourself of tragedy, my child. Take it. Free yourself from the past." He claims that happiness is better than art. She later says to Gregory, underlining the unconsciousness of her refusal to mourn, "I lived with my aunt always as if I were her own. . . . That house comes into my dreams, sometimes a house of horror. Strange. I haven't dreamed of that house since I've known you. I haven't been afraid since I've known you. . . . I've found peace in loving you." Not only is her life with her aunt already "hypothetical" (she lived only *as if* she were her own, masking the loss of the mother); it is also "theatrical." That is, stories of the past are all stories not about the mother but about the performances of Alice Alquist, about her tours, and about her great admirers, who turn out to be a tsar, a murderer, and a detective. Paula's connections to a past are foreclosed before they can even start, are put into the imaginary before they are ever real: as the first shots of the film suggest, her past begins in a loss for which she refuses to mourn, but it is already a displaced loss.

Entering later the "house of death," which looks like a mausoleum, Gregory promises to get rid of all the reminders of Paula's unhappy memory of finding her aunt's body. He says: "It's all dead in here. The whole place seems to smell of death." And then: "I wish I could have seen her." Paula happily responds: "Oh. Let me show her to you." She then reveals the portrait of Alice as the empress Theodora and reports that when her aunt played that role in St. Petersburg, the tsar used to come to every performance. Later, we suspect it is that very tsar who gave Alice the jewels that Gregory/Sergius covets and has murdered for. The jewels, which Paula knows nothing about, are already apparent in the aunt's portrait, adorning her costume, hiding in plain sight, but Gregory doesn't recognize them as an image of the real jewels. Or rather, he is incapable of recognizing that the representation in the portrait mediates the reality of the jewels and could inform him where the jewels are hidden. "How would it be if we took away all these things, took away these things that remind you so of her. The painting, the furniture. Shut it away . . . shut it away so you can't even see it. . . . We'll board it up so you'll never have to see it again." He, too, as though for her own good, says, "You must forget her." He then proceeds to shut Paula away from the world, to close her off in that mausoleum of a house, the place that locates her forgetfulness and his blindness. Gregory, the masked husband, installs himself in the attic (so commonly an image of the mind), seeking the jewels in the clutter, never recognizing the real ones on the costume. That refusal of knowledge, in other words, is *situated*: a "topos": it has a place but is inaccessible. The space of the house inters her; that is, she has entered her loss to the point that inside and outside coincide.

In a psychoanalytic narrative, Paula's refusal of mourning, which is part of maintaining or incorporating the absent mother and is displaced by the death of the aunt, accounts for her radical misrecognition of Gregory. As she says, "I don't know you. I don't know anything about you." Paula, in failing to complete the mourning process for a mother who died before Paula came to consciousness, inters the absence through identification with the murdered aunt. Paula's body serves as a memorial guardian who refuses admittance, or consciousness, even to herself and identifies with the image of the dead aunt. Inhabited by the absence of her mother, Paula is an example of the living crypt, which is mystery, code, and tomb, and which uses "Paula" as a mask to guard the place of unknowing. That mask is an imitation of Paula, who imagines authenticity in the other because she is blocked from her own authenticity. The process of the film brings Paula to a position in which the crime is outside herself: she is not imagining sounds, she is not imagining that the lights dim; she did in fact already know the murderer's name, having found his letter in a piece of her aunt's music, but did not recognize "Gregory" as Sergius: she could not put the true name on the person. The crime that she thought was behind her was, in fact, before her all the time.

The refusal that results in the failure to know who Gregory is (the murderer himself) is furthermore attached to obedience. Conceding to the exhortation to "put the past behind," Paula cannot see that the past is, in fact, right in front of her: visible, manifest, and dominating her consciousness, presiding over her actions, generating her fear of the outside (she attempts to but cannot leave the house alone) and her anxieties toward the sexual innuendos of the maid. The house does not simply represent the entombment of the murdered woman; it *is* the entombment of Paula. That is to say in semiotic terms that the mediated relationship between sign and referent (house *as* tomb) collapses into a singularity that is simultaneously sign and referent (house *is* tomb). From this perspective Paula herself is the ghost who haunts the tomb. She is caught halfway between living and dead, unable to act, unable to believe herself until an objective reality intervenes to separate her from identification with her aunt and from the tomb that encrypts the loss of her mother and to tell her who she has been.

The drama of misrecognition begins by the projection on an external other out of the failure to know oneself. The moment of recognition in the classical sense of anagnorisis constitutes a turn back to the knowledge of what one has always been. And when one has been a ghost all along, like Paula, the moment constitutes a turn toward life. That misrecognition is reversed in the 1999 film *The Sixth Sense,* which is a ghost story about a young boy who "sees dead people." The film concerns a child psychologist, Dr. Malcolm Crowe, played by Bruce Willis, who is trying to redeem an earlier failure with a patient who, he discovers too late, had also seen dead people. His redemption comes by helping the young boy, played by Haley Joel Osment, to lose his fear of the ghosts he sees and learn to talk to them.

The film initially seems to be a psychological story about redemption and overcoming fear, but at the end we discover that the psychologist has been dead all along. He is one of the ghosts the boy sees and talks to. Though Crowe is shot by a former patient in the opening scenes of the film, there is a blackout and he next appears on a bench observing the terrified young boy on his way to school. The gap between the opening scene in which he was shot and the "one year later" scene is an ordinary convention for compressing time. Interim events, presumably, are irrelevant to the relationship between the scenes. The narrative elision implies simply that Crowe has recovered from the shooting and aims now to help the young boy. Under the cover of convention, the break in the narrative enables the film to play a good trick on the audience. It plays out toward a shock of recognition that the ghost has been present all along. In retrospect, we realize there are plenty of clues, the most obvious occurs when the boy tells the psychologist that the people he sees do not know they are dead. The film's success, however, depends on the audience's unawareness that Crowe is a ghost.

The conventional gap between scenes, whose events seem to be irrelevant to the plot, has to be taken concretely, as a real gap that signifies death. More than signifying death, however, it concretizes the space of unknowing that is death. That unknowing belongs not only to the character but also to the audience, which is as wrapped in ignorance of the death as the protagonist is. It is also the space of unknowing that characterizes psychic trauma, and in that sense, every survivor of trauma is also a ghost who cannot know or recognize that very gap, the unassimilated death, the absolute lack in consciousness, that has already happened. Instead, the survivor carries on not knowing that she is already a ghost, an insubstantial image that has only the appearance of life. The trauma survivor, like the character of Dr. Malcolm Crowe, may behave normally. The only evidence that something is wrong is the sense that people do not seem to acknowledge or see, just as Crowe's wife in the film seems, for some unknown reason, to ignore, dismiss, and refuse to speak to him, and just as later the audience realizes that the only one who actually speaks to Crowe is the boy. Crowe shows up late to an anniversary dinner, apologizing, not realizing that his wife cannot see him, and seeming to assume she is simply angry at his being late. The gap in the ghost-survivor's memory is concealed by the habits of life, by psychology, by convention. The unknowing of the traumatic absence appears in the film narrative as a cut between scenes, but it is the same absence characterized in optics and in psychoanalysis by the blind spot of the eye and the ego. His wife and the mother of the boy cannot see Crowe because, as a ghost who does not know he has died, he occupies his own blind spot and hides from himself behind the ego's role as "fabricator and fabrication," in Jacqueline Rose's term.[17] The ego is the survivor of a psychic death that fabricates the appearances of life for itself and others.

The hole in the narrative turns out to have been not only the site of death but also an initiation into a liminal space where the living communicate with the dead. But that liminal space is constituted by the film itself and arises from the formal arrangement of the visible and invisible, the lighted, talking figures and the blackout. It is a privileged space in the sense that only some few, like the boy, realize only ghosts are talking. At a narrative level the film is merely clever. The import of the gap, however, is connected to the effect of the film medium that plays out and explodes the habits to take as real what is fundamentally fabricated by the desire to know and understand what one is dealing with, particularly in confronting our personal deaths, our own ghostliness. The gap in the narrative, in other words, replicates the absences behind appearances as well as the fabrications that constitute appearances. The formal elements of the medium situate a meeting place for the living and the dead at the level of surfaces, in the non-human dimension of the film itself. Visual representation itself, not the subject matter of representation, constitutes the appearance of the ghost, the uncanny thing that has unfinished business among the living, behind which is no-thing.

Living-dead ghosts stories, such as *The Sixth Sense,* produce neither the aesthetic estrangement of modernist abstraction nor the techniques of alienation that reveal ideology, though they are related to both. Abstraction often serves to revise habits of perception or to critique norms of behavior, thought, and action, but the formal elements so obvious in abstraction tend to disappear in the popular entertainments of ghost stories. The ghost in *The Sixth Sense,* that is, appears initially as a normal (i.e., living) figure of realistic representation. Through the course of the narrative, that realistic figure turns into its own double, the ghost of itself. The shock in the film is not simply that the character Malcolm Crowe has been dead all along—like the film image itself—but also that the film has pleasurably double-crossed both him and the audience into a recognition of unknowingness. The pleasure of the double cross comes largely from being startled into an awareness of the formal aspects of representation in which the unknowable resides as a blank space and a leap over time. One comes to see the film as a clever and successful manipulation. The tie between the artifice of representation and the unknowingness of trauma is nascent in virtually any kind of representation, making all representation in some sense uncanny, both familiar and strange, both pointing to the known and standing apart as an autonomous, nonhuman product, covering the gap that lies between.

For as that which is most utterly unrepresentable, death is known only by its fake double, the effigy that stands at a portal to identify what death is like but not what death is. Real death is always elsewhere, but its double is found hiding in the plain sight, both visual and narrative, of representational habits. The questions raised by such films as *The Sixth Sense,* as for representation in general, are: How do we know a ghost when we see one? How, especially, do we know the ghost is us? How do I live with my own unknowing?

These ghost stories act out suspensefully the projects of estrangement by which habits of perception are shocked into a recognition of the reality of death, which has been present all along, unseen, unfelt, unheeded, yet obvious to those who know how to look. For the reality of death is the most basic version of the real encounter, of an encounter with the Real, which, in Lacan's terms, is an encounter that is always missed. Death is a singularity that is always other than what presents itself, yet it is precisely not beyond or outside what presents itself. But who knows how to look? By what means does someone see not only what appears but also more or other than what appears? Is there anyone who can see what it is that ghosts the living or what ghosts dwell among the living? The perception of the uncanny requires a capacity to recognize the simultaneity of both familiarity and strangeness and the binding of the living and the dead. That perception usually comes too late, only after the fact, as an explanation for what happened and why.

Alfred Hitchcock's 1958 *Vertigo* is another film that uses a blackout to expose the limits on an encounter with death. And like *Gaslight* it also uses a jewel as an image of a desired object that captures a gaze but is misrecognized because it is first seen in representation, such that the reality of the jewel is missed. The truth of a valuable object of desire, the jewel, is missed because it is first seen as a duplicate whose original seems to be elsewhere. Only in the second viewing does the truth in the image appear. Representation itself ensures that the real thing is missed but has been present in front of the viewer all along.

In the famous opening scene that presumably initiates his case of vertigo, Scottie Ferguson (James Stewart), along with a uniformed policeman, is chasing someone across the rooftops of San Francisco. The sequence is largely shot in silhouette against a dark blue sky as the criminal—already an imaginary figure for the guilty self in dreams—and the policeman make successful leaps onto a steeply pitched roof. But Scottie slips, catching hold only of a gutter pipe on the edge of the roof. As the policeman returns to help, he slips off the roof, leaving Scottie clinging to the gutter pipe and staring terrified at the street below. Blackout.

In the next shot, Scottie is recovering in the studio of his motherly pal, Midge. He is playing with a decidedly phallic cane, which falls as he holds it out. "Ouch," he says. Reference to his protective corset, which, he says, will come off tomorrow, further emasculates him. As witness to the falling policeman, the figure of father and authority alike, Scottie is doubly guilty, first for being the cause of the fall and second for surviving it. Expositional, the scene reveals that Scottie has retired from the police force, that he is independently wealthy, that he is ignorant that Midge loves him, that he has acrophobia. It is an emasculated Scottie, wearing a corset and carrying a cane that he can't keep up. Absent from the exposition is a story for his escape from the roof. We are left to infer his fall, his rescue, and his recovery. Convention allows the presumption of a logical connection between the two scenes, as it does in *The Sixth Sense*. Somehow Scottie was rescued from the rooftop, leaving him with a limp and acrophobia. Film is particularly adept at both implying and breaking the continuity of cause and effect. The break between these scenes expressly elides causality and replicates the ellipsis of traumatized consciousness. It both formally and narratively iterates the nature of trauma. As Robin Wood and Donald Chankin noted of the elision: "The lack of any explanation for his escape creates the effect of the protagonist remaining 'metaphorically suspended over a great abyss' throughout the film."[18]

But it is the shared space of the conventional film logic and the formal film cut that more fully express the trauma. Convention and our elision of causality by habits of reading film provide exactly the kind of alibis that conceal trauma. They constitute the disbelief and disavowal that characterize the misrecognition of a traumatic event and its further concealment by an interpolated narrative. In fact "nothing" happened. And to take that nothing literally rather than to interpolate possible stories is to recognize the radical nothing that is trauma. The juxtaposition of the two scenes, in other words, replicates a more precise sense of trauma and its therapeutic unfolding in the film's process. The unknown blank between scenes is the "X factor," which Žižek says "is ultimately the subject's birth and/or death, so the fantasy object is the impossible gaze which makes the subject into a witness to his/her own conception or death."[19]

As Cathy Caruth points out, reflecting on Freud, the nature of trauma is not simply in an event itself but in the "structure of experience" formed by an absence of consciousness. Not merely a forgetting, a traumatic experience registers only as a loss of consciousness. "The event is not assimilated or experienced fully at the time but only belatedly, in its repeated *possession* of the one who experiences it. To be traumatized is precisely to be possessed by an image or event."[20] Trauma manifests itself as a lost time and makes its appearances in the "dreams, hallucinations and thoughts that are absolutely literal, inassimilable to associate chains of meaning."[21] Trauma, that is, is not carried simply as a repressed experience whose retrieval will solve a mystery. Rather, it carries or possesses the person, independently of will, of language. It returns of its own accord, in its own time, in its own forms of refusal to assimilate. Without language, it is also without temporality. Unmoving, unchanging, "nothing" recollects, sustains, and anticipates death. The survivor of trauma is therefore an unknowing witness to her own death, one who recalls, anticipates, and is possessed by it. Žižek, again, points out that "*the space of 'what can be said,' the subject's universe of meaning, is always 'curved' by traumatic blanks,* organized around what must remain unsaid if this universe is to retain its consistency. The subject necessarily misrecognizes the *constitutive* nature of these blanks."[22]

Psychoanalytic readings of *Vertigo* have been well rehearsed before now.[23] After an initially confused reception, it seems an almost transparent film about a crisis of masculinity and representation, about optical fantasy in which the woman on the screen is the screen for the obscure object of desire, the object always out of reach, always beyond the celluloid, and all the more perfect because of it: a love story, a story of obsession with death, with love, with image. "Love at first sight, wild love, immeasurable love, fiery love," writes Julia Kristeva. "A vertigo of identity, vertigo of words: love, for the individual, is that sudden revelation, that irremediable cataclysm, of which one speaks only *after the fact.*"[24] That so many "love" the film itself now suggests that it always has been a phantasm replicating an obsession with the phantoms of love and death. The phantasmic nature of Hitchcock's filmic eye is exemplary of the phantasmic nature of spectacle itself, insofar as spectacle, Medusa-like, transfixes the one who sees. The vertigo of the title is repeated in the motif of the multiple falls that are characterized by loss of orientation, loss of self, as the eye is transfixed by an image. Repeatedly falling in love with an image, falling to one's death, witnessing the faux fall of the image, and failing to recognize the real death: all are organized around the absence of the real wife whom Scottie is charged to follow.

Scottie is clearly a detective voyeur, following his imaginary Madeleine from her first full-screen, soft-focus image appearing at Ernie's to sites around San Francisco. His is a prosthetic rebirth sustained only by fantasy, the imagination of the viewer, and the apparatus of the medium. Scottie himself becomes the empty signifier, a ghost of himself, following a desire whose origin is in the fall. In Lacanian terms, the fall, for individual cases of traumatic absence as well as in historical loss (the loss of presence in time), is the occasion for the appearance of phantasmagoric entities, like the figures on the cinematic screen. Falling between the real and the symbolic, these figures generate impossible desires to re-create the object of desire as a real object. But part of that impossibility belongs to the fact that the figures themselves are ghosts of the real. From within the fall from consciousness, however long or short the duration, the consciousness of the living being is in communion, so to speak, with the dead, is at one with the dead. When Scottie becomes catatonic after the imagined death (fall) of Madeleine, the lure of the detective narrative collapses and his reappearance in the second half only makes his emptiness more explicit. If, after a breakdown, he is seen to be "getting on" with his life, it is only as a cover for his suspension in time, for his suspension over a trauma that has been disavowed. His suspense is no metaphor but an affective condition of the film, within which both he and the viewer are hard pressed to distinguish the real from the imaginary.

Scottie himself has come *d'entre les morts,* "from among the dead," which was the title of the book by Pierre Boileau and Thomas Narcejac written expressly for Hitchcock after he missed directing their previous work, *Diabolique.* The ambiguity of the French title is telling. "From among the dead" suggests a return from a community of the dead, but it could also say "from between deaths." The second suggests a scene between two deaths, the symbolic and the real, which is to say the double death that representation entails. For the film is full of death's doubles: Madeleine/Judy dies twice; the first is already a double as the real, if unknown, Madeleine dies, and the surrogate Madeleine dies symbolically and returns as the real Judy Barton. Her first fall is fake, the second real. The second, because an accident, touches on the real. Scottie also dies twice, falling into and out of his symptomatic vertigo, between the imaginary and the real.

A series of shots at Ernie's, one of San Francisco's now long-gone elegant eateries, shows through Scottie's eyes the imaginary Madeleine (Kim Novak) reflected in mirrors. There is no language in this famous interlude. Bernard Hermann's music, which dominates most of the scenes between Stewart and Novak, follows her emergence into a full-frame close-up, a profile held long enough to change the background colors that isolate the image of her face from any context. And her face is luminous. It makes clear how the "scopic drive," named by Freud, is so closely aligned with film's capacity to inaugurate desire in the image. The image of Kim Novak on the screen works as a veil for the absences of both the person and the character. The image is, simply put, stunningly beautiful. If it invokes a desire to see and possess that which is beyond the screen, it does so only after one falls in love with the image on the screen. If the drive produces the fall in and out of love, through the abyss of desire, one is momentarily at the site/sight of love on the surface of the screen.

Scottie, like the film, goes quickly toward an identification with the "fallen woman" Carlotta, whose image in a painting appears as the object of Madeleine's own obsession with a past. The trance of looking overtakes Scottie as well as the camera. Point of view belongs equally to everyone, with the portrait of Carlotta, the object, looking back at Madeleine, Scottie, and a viewer. The camera, in holding on Carlotta, takes a long time with the parallels between Madeleine's nosegay and the one in the picture. It focuses on the similar whorls in their hair, spirals that look like an eye or the aperture of a lens and invite another vertiginous fall into empty space, where the view disappears into nothingness. Finally, the camera focuses on a gaudy jeweled necklace that Carlotta wears in her portrait. Eventually, it appears that Madeleine's fake attempt at suicide is modeled on Carlotta's suicide. The camera becomes the rhetorical device of the unconscious, asking, Who is looking? Who is dead? An imaginary identification within an imaginary identification, the portrait looks back at Hitchcock's camera, which joins Scottie and the viewer in fascination with the matching whorls in the hair of Madeleine and portrait. Novak's face is never shown in the scene: the camera looks through her to the portrait. The line of sight follows the eyes of both Scottie and Madeleine—now joined with the viewer— to the mystery woman in the portrait.

Later, after the true/false death of Madeleine and the transformation of Judy Barton back into the image of Madeleine, she (who? Judy? Madeleine?

both?) is dressing for dinner. She asks Scottie for help putting on the neck-lace, and he sees it in the mirror. He sees it for the second time, in other words, within the frame of a visual representation, and has another shock. Only this time it is the shock of recognition of the image coming into "itself" as an object. It now appears to Scottie's glance as an image of a real object, and from there it enters consciousness, which separates the mate-rial reality from the representational image, showing the reality of the false image. He is no longer in love. At this point, he perceives the truth of the Judy/Madeleine pretenses and breaks the trance of the imaginary. The neck-lace, the object first found within representation, has circulated through all the degrees of an absent woman's identity. It belonged to the real wife, who is now dead. It is the kind of Hitchcock object that, as Žižek remarks, "circulates among the subjects and, by its very circulation, makes out of them a closed intersubjective community. . . . [It is] . . . the tiny 'piece of the real' which keeps the story in motion by finding itself 'out of place.' . . . This object embodies, gives material existence to the lack in the Other, to the constitutive inconsistency of the symbolic order."[25]

Why does Judy put on the necklace? A psychological lapse, perhaps, but it really makes no sense. But that lack of sense and the obdurate material-ity of the necklace, which Scottie's gaze finally sees in the mirror, is where, for both Scottie and the film, the Real looks back at the viewer from within the field of representation. Scottie calls it a "sentimental" act. If sentimen-tally she has consented to becoming an image for him, putting on the necklace is an accident that leads to an unmasking. She tries, it seems, to keep the necklace in the dimension of the illusion that has made her happy, when all it can do is bring the misrecognized reality of the real death into the foreground. When she says in a farewell note that she never delivers, "I hoped you would love me for myself," she mistakenly believes that a "real" Judy Barton self could ever equal the idealized illusion and imaginary pro-duction of Madeleine. It is never clear who the "real" person might have been or might be, because she is posited, even at the end, as "always already" having been a product of the older man, of Elster.

Indeed, even for me as an audience member, the "real" Judy Barton, now back being the sales clerk she was before taking up with Gavin Elster, is a disappointment, not only because of her appearance and behavior, some-where between crass and naive, but also because Kim Novak seems sud-denly to have turned into a not very good actress. I, too, have been seduced by the idealized image of the actress. By comparison, the "real" Judy seems false, perhaps trying too hard to be real and failing. More likely, I would have to admit being taken in by Hitchcock's own imaginary manipulations of Kim Novak. As she puts on the necklace in her moment of reckless confidence in love, Kim Novak/Judy Barton suddenly appears as a kind of Lacanian "stain" from within the film. The stain, like the necklace, is that which is suddenly out of place, no longer at home within the representative field but sticking out, like a real object on a painted canvas. Just as what I perceive to be Kim Novak's suddenly bad job of acting leaps out at me from within the representation, that moment in the film represents the recognition of the stain of the Real from within the film. It is the thing, the object, within a visual field, by which the "frame" of the image is being "framed by part of its content."

The trajectory of the object follows the course of perception between the living and the dead, between representation and reality, among narrative lie, imagistic trance, and the truth of its material existence. And between those extremes is the death of the real wife, the death that is witnessed only in effigy, in a misrecognition that the death of Elster's wife really was the death of his wife. Her unwitnessed death, the extreme version of the traumatic fall, becomes the organizing principle of all other events in the film. The drama of misrecognition forms around the unrecognized death that occurs between the Imaginary and the Real. The vertigo of the film is thus a matter not simply of the subjective construction of the "hero" but of a systematic vertigo within the filmic apparatus itself, in which the eye of the audience is also seduced by the image and fails to recognize the scene of death at which it gazes. The vertigo of the film thus reaches the inclusive, impersonal dimension that Žižek has called "the subject without subjectivity."[26] Scottie's inevitable failure to encounter the first real death of the wife, as he has failed to encounter his own, results in a misrecognition of the reality of that death. More paradoxically it was a misrecognition of the truth of the falsehood, the truth of the ruse, a real death disguised as a false one: it was not "Madeleine" who died but rather Madeleine, just as in terms of the trauma, it was not only the policeman who fell but also Scottie, who misrecognized the death of another as his own. It is only in the second death, the death of the doubly false "Madeleine," that the debt to the Real is paid and the encounter with the Real takes place. The first fall to death is hidden in plain sight. Because all the figures of the film participate intersubjectively in the circulation of falsehoods, they are not so much characters as "little wheels in a nonsubjective machinery" that is equivalent to the "symbolic order," which is the film *Vertigo* itself, a "transsubjective mechanism which regulates the process."[27]

All three of these films, *Gaslight, The Sixth Sense,* and *Vertigo,* are simply examples of those (and there could be hundreds more) that thematically and narratively trace the ghostly aspects of visual representation through a filter of characters who misrecognize their own ghostliness and confront death through the devices of representation and its return. Though visually realistic, the narratives emerge in concert with the phenomenal and formal absences that constitute the filmic medium, which is itself ghostly. Onto the screen of images made of color, light, and shadow one projects the impossible desires reflected there and misrecognizes the truth of the ghosts as fabrications. The visual medium is the mechanism that produces such errors, and in the belief that a film is no more than a representation we fail to see that its imaginary aspect is also, actually, the real thing, a substitute hiding its reality in plain sight. The void in consciousness and in sight produces the contours of "character," which in turn is produced by failure to see oneself. The coincidences between the technology of film and the technology of character manifest what Lukács above called the "new drama," in which character is both an intersection and an empty center, that is, a "transsubjective mechanism" onto which subjects project objectivity.

Ghosts return through the aperture of the eye. Just as Scottie mourns an effigy by failing to recognize that the real wife and her substitute have exchanged places, we find only by repetition of a second death that we have been mourning the imagined loss of the real all along. Time unfolds the realization that the relationship between the real thing and the fabrication is not a matter of either/or but a matter of both/and. The contrast between the show of death, like the Player's in *Rosencrantz and Guildenstern Are Dead,* and death as disappearance shapes a space of difference between life and death and shows them to be entwined in an endless, stochastic repetition of imagination and reality, out of which we produce the truth of ghosts.

After Words

A young colleague not too long ago said she was awfully tired of all the talk about loss and death and trauma. And, indeed, it seems these concerns may have run the critical course in academia, especially in the fading light of Derrida and Lacan and poststructural fever. I sympathize with her. How many times can one read or write about trauma before fatigue sets in and it becomes one more item in the history of critical perspectives? Theatre, after all, is positive and productive. It is a material, functional, social, and aesthetic phenomenon; it means things. It's tiresome to keep repeating that we don't know what we don't know, can't know. Let's get on with it. Of what cannot be said, must we, with Wittgenstein, remain silent?

But the unknown, the dead, the lost, will speak through us even if they don't speak directly to us. We will act out their demands even if we cannot hear their voices, even if too many voices are clamoring for attention. Denial is a strong force and keeps us functioning, but the desire for reality, the desire to be real, the desire to live really is also a strong force, and the authentic and real encounter with life includes an encounter with death. Death is our common fatality; the death of others, our common sorrow. How do we live *d'entre les morts?*

Theatre is a means of creating a real encounter even when it is not always made or perceived to do that. The habits of thought that run through a system of either/or realities equate life and death with being and nonbeing. If anything, the production of theatre suggests that even amid the operations of the duality, say, of on- and offstage, the third element, which is

183

production itself, breaks them down to indicate conceptual limits. Non-being is an unrealizable concept. To put it another way, death, loss, and absence are already what we live within, what already exists in the world and constitutes it. Denial is what puts them into the crypt, into the realm of imaginary nonbeing, when we already live concretely among what Robert Harrison calls "the dominion of the dead" that is the earth. So when we encounter absence, loss, even death, we are encountering reality. The conceptual paradox is both revealed and surmounted by practice, because it is through practice that the world keeps emerging and representing itself. I suspect with careful enough attention almost any instance of theatre would reveal its part in creating a real encounter, an encounter with the real, because it is a real practice that reveals its own emergence from the space of difference that is not wholly different, just offset, syncopated in time.

That is why I have tried to pull from the least critically available aspects of theatre some way of seeing that its ghostliness is as real as creamed chipped beef on toast. From the widest formulation of phenomena, time and space, the particularities of the real past and present, of material objects, of the hidden and revealed, are put into play in theatre. Practice takes conceptual dualities and transforms them into something other than what we can think, but it is nonetheless possible to act in the midst of the transformation. These are the elemental aspects that inform the chapters of this book: time, things, and the acts of making the invisible visible. As Merleau-Ponty indicated, by our bodily insertion into the world we tend to equate what is perceived with what is true, and it takes a complication of perception to allow the life and death of the world to reveal themselves. Theatre complicates perception by asking for an encounter outside our customary and daily habits and yet is never really outside. It demands one more appointment to be on time, to be present, in a world of appointments in which the present always escapes. It asks that we hear the voices of the dead in the sound of the living. It suspends the usefulness of the objects we surround ourselves with and allows us to attend to the touch of the world and its flesh. It gives us a place to sit and watch the world go by, in chairs that catch us halfway to falling. It shows how we keep secrets and lets us take pleasure both in momentary revelation and in the labor by which we produce and reproduce such revelation. It screens our consciousness to show us the blind spots. In all these ways theatre increases perception, not so much to give us truth as to enable us to encounter the otherwise unseen, unacknowledged, and denied reality of what is not otherwise apparent.

For all those grand notions, these chapters, as I read them back, seem both repetitious and incomplete. Examples are sparse. If there is a reason beyond inadequacy to the task, it is that there is a terrible sameness to loss in the experiences of any one individual and an equal sameness in the need for attachment and connection. It is also because almost any example of theatre would serve. Only when absences are compared in terms of scope, depth, or duration do they separate between trivial and profound, temporary and final. The infant who mourns the loss of the mother, the teen who moans the loss of love, the parent who wails the loss of a child, the country who mourns the loss of its young in war: each one will know loss and will either successfully mourn or incorporate it in an endless melancholy of denial or reactive aggression. Personal losses and their constitution of the psyche are replicated in historical losses such that historiography is both a personal and a public matter. What is written and remembered depends critically on how it is written and remembered. Yet the unwritten will return and demand revenge, which is why the encounter is both necessary and inevitable but can be done only "in effigy," the second time around. It is then that the fake, the substitute, the double, achieves its truth, and ghosts are released from their hauntings.

Notes

INTRODUCTION

1. Goesta M. Bergman, *Lighting in the Theatre* (Totowa, NJ: Littlefield, 1977), 68. Ingegnieri was a member of the Academia Olimpico and created the mise-en-scène for the *Oedipus Rex* that opened the Teatro Olimpico in 1585. His treatise "Il discuro della poesia rappresentative e del modo di rappresentare le favole scenich" is quoted in Bergman.

2. Saint Augustine, *Confessions,* trans. Henry Chadwick (Oxford: Oxford University Press, World Classics, 1992), 230 (11.14.17).

3. Robert Pogue Harrison, *The Dominion of the Dead* (Chicago: University of Chicago Press, 2003), 36.

4. *The Riverside Shakespeare,* ed. G. Blakemore Evans (Boston: Houghton Mifflin, 1974), 5.1.216–17. I quote from this edition throughout my study.

5. Elin Diamond, *Unmaking Mimesis: Essays in Feminism and Theater* (New York: Routledge, 1997).

6. Herbert Blau, *Take Up the Bodies: Theater at the Vanishing Point* (Urbana: University of Illinois Press, 1982), 282–83.

7. Eric Partridge, *Origins: A Short Etymological Dictionary of Modern English,* 2nd ed. (New York: Macmillan, 1958), 404. The extensive entry for "mind" includes, from the Greek, Latin, and Indo-European, derivatives for remembrance and understanding as well as verb forms, *to think, to mention, to warn. Menos* includes mind, intention, and force but is related to the verb form *mnasthai,* "to remember," and *mnainesthai,* "to rave," all rooted in the Sanskrit *manas,* "mind, spirit."

8. Herbert Blau, *The Eye of Prey: Subversions of the Postmodern* (Bloomington: Indiana University Press, 1987), 171.

9. Ibid., 171–72.

10. Ibid., 173.

11. Avery F. Gordon, *Ghostly Matters: Haunting and the Sociological Imagination* (Minneapolis: University of Minnesota Press, 1997), 179.

12. "What interests us most in the long extract [of definitions] is to find that among

its different shades of meaning the word *Heimlich* exhibits one which is identical with its opposite, *unheimlich*. What is *Heimlich* thus comes to be *unheimlich*. . . . In general we are reminded that the word *Heimlich* is not unambiguous, but belongs to two sets of ideas, which without being contradictory are yet very different: on the one hand, it means that which is familiar and congenial, and on the other, that which is concealed and kept out of sight. The word *Heimlich* is only used customarily, we are told, as the contrary of the first signification and not of the second. . . . We notice that Schelling says something which throws quite a new light on the concepts of the 'uncanny,' one which we had certainly not awaited. According to him everything is uncanny that ought to have remained hidden and secret, and yet comes to light." Sigmund Freud, "The Uncanny," *Papers on Applied Psycho-Analysis*, in *Collected Papers*, trans. Joan Rivière, ed. Ernst Jones, reprinted in Freud, *On Creativity and the Unconscious*, ed. Benjamin Nelson (New York: Harper and Row, 1958), 129–30.

13. Edward Gordon Craig, *On the Art of the Theatre* (London: Seven Arts, Heinemann Ltd., 1958), 85. However nostalgic for an imaginary past he seems, Craig saw realism as "the blunt statement of life, something everybody misunderstands while recognizing" (89), in distinction from Asian actors who "have permeated every thought, every mark, in their work with this sense of calm motion resembling death" (86). "And in that picture, if the form be that of the living, on account of its beauty and tenderness, the colour for it must be sought from that unknown land of the imagination, and what is that but the land where dwells that which we call Death" (89).

14. Ibid., 85.

15. Marvin Carlson, *The Haunted Stage: Theatre as Memory Machine* (Ann Arbor: University of Michigan Press, 2001), 7.

16. Margery Garber, *Shakespeare's Ghost Writers: Literature as Uncanny Causality* (New York: Methuen, 1987), 174.

17. Bert O. States, *Great Reckonings in Little Rooms: On the Phenomenology of Theater* (Berkeley: University of California Press, 1985), 7. States goes on to quote Merleau-Ponty: "It is impossible . . . to decompose a perception, to make it into a collection of sensations, because in it the whole is prior to the parts." Quoted from *The Primacy of Perception and Other Essays on Phenomenological Psychology, the Philosophy of Art, History, and Politics*, ed. James M. Edie (Evanston, IL: Northwestern University Press, 1964), 15.

18. Rebecca Schneider, "After Us the Savage Goddess: Feminist Performance Art of the Explicit Body Staged, Uneasily, across Modernism Dreamscapes," in *Performance and Cultural Politics*, ed. Elin Diamond (New York: Routledge, 1996), 155.

19. Gordon, *Ghostly Matters*, 7, 23.

20. Walter A. Davis, *Get the Guests* (Madison: University of Wisconsin Press, 1994).

21. Jacques Lacan, "Desire and the Interpretation of Desire in *Hamlet*," in *Literature and Psychoanalysis: The Question of Reading Otherwise*, ed. Shoshana Felman, trans. James Hulbert (Baltimore: Johns Hopkins University Press, 1980), 25.

1. TONIGHT AT 8:00

1. Peter Handke, *Offending the Audience*, in *Kaspar and Other Plays*, trans. Michael Roloff (New York: Farrar, Straus and Girous, 1969), 22.

2. Ibid., 29.

3. Ibid., 32.

4. Ibid., 25.

5. Virginia Woolf, *The Waves* (New York: Harvest/HBJ, 1959), 255.

6. Augustine, *Confessions*, 231 (11.14.17).

7. Ibid., 231 (11.15.18).

8. Ibid., 233 (11.18.23).

9. Ibid., 235 (11.20.26). "What is by now evident and clear is that neither future nor past exists, and it is inexact language to speak of three times—past, present, and future. Perhaps it would be exact to say: there are three times, a present of things past, a present of things present, a present of things to come. In the soul there are these three aspects of time, and I do not see them anywhere else. The present considering the past is memory, the present considering the present is immediate awareness, the present considering the future is expectation. If we are allowed to use such language, I see three times, and I admit they are three. Moreover, we may say, There are three times, past, present, and future. This customary way of speaking is incorrect, but it is common usage. Let us accept the usage." Paul Ricoeur's three-volume *Time and Narrative* (Chicago: University of Chicago Press, 1984) begins with Augustine's questions and sets them off against Aristotle's notion of mimesis to construct his own sense of a "threefold mimesis."

10. Augustine, *Confessions*, 243 (11.27.36).

11. Ricoeur explains: "The whole last part of Book 11 (26:33–28:37) is directed at establishing this connection between the two basic themes of the investigation: between the thesis of the threefold preset, which solved the first enigma, that of a being that lacks being, and the thesis of the distension of the mind, summoned in order to resolve the enigma of the extension of a thing that has no extension." Ricoeur, *Time and Narrative*, 1:16.

12. Augustine, *Confessions*, 243 (11.28.37).

13. Ibid., 233 (11.17.22).

14. Sigmund Freud, *The Interpretation of Dreams*, trans. James Strachey, reprint ed. (New York: Basic Books, n.d.), 511.

15. Ibid., 509.

16. Ibid., 510.

17. Jacques Lacan, *Four Fundamental Concepts of Psychoanalysis*, ed. Jacques-Alain Miller, trans. Alan Sheridan (New York: Norton, 1981), 56.

18. Ibid., 56.

19. Ibid., 58–59.

20. Samuel Beckett, *Waiting for Godot* (New York: Grove Press, 1954), 58.

21. Cathy Caruth, *Unclaimed Experience: Trauma, Narrative, and History* (Baltimore: Johns Hopkins University Press, 1996), 100. Caruth investigates the links between literature and psychoanalytic theory for the fruitful revelations of how "literature, like psychoanalysis, is interested in the complex relation between knowing and not knowing" (3). She relates Freud's account of Tasso's story of Tancred, who unknowingly "kills his beloved Clorinda in a duel while she is disguised in the armour of an enemy knight. After her burial he makes his way into a strange magic forest which strikes the

Crusaders' army with terror. He slashes with his sword at a tall tree; but blood streams from the cut and the voice of Clarinda, whose soul is imprisoned in the tree, is heard complaining that he has wounded his beloved once again" (2). Caruth is particularly interested, beyond Freud, in the voice that constitutes a witness to both killings. The story "thus represents traumatic experience not only as the enigma of a human agent's repeated and unknowing acts but also as the enigma of the otherness of a human voice that cries out from the wound, a voice that witnesses a truth Tancred himself cannot fully know" (3).

22. Freud, *Interpretation of Dreams,* 513–14.

23. Ibid., 509.

24. Ibid., 538.

25. Ibid., 542.

26. Ibid., 538.

27. Caruth, *Unclaimed Experience,* 91.

28. Ibid., 102.

29. Lacan, *Four Fundamental Concepts of Psychoanalysis,* 55.

30. "Should this be the end of the story? a kind of sigh? a last ripple of the wave? a trickle of water to some gutter where, burbling, it dies away? Let me touch the table— so—and thus recover my sense of the moment. A sideboard covered with cruets; a basket full of rolls; a plate of bananas—these are comfortable sights. But if there are no stories, what end can there be, or what beginning? Life is not susceptible perhaps to the treatment we give it when we try to tell it. Sitting up late at night it seems strange not to have more control. Pigeon-holes are not then very useful. It is strange how force ebbs away and away into some dry creek." Woolf, *The Waves,* 267.

31. James Knowlson, *Damned to Fame: The Life of Samuel Beckett* (New York: Simon and Schuster, 1996), 447.

32. Samuel Beckett, *Happy Days* (London: Faber and Faber, 1961), 33–34.

33. Ibid., 8.

34. Lacan, "Desire and the Interpretation of Desire in *Hamlet,*" 17.

35. Maria Torok, "The Lost Object—Me," in Nicolas Abraham and Maria Torok, *The Shell and the Kernel,* vol. 1, ed. and trans. Nicholas T. Rand (Chicago: University of Chicago Press, 1994), 141.

36. Ibid.

37. Ibid., fn. 140.

38. Nicholas Abraham, "The Phantom of Hamlet or The Sixth Act *preceded by* 'The Intermission of Truth,'" in Abraham and Torok, *The Shell and the Kernel,* 188.

39. Ibid., 189.

40. Marjorie Garber, *Shakespeare's Ghost Writers: Literature as Uncanny Causality* (New York: Methuen, 1987), 157.

41. Ibid., 157–58.

42. Written on the outside wall of the memorial built to the 168 dead of the Oklahoma City bombing of the Alfred P. Murrah Federal Building on April 19, 1995, in large numerals, is: 9:03. That empirical datum of time faces up directly to the uncanny impossibility of comprehending the moment of the bombing itself, and therefore of comprehending the reality of death, whether that of the victims or the state-sanctioned

death of Timothy McVeigh, the bomber. The sign is graphic and mute placement for the failure of any signifier to point adequately to the event. At most, the moment of the explosion is marked as a moment that remains, in the aftermath, uncanny, inhuman, incomprehensible, and heartbreaking. No explanation suffices; no memorial matches the horror. The digital mark of time, not its spatial analogue, sets out the failure of markings to organize the moment around which "before" and "after" constitute themselves. On the memorial wall, the time insists that the visitor confront the moment as a failed, insufficient signifier, even as he or she passes through it into the memorial space.

43. Caruth, *Unclaimed Experience,* 60.

44. Catherine Clément, *Syncope: The Philosophy of Rapture,* trans. Sally O'Driscoll and Deirdre M. Mahoney (Minneapolis: University of Minnesota Press, 1994), 5.

2. ALL THE DEAD VOICES

1. Michel de Certeau, *The Writing of History,* trans. Tom Conley (New York: Columbia University Press, 1988), 1.

2. Ibid., 2.

3. Ibid., 5.

4. Ibid., 4.

5. Søren Kierkegaard, *Fear and Trembling/Repetition,* ed. and trans. Howard V. Hong and Edna H. Hong (Princeton: Princeton University Press, 1983), 275.

6. Ibid., 174.

7. Slavoj Žižek, "Why Is Every Act a *Repetition?*" in *Enjoy Your Symptom! Jacques Lacan in Hollywood and Out,* 2nd ed. (New York: Routledge, 2001), 79.

8. Kierkegaard, *Fear and Trembling/Repetition,* 210.

9. Ibid., 212.

10. Žižek, "Why Is Every Act a *Repetition?*" 75.

11. Ibid., 75.

12. Ibid., 77.

13. Ibid., 91.

14. Roland Barthes, *The Pleasure of the Text,* trans. Richard Miller (New York: Hill and Wang, 1975), 22.

15. Ibid., 21.

16. Ibid., 52.

17. Jacques Lacan, *Écrits: A Selection,* trans. Alan Sheridan (New York: Norton, 1977), 86.

18. Kierkegaard, *Fear and Trembling/Repetition,* 212.

19. Lacan, *Écrits,* 124–25.

20. Ibid., 160.

21. Slavoj Žižek, *The Plague of Fantasies* (London: Verso, 1997), 93–94.

22. Beckett, *Waiting for Godot,* 58.

23. Anthony B. Dawson, *Shakespeare in Performance: Hamlet* (Manchester: Manchester University Press, 1995), 61. Dawson is quoting Edward R. Russell, *Arrested Fugitives* (London, 1912).

24. Ibid., 61, quoting Russell again.

25. Nigel Alexander, *Poison, Play, and Duel: A Study in Hamlet* (Lincoln: University of Nebraska Press, 1971), 47.

26. Jonathan Goldberg, *Voice Terminal Echo: Postmodernism and English Renaissance Texts* (New York: Methuen, 1986), 98–99.

27. Garber, *Shakespeare's Ghost Writers,* 149. Garber is quoting de Man's definition of the different forms of memory taken from Hegel.

28. Ibid., 151.

29. Ibid.

30. Augustine, *Confessions,* 186–88 (10.8.13–10.9.16).

31. Ibid., 193 (10.16.24).

32. Frances A. Yates, *The Art of Memory* (Chicago: Chicago University Press, 1966), 6–7.

33. In contrast to the artificial memory, "the natural memory is that which is engrafted in our minds, born simultaneously with thought." Ibid., 5.

34. Ibid., 137.

35. Ibid., 144–45.

36. Barbara Johnson, "The Frame of Reference: Poe, Lacan, Derrida," in *Literature and Psychoanalysis,* ed. Felman, 458.

37. de Certeau, *The Writing of History,* 1.

38. Ibid., 47–48.

39. Ibid., 1–2.

40. Ibid., 101.

41. Herbert Blau, *The Eye of Prey: Subversions of the Postmodern* (Bloomington: Indiana University Press, 1987), 181.

42. Jacques Derrida, "Foreword: *Fors:* The Anglish Words of Nicolas Abraham and Maria Torok," in Nicolas Abraham and Maria Torok, *The Wolf Man's Magic Word: A Cryptonomy* (Minneapolis: University of Minnesota Press, 1986), xviii.

43. Nicolas Abraham and Maria Torok, "The Topography of Reality: Sketching a Metapsychology of Secrets," in Abraham and Torok, *The Shell and the Kernel,* vol. 1, 157.

44. Ibid., 158.

45. Derrida, "Foreword," xix.

46. Ibid., xxii.

47. Jacques Derrida, "La parole soufflée," in *Writing and Difference,* trans. Alan Bass (Chicago: University of Chicago Press, 1978), 174–75.

48. Derrida, "Theater of Cruelty and the Closure of Representation," in *Writing and Difference,* 249.

49. Sigmund Freud, *The Standard Edition of the Complete Psychological Works of Sigmund Freud,* vol. 11, ed. James Strachy (London: Hogarth Press, 1966), 16.

50. Ibid., 16–17.

51. Lacan, *Écrits,* 50.

52. Claude Lanzmann, "The Obscenity of Understanding: An Evening with Claude Lanzmann," in *Trauma: Explorations in Memory,* ed. Cathy Caruth (Baltimore: Johns Hopkins University Press, 1995), 205; Maurice Blanchot, *The Writing of the Disaster,* trans. Ann Smock (Lincoln: University of Nebraska Press, 1995), 41.

3. OBJECTS

1. States, *Great Reckonings in Little Rooms*, 29.

2. Tadeusz Kantor, "The Post Office," in *A Journey through Other Spaces: Essays and Manifestos, 1944–1990*, ed. and trans. Michal Kobialka (Berkeley: University of California Press, 1993), 82–83.

3. Susan Stewart, *On Longing: Narratives of the Miniature, the Gigantic, the Souvenir, the Collection* (Durham, NC: Duke University Press, 1993), 135.

4. Ibid., 135.

5. Eve Kosofsky Sedgwick, *Touching Feeling* (Durham, NC: Duke University Press, 2003), 13–14.

6. Suzan-Lori Parks, *The America Play and Other Works* (New York: Theatre Communications Group, 1995), 185–86.

7. For a more thorough discussion of the play, please see Harry Elam and Alice Rayner, "Echoes from the Black (W)hole: An Examination of *The America Play* by Suzan-Lori Parks," in *Performing America: Cultural Nationalism in American Theatre*, ed. Jeffrey D. Mason and J. Ellen Gainor (Ann Arbor: University of Michigan Press, 1999), 178–92.

8. Stewart, *On Longing: Narratives of the Miniature*, 135.

9. Ibid., 151.

10. Žižek, *The Plague of Fantasies*, 7.

11. Parks, *The America Play*, 193–94.

12. Paul Zielbauer, "Found in the Clutter, a Relic of Lincoln's Death," *New York Times*, July 5, 2001, A1.

13. Brigitte Peucker, *Incorporating Images: Film and the Rival Arts* (Princeton, NJ: Princeton University Press, 1995), 113.

14. Kantor, "The Poor Object," in *A Journey through Other Spaces*, 74.

15. Ibid., 73–74.

16. Michal Kobialka, "The Quest for the Self/Other: A Critical Study of Tadeusz Kantor's Theatre," in *A Journey through Other Spaces*, 275.

17. Ibid., 275.

18. Kantor, "Emballage Manifesto," in *A Journey through Other Spaces*, 78.

19. Ibid., 79.

20. Ibid., 82.

21. Martin Heidegger, "The Thing," in *Poetry, Language, Thought*, trans. Albert Hofstadter (New York: Harper Colophon, 1971), 165–86.

22. For the quoted fragment, see ibid., 168.

23. Ibid., 169.

24. Ibid., 170–71.

25. Ibid., 173.

26. Ibid., 174.

27. For this and the following quotations, see ibid., 178.

28. "The gift of the outpouring is a gift because it stays earth and sky, divinities and mortals. Yet staying is now no longer the mere persisting of something that is here. Staying appropriates. It brings the four into the light of their mutual belonging. From

out of staying's simple onefoldness they are betrothed, entrusted to one another, they are unconcealed." Ibid., 173.

29. Ibid., 177.

30. Bert States gets around any theological sense of the appearance of the gods in the work of art by pointing out: "What Heidegger means here is not a literal presence of the god, but a presence that makes it unnecessary to refer elsewhere for the god. It is the truth of the god that arrives on the stage and not the stage that refers to a real god beyond it, existing in some unavailable form" (States, *Great Reckonings in Little Rooms*, 3).

4. EMPTY CHAIRS

1. See Partridge, *Origins*, 90.

2. States, *Great Reckonings in Little Rooms*, 73.

3. Ibid., 72.

4. John Rockwell, "Robert Wilson's Stage Works: Originality and Influence," in *Robert Wilson: The Theater of Images* (Cincinnati: Contemporary Arts Center, 1980), 39.

5. Ibid.

6. I am grateful to Jon Erickson for pointing out an essay by Rudolph H. Weingartner on the philosopher of culture, Georg Simmel. In that essay he writes about Simmel's idea of the "undifferentiated state," *Erleben*, or "experience" in which "the self and its objects still remain undifferentiated, in which impressions or representations fill up consciousness, while the bearer of these contents has not yet separated himself from the contents" (43). He writes further: "The obstacle . . . which leads to the disintegration of *Erleben* stands in the way of a *particular* human function. It prevents the fulfillment of a certain lack, or it blocks the expression of a particular kind of energy. In every case, a gap is opened between subject and object, but the relation between them may vary from case to case. Depending on the impulses and capacities involved and on the character of the stimulus, the contents of which the subject becomes aware are 'felt' in different ways, the 'attitude' toward them varies, the subject 'presents' content to itself differently. As the unity of *Erbelen* breaks up, contents are experienced in different modes." Rudolph H. Weingartner, "Form and Content in Simmel's Philosophy of Life," in *Georg Simmel, 1858–1918: A Collection of Essays, with Translations and a Bibliography*, ed. Kurt H. Wolff (Columbus: Ohio State University Press, 1959), 45.

7. See Richard Schechner, *Between Theater and Anthropology* (Philadelphia: University of Pennsylvania Press, 1985), 36–38.

8. One of the clearest summaries of this idea, stemming from Freud but pervasive in the work of Lacan and Derrida, is Cathy Caruth's book *Unclaimed Experience*. Her chapter on the film *Hiroshima, mon amour* is particularly acute in detailing the "missing of the event" of the death of the other.

9. Eugene Ionesco, *The Chairs*, in *The Bald Soporano and Other Plays*, trans. Donald M. Allen (New York: Grove, 1958), 138.

10. Kenneth Tynan in Eugene Ionesco, *Notes and Counternotes*, trans. Donald Watson (London: John Calder, 1964), 92.

11. Ionesco, ibid., 95.

12. Ionesco, *The Chairs*, 113.

13. Ionesco, *Notes and Counternotes*, 112.

14. Ionesco, *The Chairs*, 118. Hereafter in this discussion of *The Chairs*, the pertinent page numbers are cited parenthetically in the text.

15. Jacques Derrida, "The First Session," in *Acts of Literature*, ed. Derek Attridge (New York: Routledge, 1992). This essay outlines the multiple uses of "mimesis" in Plato and (therefore) in the history of interpretation. Customarily and habitually related to ideas of truth, he says, mimesis can designate the appearance of the thing in *phusis* (nature) that must be doubled in order to make its appearance as it is. I take this to mean the necessity of consciousness within nature in order to make nature known to itself (i.e., primarily human consciousness). Therefore, he implies, truth is that which appears, is unveiled, emerges to shine (here an implicit critique of Heidegger). Or, mimesis can more usually designate the idea of a copy of an original, whose relationship is primarily one of adequacy between the terms.

The later part of the essay engages a passage of Mallarmé's that concerns a text and possible performance of a mime, *Pierrot Murderer of His Wife*. It argues that the textual strategy of Mallarmé's piece in some sense reiterates the "nothingness" that is both the source of the mime and the content of the mime (murder by syncope: by the gap and gasp in consciousness caused by tickling his wife to death). Mime and text alike reperform a nonexistent past. The internal division within mimesis evacuates the sense of mimesis as a productive as well as a copy-original model. Derrida in this early essay "harkens forward" to his statement later in *Specters of Marx* that "there has never been a scholar, as such, who believes in ghosts." Pierrot, Mallarmé's texts, the performance and its history, are the ghostly aspects of mimesis that are and are not productive, are and are not copies, real and unreal, texted and performed, living and dead: none of which are conditions of being.

16. Kobialka, "The Quest for Self/Other," 387 n. 1.

17. Ibid., 383.

18. Jacques Derrida, "The First Session," in *Acts of Literature*, ed. Derek Attridge (New York: Routledge, 1992), 164.

19. "An undecidable proposition, as Göedel demonstrated in 1931, is a proposition which, given a system of axioms governing a multiplicity, is neither an analytical nor deductive consequence of those axioms, nor in contradiction with them, neither true nor false with respect to those axioms. *Tertium datur,* without synthesis." Ibid., 173.

20. Kantor, "The Theatre of Death," in *A Journey through Other Spaces*, 112.

21. Ibid., 109.

5. DOUBLE OR NOTHING

1. Marguerite Bieber, *The History of the Greek and Roman Theater* (Princeton, NJ: Princeton University Press, 1961), 179–80.

2. Ibid., 48.

3. Ibid., 82 and 92.

4. Among other places: Herbert Blau, *The Audience* (Baltimore: Johns Hopkins University Press, 1990).

5. O. Mannoni, *Clefs pour l'imaginaire ou l'autre scène* (Paris: Éditions du Seuil, 1969), 11. "Le fétishiste a répudié l'expérience qui lui prouve que les femmes n'ont pas de phallus, mail il ne conserve pas la croyance qu'elles en ont un, il conserve un fétiche *parce qu'*elles n'en ont pas. Non seulement l'expérience n'est pas effacée, mais elle devient à jamais ineffaçable, elle laisse un *sigma indélébile* dont le fétishiste est marqué à jamais. C'est le souvenir qui est effacé." (The fetishist has repudiated the experience that proved to him that women do not have the phallus, but he does not maintain the belief they have one; he maintains the fetish *because* they don't have one. Not only is the experience not erased, it becomes ineradicable; it leaves an *indelible stigma* with which he is forever marked. It is the memory that is erased); my translation.

6. Gaston Bachelard, *The Poetics of Space,* trans. Maria Jolas (Boston: Beacon Press, 1969), 211–12.

7. Frank Kafka, "Before the Law," in *The Penal Colony: Stories and Short Pieces,* trans. Willa and Edwin Muir (New York: Shocken, 1961).

8. Martin Heidegger, *Being and Time: A Translation of "Sein und Zeit,"* trans. Joan Stambaugh (Albany: State University of New York Press, 1996), 6.

9. Ibid., 6.

10. ". . . when the curtain goes up on the market and the table plays actor and character at the same time, when the commodity-table, says Marx, comes on stage *(auftritt),* begins to walk around and put itself forward as a market value. *Coup de théâtre:* the ordinary, sensuous thing is transfigured. . . . It becomes someone, it assumes a figure. This woody and headstrong denseness is metamorphosed into a supernatural thing, *a sensuous non-sensuous* thing. . . . The commodity is a 'thing' without phenomenon, a thing in flight that surpasses the senses." Jacques Derrida, *Specters of Marx: The State of the Debt, the Work of Mourning and the New International,* trans. Peggy Kamuf (New York: Routledge, 1994), 150–51.

11. Ingegneri quoted in Allardyce Nicoll, *Stuart Masques and the Renaissance Stage* (New York: Harcourt Brace, 1938), 204.

12. States, *Great Reckonings in Little Rooms,* 35.

13. Beckett, *Waiting for Godot,* 58.

14. States has written extensively on dreams and their connection to storytelling and art. He makes a case for the point that however much dreams seem to be part of an alternative world, they belong to the same realm of human capacity as those for image making, storytelling, and metaphor. See, for instance, Bert States: *The Rhetoric of Dreams* (Ithaca, NY: Cornell University Press, 1988); *Dreaming and Storytelling* (Ithaca, NY: Cornell University Press, 1993); and *Seeing in the Dark* (New Haven, CT: Yale University Press, 1997).

15. Martin Heidegger, *Identity and Difference,* trans. J. Stambaugh (New York: Harper and Row, 1969), 19.

6. GHOSTS ONSCREEN

1. Tom Stoppard, *Rosencrantz and Guildenstern Are Dead* (New York: Grove Press, 1967), 125.

2. Georg Lukács, "The Sociology of Modern Drama," trans. Lee Baxandall, in *The Theory of the Modern Stage,* ed. Eric Bentley (New York: Penguin, 1968), 435–36.

3. Frederick Penzel, *Theatre Lighting before Electricity* (Middletown, CN: Wesleyan University Press, n.d.), 70.

4. Quoted ibid., 72.

5. Ibid., 71.

6. But safety came first, and electricity seemed far safer than the volatile gas. By 1887, according to Penzel, most American and Continental theaters used electricity. Sometime after 1887, Spain mandated the use of electric lights, and in 1897, German theatre regulations banned gas or oil lamps altogether (Penzel, *Theatre Lighting before Electricity,* 74).

7. *San Francisco Journal,* April 8, 1921.

8. Maurice Merleau-Ponty, *The Visible and Invisible,* trans. Alphonso Lingis (Evanston, IL: Northwestern University Press, 1968), 28.

9. Peggy Phelan, *Unmarked* (New York: Routledge, 1993), 106–7.

10. Ibid., 107.

11. Stanley Cavell, "Naught Orators: Negation of Voice in *Gaslight*," in *Languages of the Unsayable: The Play of Negativity in Literature and Literary Theory,* ed. Sanford Budick and Wolfgang Iser (Stanford: Stanford University Press, 1987), 356.

12. Ibid., 357.

13. Ibid., 361.

14. Ibid., 372.

15. Ibid., 352. Further on Cavell writes: "The extent to which, or sense in which, such domestic melodramas are ghost stories—a matter coming to another head, in Ibsen, in *Ghosts*—is laid out in the question the detective asks the constable after they have followed Gregory only to have him disappear into the fog, like a ghost: 'You don't suppose he could have gone into his own house do you? . . . Why should a man walk out of his own house, all the way around the corner, just to get back where he started from?' If we translate this as 'Why would he wish to enter his house unseen?' the answer is irresistible: in order to haunt the house, which is a way of inhabiting it. Here the path is opening for considering Paula to be responding to lowering lamps and noises in the attic as to a ghost story, or ghost play. . . . This suggestion is confirmed by Gregory's last accusation of Paula, that her madness is inherited from her mother, who, he claims to have discovered, died in an insane asylum—himself now the fabricator of a ghost story, fictionalizing Paula's history as well as her perceptions. . . . She attaches great feeling and significance to the memory of her aunt's going over for her, on special occasions, the stories associated with her collection of theatrical mementos; but the child seems not to have asked about, nor to have had, mementos associated with the figure she calls mother. As if she does not feel she has the right to know something, or as if she already knows something. Now consider again: Who does Paula know to be in the attic? And before all: Who did she know was there before she knew?" (374).

16. Derrida, "Foreword" in Abraham and Torok, *The Wolf Man's Magic Word,* xxxv. Citations in the remainder of this discussion appear parenthetically in the text.

17. Jacqueline Rose, "The Imaginary," in *Sexuality in the Field of Vision* (London: Verso, 1986), 171. Quoted in Victor Burgin, *In/Different Spaces: Place and Memory in Visual Culture* (Berkeley: University of California Press, 1996), 46.

18. Donald O. Chankin, "Delusions and Dreams in *Vertigo*," in *Hitchcock Annual* (Gambier, OH: Hitchcock Annual Corp., 1992–93), 29. See also Robin Wood, *Hitchcock's Films Revisited* (New York: Columbia University Press, 1989), III.

19. Slavoj Žižek, *Everything You Always Wanted to Know about Hitchcock but Were Afraid to Ask Lacan,* ed. Žižek (London: Verso, 1992), 242.

20. Cathy Caruth, "Introduction," *Trauma: Explorations in Memory,* ed. Caruth (Baltimore: Johns Hopkins University Press, 1995), 4. Elsewhere Caruth writes: "But what seems to be suggested by Freud in *Beyond the Pleasure Principle* is that the wound of the mind—the breach in the mind's experience of time, self and world—is not, like the wound of the body, a simple and healable event, but rather an event that, like Tancred's first infliction of a mortal wound on the disguised Clorinda in the duel, is experienced too soon, too unexpectedly, to be fully known and is therefore not available to consciousness until it imposes itself again repeatedly, in the nightmares and repetitive actions of the survivor. . . . Trauma is not locatable in the simply violent or original event in an individual's past, but rather in the way that its very unassimilated nature—the way it was precisely *not known* in the first instance—returns to haunt the survivor later on." Caruth, *Unclaimed Experience,* 4.

21. Caruth, "Introduction," *Trauma,* 5.

22. Slavoj Žižek, "In His Bold Gaze My Ruin Is Writ Large," in *Everything You Always Wanted to Know about Lacan but Were Afraid to Ask Hitchcock,* ed. Žižek, 242.

23. Both Tania Modleski and Robert Samuels locate Scottie's subjective experience in a certain kind of identification with the female. Samuels suggests that it is the lack of an explicitly (hetero)sexual orientation that most fundamentally horrifies Scottie: "I would like to argue that in Lacan's theory of castration anxiety, the male subject is not primarily afraid of recognizing the female's genitals because they represent the possibility that he can lose his own genitals or phallus, but rather because he is afraid of seeing in the other a reflection of his own nothingness. . . . By equating the female with the Real that cannot be symbolized, Lacan places this female subject in a position of unknowability. However, I would like to affirm that, if we maintain Freud's theory of foundational bisexuality, the horror of the Real is fundamentally a horror of the lack of sexual orientation." Robert Samuels, *Hitchcock's Bi-textuality: Lacan, Feminisms, and Queer Theory* (Albany: State University of New York Press, 1998), 81–82.

Similarly, Modleski writes of Scottie's identification with the female as a lack within heterosexual desire: "Scottie's failure to cure Madeleine deals a mortal blow to his masculine identity, as the dream that he has shortly after Madeleine's presumed death indicates. . . . What is most extraordinary in this dream is that Scottie actually *lives out Madeleine's hallucination,* that very hallucination of which he had tried so desperately to cure her, and *he dies Madeleine's death.* His attempts at a cure having failed, he himself is plunged into the 'feminine' world of psychic disintegration, madness, and death. Even the form of the dream, which is off-putting to many viewers because it is so 'phoney,' suggests the failure of the 'real' that we have seen to be at the stake of Scottie's confrontation with Woman." Tania Modelski, *The Women Who Knew Too Much* (New York: Methuen, 1988), 95.

24. Julia Kristeva, *Tales of Love,* trans. Leon S. Roudiez (New York: Columbia University Press, 1987), 2–3.

25. Žižek, *Enjoy Your Symptom!* 18.

26. Žižek, "In His Bold Gaze My Ruin Is Writ Large," 253.

27. Žižek, *Enjoy Your Symptom!* 19.

Index

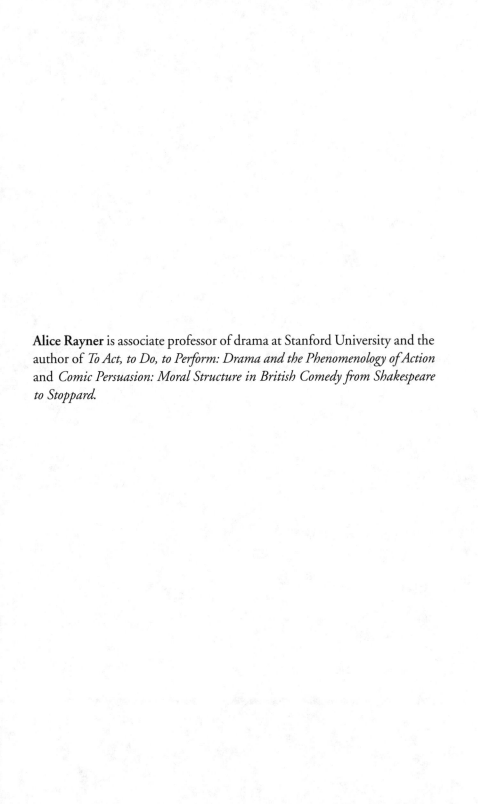

Alice Rayner is associate professor of drama at Stanford University and the author of *To Act, to Do, to Perform: Drama and the Phenomenology of Action* and *Comic Persuasion: Moral Structure in British Comedy from Shakespeare to Stoppard.*